LITCHFIELD COUNTY AND THE CIVIL WAR

Peter C. Vermilyea

Published by The History Press
Charleston, SC
www.historypress.com

Cover: Collection of the Litchfield Historical Society, Litchfield, Connecticut.

First published 2024

Manufactured in the United States

ISBN 9781467156219

Library of Congress Control Number: 2023947101

Notice: The information in this book is true and complete to the best of our knowledge. It is offered without guarantee on the part of the author or The History Press. The author and The History Press disclaim all liability in connection with the use of this book.

For Gabor S. Boritt, "Forever am I thy debtor…."

And in memory of my father-in-law, Dennis Hovland.

Contents

Acknowledgements

The seed for this book was planted about fifteen years ago on a Memorial Day run past a local cemetery where flags marked the graves of veterans. One grave stood out: an obelisk with flags on three sides. This was the grave of Edward, Henry and Luman Wadhams, brothers and Civil War soldiers from Goshen, Connecticut, who served in three different regiments and were killed in three different battles, within ten days of one another. I set out to research this story but soon became fascinated by how Litchfield County sent those men off to war in the first place. The pages that follow tell that story. I would not have been able to do so without the help of those listed here. I am responsible for any mistakes.

I am greatly indebted to the staff at the Litchfield Historical Society. Cathy Fields, now retired as director, is a bastion of support for all who research the town's history. Lee Swift is unfailingly generous in sharing her wealth of knowledge about Litchfield's history. Kate Zullo offered opportunities to share my research. Alex Dubois provided key assistance with sources and images. Sean Kunic helped gather archival material and listened patiently to me talking about this book over bocce games. Jessica Jenkins, new director in Litchfield, shared research on the Wide Awakes and read portions of the manuscript. My colleagues on the board of trustees of the Litchfield Historical Society have long supported my work.

I am deeply appreciative of all Litchfield County historical societies and libraries, especially Stephen Bartkus at the Gunn Historical Museum, Marge Smith at the Kent Historical Society and Jerry Milne and Louise

Strange at the Plymouth Historical Society. Equally essential have been the county's librarians. My friend Audra MacLaren at the Gunn Memorial Library offered support and opportunities to share my research. The entire staff of the Oliver Wolcott Library is incredibly helpful, especially Caitlin Costa. I can't thank Verna Gilson of the Beardsley and Memorial Library in Winsted enough for sharing her unsurpassed knowledge of that town's history. Thanks go as well to the New Milford Public Library and Lukas Hyder of the White Memorial Conservation Center.

Beyond Litchfield County, I am indebted to Sierra Dixon and the staff at the Connecticut Museum of Culture and History. Mel Smith, Jeannie Sherman and Lizette Pelletier at the Connecticut State Library and Archives provided essential assistance, as did Dave Corrigan at the Museum of Connecticut History. Jessica Baker at Yale University and Benjamin Panciera at Connecticut College both provided materials about Homer Curtiss. Robb Hill helped with research at the National Archives, and Lisa Newman provided images from the United States Army History and Education Center.

I am very thankful to the historians who took time away from their own research to assist me. Peter Carmichael, Jill Titus and Ashley Luskey at the Gettysburg College Civil War Institute have been great supporters of this project; I am lucky to work with them each summer. I am also grateful to Gary Gallagher of the University of Virginia, Jason Philipps and Brian Luskey of West Virginia University and Bert Dunkerley of the Richmond National Battlefield Park. John Banks, Dan Keefe, Eileen Schmidt, David Ward and Fenton Williams graciously shared their own research. Eric Wittenberg offered important advice.

Colleagues Scott Fellows and Ian Strever at Housatonic Valley Regional High School were especially helpful. Scott helped me better understand the statistical data in my research, and when I faced a severe case of writer's block, Ian contributed a project-saving suggestion.

It was a pleasure to work with Michael Kinsella and Ryan Finn of The History Press. They believed in my vision for this project and shepherded it to completion. I am grateful for all their work!

Two individuals merit special acknowledgement. First, Linda Hocking, curator of archives at the Litchfield Historical Society, has been an enthusiastic supporter of this project since its inception, answering questions, fielding endless archival requests and reading several chapters of the manuscript. I simply could not have written this book without Linda's help. Second, my great friend and colleague Jared Peatman has been a rock of support and encouragement. From reading the first draft of my idea for this book to reviewing the completed manuscript, Jared has taken time away from his own project to make this one better.

This project would never have gotten off the ground without the support of my family. My mother-in-law, Sandy Hovland, remains my first-rate copy editor. My parents, Pete and Kathy Vermilyea, and my sister, Megan Lambert, continue to foster my love of history. My sons, Ben and Luke, have graciously put up with a lifetime of being dragged to see wagon ruts or abandoned railroad tracks at remote places inhabited only by tumbleweeds. My wife, Jill, has blessed my life in ways much more important than in her support of this project. I am indeed lucky to have them all in my life.

This book is dedicated to two individuals who have greatly impacted me. My father-in-law, Dennis Hovland, passed away as this project neared completion. An engineer, he grew to love history. Gabor Boritt, once and always my teacher and my oldest friend in the history business, has provided countless opportunities to me. This is a small token of appreciation for all they have done for me.

Introduction

September 12, 1912

They were old men now. Once they numbered nearly one thousand, young men who left their homes and families for war. There were far fewer on this day, but the site was the same: the farmer's field, atop Chestnut Hill, about a mile southeast of Litchfield, Connecticut. And their military bearing remained, even though fifty years had elapsed since they first gathered to begin their military training. Photographs of that day show men with gray hair and weathered faces, but their posture recalls soldiers standing at attention.

Fifty years earlier, most of the men had walked to this spot. They had not yet learned to march like soldiers. Others were driven there in carriages or wagons by loving family members, friends or neighbors. They were, as many would later call them, the "flower" of Litchfield County. On this day, a march was deemed too difficult for these men, most of whom were now in their seventies. Instead, they piled into automobiles for the short ride from town to the field.

Many men wore medals that bespoke the day's purpose. A bronze medal with two crossed cannons and a red ribbon reminded spectators that these men were once artillerymen, members of the 2nd Connecticut Heavy Artillery Regiment. Also etched on the medal was the image of a monument. That was the reason why they had gathered here on this day. Fifty years earlier, they assembled there—at what was known as Camp Dutton—as strangers,

Veterans of the 19th Connecticut at the Camp Dutton monument dedication, 1912.
Collection of the Litchfield Historical Society, Litchfield, Connecticut.

with the common goal of enlisting in the Union army but motivated to do so for different reasons. Over the next two and a half years, they would share sufferings and sacrifices, triumphs and tragedies. These experiences turned these one-time strangers into a band of brothers. Speeches preceded the unveiling of the monument, although the crowd—which included Governor Simeon Baldwin, the Governor's Foot Guards and other civic organizations—could likely make out that it was a stone about six feet high. Following a speech by former regimental officer Dwight C. Kilbourn, the monument was revealed. Its inscription read:

> *Camp Dutton*
> *The 19th Conn. Infantry*
> *Afterwards*
> *2nd Conn. Heavy Artillery*
> *Mustered Into U.S. Service On This Field*
> -------------------
> *Erected A.D. 1912*
> *Erected by the Survivors*

This was the second monument erected to commemorate the regiment. The first, erected by the State of Connecticut at Arlington National Cemetery sixteen years earlier, largely recognized the combat experience of the men. The 1912 Litchfield monument was the work of the veterans, who, with great poignancy, termed themselves "the survivors." The regiment—which had begun its career as the 19th Connecticut Infantry before being converted into a heavy artillery unit—suffered terribly in its first battle at Cold Harbor, Virginia, on June 1, 1864, sustaining more than 300 casualties in approximately one hour of fighting. At Winchester, Virginia, in September 1864, the regiment performed heroically in a great Union victory, as it would again one month later at the strategically important triumph at Cedar Creek. More than 420 of the regiment's men would die in the war, with hundreds more wounded or the victims of debilitating diseases.

Why construct a monument in a farmer's field in Connecticut rather than on the battlefields of Virginia? That is the question at the heart of this book. Camp Dutton represented something significant to these men and their community. Of the monument's dedication, Governor Baldwin said, "So from Camp Dutton, 50 years ago, went out some who are here before me, and many another who was never to return."[1] Baldwin hints that at Camp Dutton the men began the shared experience that defined their lives: the transformation from civilians to Union army soldiers. Here they formed friendships that lasted half a century or were, perhaps, ended in a flash of Confederate rifle fire. Here the enormous exertions of the county—financial, political and in human resources—resulted in the great patriotic act of sending its men off to war. Here the debate and dissent that had marked the previous two years transformed into a brief moment of unity in support of the war effort.

The story of the raising of the 19th Connecticut Infantry is both a remarkable one and one that took place in virtually every county in the North in the summer of 1862. For mobilization to be successful, all members of the community needed to be involved. Obviously there was a role for military leaders, but there were also roles for women. Teachers and ministers made fine military recruiters. Successfully raising a regiment required enormous financial commitments, both from a community at large and from wealthy residents who pledged funds from their own fortunes. Additionally, during the Civil War, political leaders made a decision that dissent needed to be stamped out for the war effort to succeed. This book explores how one Northern community—Litchfield County, Connecticut—carried out these processes of mobilization. In doing so, it provides a better understanding not only of the Northern homefront but also of how the role of the community in raising a Civil War regiment established a strong connection between that homefront and the men on the battle lines. The efforts and sacrifices made by civilians to send others to war led to a deep and personal connection with the regiment. Those at home actively sought news about the men at war. Newspapers pleaded with their readers to share soldier letters for the entire community to read. Great effort and organization was put into sending what would later be called care packages to soldiers on a regular basis. Civilians shared the soldiers' triumphs and ached over their defeats. At the heart of these connections was the shared experience of mobilization. It was not just a military event; it involved all aspects of a community.

During the course of the Civil War, President Abraham Lincoln made twelve separate calls for troops. This book touches on five of those, with an emphasis on two: the July 1, 1862 call for 300,000 volunteers to serve for three years and the August 4, 1862 call for another 300,000 men to serve for nine months. It begins by examining how Litchfield County reacted politically to Lincoln's election, the secession crisis and the coming of the war. The earliest days of the war brought the expected surge of patriotism but also dissent from almost every corner of the county. The service to the country by the first volunteers was supported by the extraordinary efforts of women, which occasionally took on political tones. The story climaxes in the summer of 1862, as a military crisis for the Union necessitated an unprecedented call for manpower. Juxtaposed with the calls for patriotism and duty were financial incentives at levels previously unseen, and for every man who rallied to the flag, seemingly another sought out an examining surgeon for an exemption from service.

A note on sources is necessary. Because the 19th Connecticut was conceived as a regiment raised within a single county, and because its training took place in the center of that county, the men did not travel far upon first enlisting. This allowed for thousands of people—family, friends and the curious—to travel to the camp to see the regiment train. Consequently, there are few soldier letters that cover this period. Therefore, this study's exploration of enlistment and training is heavily dependent on the letters or diaries of six men: Homer Curtiss, a farmer from Warren; James Deane, an East Canaan minister; Michael Kelly, an Irish immigrant who worked in manufacturing in Sharon; Edward Roberts, a Canaan carriage maker; David Soule, a New Milford carpenter; and Theodore Vaill, a Litchfield farmer. All were in their twenties except for the thirty-year-old Vaill.

These men represent different backgrounds, levels of education and towns within the county. To establish the cultural and political climate of the county, I read deeply into the three newspapers that serviced the region. These were the *Housatonic Republican*, based in Falls Village; the *Litchfield Enquirer*; and the *Winsted Herald*. While all three were supportive of the Republican Party, they were also highly parochial; there was no love lost between the *Enquirer* and the *Herald*. Archival materials—enlistment records, financial information, diaries, sermons and more—and the 1860 census help us understand, in broad strokes, the motivations of those who enlisted and those who did not.

Chapter 1

"Wide Awake"

The scene was surreal, even to the oldest residents of Winsted, Connecticut, who may have cherished faint memories of the Revolutionary War. An eerie glow reflected off the houses and storefronts, windows mirrored the flames that burned in the streets and whiffs of burning oil wafted across air already heavy with smells of an industrial community. Gray-clad men intoning ritualized songs capped off the panorama. Politics in the mid-nineteenth century was rambunctious, intensely competitive and sometimes violent. Voters could expect candidates to launch libelous assaults on their opponents, while the newspapers—creatures of political parties—joined the fray. But those who heard the commotion outside and rushed to their windows on Saturday, September 1, 1860, witnessed something completely different—inspiring or apocalyptic, depending on one's political views. There, on Main Street, were the Wide Awakes, spirited young Republicans clad in quasi-military uniforms, carrying flaming torches while marching in step with the songs they were singing. Devoted to their party and its presidential nominee, Abraham Lincoln, these Wide Awakes were part of a national movement, born in Hartford, designed to whip up excitement for the coming election. "The boys are getting enthusiastic," the *Winsted Herald* reported, "and are bound to have some torches which will *burn*....All Republicans are requested to come out and aid in kindling the camp-fires on Saturday evening."

While political rancor was to be expected, this combination of party activism and militancy was something new, perhaps even frightening,

A membership certificate for a Wide Awake club. Note the military appearance of their uniforms. *Library of Congress.*

in Connecticut, known even then as the Land of Steady Habits. And if Connecticut was a state that prided itself on its traditions and reluctance to change, those sentiments were especially true of its far northwest corner, Litchfield County. This was rugged country, and its apparent economic worthlessness has led historian Rachel Carley to term it "the last, worst acreage" in Connecticut. Still, the county's enterprising settlers used its swampy meadows to fatten cattle for sale in New York City. Later, iron ore was discovered, and with ample supplies of trees for charcoal, the economics of the northwestern reaches of the county became tied firmly to the iron industry, earning the region the nickname "Arsenal of the Revolution."[1]

By 1860, however, the county's population and economy had somewhat stagnated. In the wake of the Revolution, many Litchfield County residents fled the region's rocky soil for the presumed greener pastures of Ohio. Between 1800 and 1860, the population of Litchfield County grew by only 15 percent, compared to an 83 percent increase in the state of Connecticut and a whopping 500 percent climb in the population of the United States. The county's population as a whole stood at 47,318 in 1860, with its largest towns being New Milford (3,535), Winchester (3,513) and Plymouth (3,244). But while the towns that were at the heart of the iron industry—Salisbury, Cornwall, Canaan, Kent and Warren, for example—saw their populations stay flat or even decrease, towns like Winsted, Torrington and Plymouth, which had developed industries linked to water-driven manufacturing, were growing.

New industries required new workers, and in many cases employers looked to immigrants to fill their ranks. Soon, echoes of French, Cockney accents and Irish brogues lilted among the hills and valleys of Litchfield County. The town of Sharon, for example, had 2,566 residents in 1860; about 300 of them were foreign-born, with the majority of those being from Ireland. Despite these new dynamics, Litchfield County residents had justifiable reasons for believing that their towns were being left behind in the whirlwind of growth—especially urbanization and industrialization—that marked Northern society in the antebellum years.

Outside of the emergence of new industrial centers, few of these trends were evident in Litchfield County. The iron industry, which had fueled much of the region's economic growth over the previous century, was being consolidated. The acquisition of the county's mines and furnaces by the Barnum and Richardson Company mirrored a nationwide trend in which wealth was increasingly concentrated in the hands of a few. Furthermore, other parts of the country were now producing higher-quality iron, superior for producing the precision products now in demand in the nation's factories. The Panic of 1857, which led to widespread bankruptcies and unemployment, hit Connecticut's industries particularly hard, with production and wages still at recessed levels when the Wide Awakes paraded through Winsted in September 1860.[2]

The rising political turmoil of the 1850s led to further concern for Litchfield County's industries. Would the political rifts opened by the issue of slavery lead to economic rifts between North and South? If so, the South might look elsewhere to purchase the clocks, cutlery and iron products that powered the county's economy. Signs that the political upheaval sweeping the nation could have economic ramifications for the Nutmeg State abounded, especially after Torrington native John Brown's October 1859 raid on Harpers Ferry, Virginia. While the *Litchfield Enquirer* referred to Brown as the "Hero of the Drama," many Connecticut business leaders expressed concerns about the degree to which the raid might increase the rift between North and South and speculated on its potential financial impact.[3]

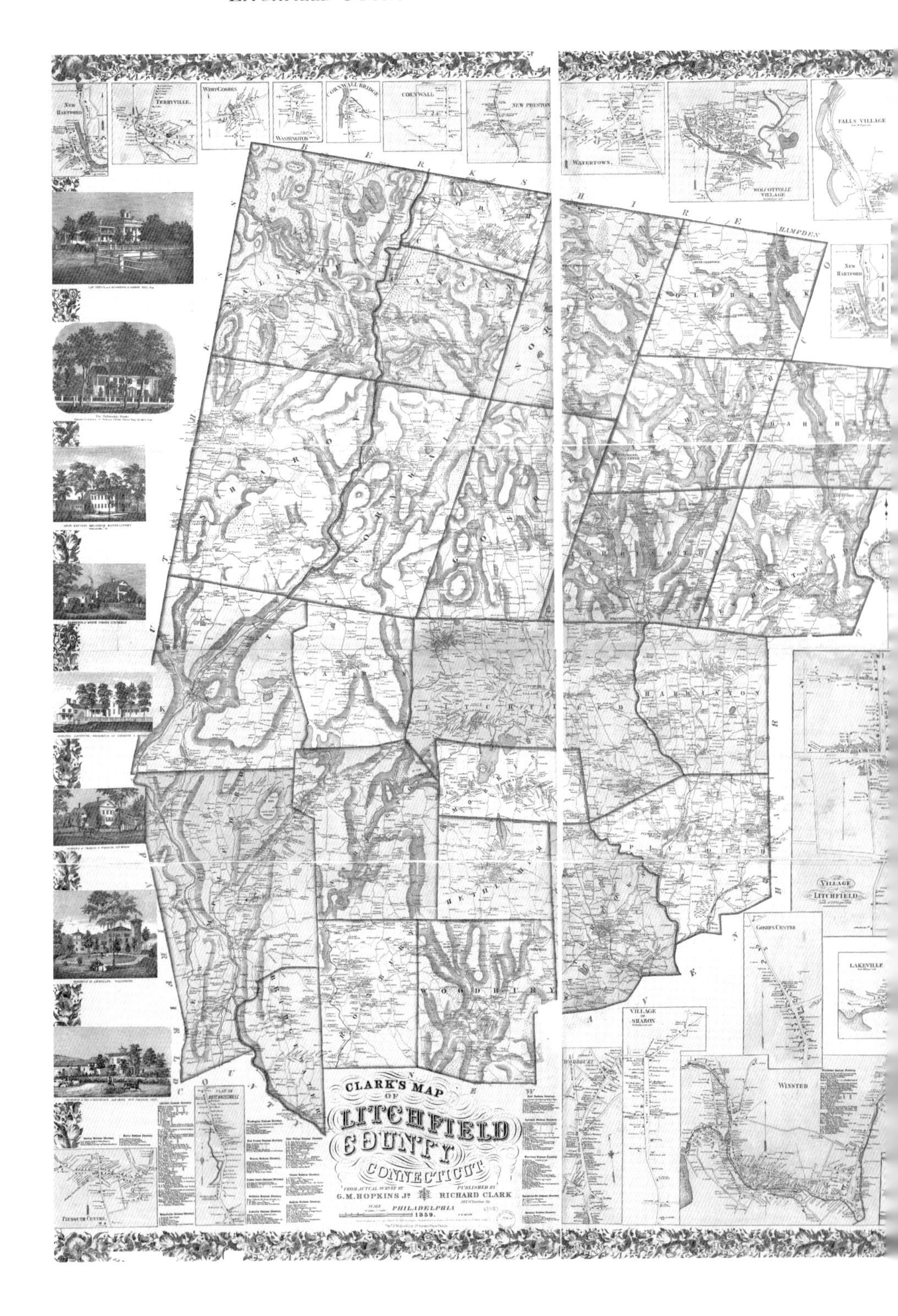
NEW HARTFORD
TERRYVILLE
WEST GOSHEN
CORNWALL BRIDGE
CORNWALL
WASHINGTON
NEW PRESTON
WATERTOWN
WOLCOTTVILLE VILLAGE
FALLS VILLAGE
HAMPDEN
NEW HARTFORD
VILLAGE OF LITCHFIELD
GOSHEN CENTRE
LAKEVILLE
VILLAGE OF SHARON
WOODBURY
WINSTED
PLYMOUTH CENTRE
CLARK'S MAP OF LITCHFIELD COUNTY CONNECTICUT
FROM ACTUAL SURVEY BY G.M. HOPKINS Jr.
PUBLISHED BY RICHARD CLARK
PHILADELPHIA
1859.

Along with stagnant populations and economic concerns, religious changes added to the societal anxiety of the region. In no other arena had Litchfield County contributed as much to the nation's history as in religion. The county had been home to noted Congregational ministers Joseph Bellamy and Lyman Beecher. It was the birthplace of the famed Second Great Awakening preacher Charles Grandison Finney and of liberal theologian Horace Bushnell. The county's fathers, descendants of the Puritans, sought to bring the notion of the "City on the Hill" with them to their new home, establishing churches, schools and a social safety net. By the mid-nineteenth century, however, the increasing number of Catholic immigrants and the fading hold of the Second Great Awakening was threatening the religious fabric of the county. A survey completed by ministers in 120 of the state's nearly 170 towns found that close to one-third of native-born residents of Connecticut's rural areas never attended church, while in the manufacturing centers, that number was only one-sixth.[4]

Meanwhile, other civic institutions grew in prominence. Education was deeply valued, with many towns having more than a dozen one-room schoolhouses. Furthermore, most communities had an academy that specialized in preparing young men for college. In the case of towns in northwestern Connecticut, these colleges were often Williams College or Yale. Sarah Pierce's Litchfield Female Academy and the Morris Academy in the South Farms section of Litchfield (after 1859 the town of Morris) were revolutionary in their education of young women. Civic organizations and sports teams were growing in number and were frequently reported on in newspapers.[5]

Northerners were also deeply invested in their increasingly democratic government. In northwestern Connecticut and across the North, "a high percentage of the eligible male population of any town was very likely to have been a member of the town council, commissioner of roads, or mayor." With no formal law enforcement below the level of county sheriff, citizens formed posses to keep the peace. They cared for their poor through the creation of town farms, served on juries and participated in town meetings. But more than anything, they voted. Voter participation rates across the North often approached 85 percent in the two decades

Clark's Map of Litchfield County, Connecticut, 1859. *Library of Congress.*

Torrington native John Brown, whose 1859 raid on Harpers Ferry, Virginia, was a catalyst of the war. *Library of Congress.*

before and after the Civil War. These voters strongly identified with their political party, and splitting a ticket was extremely rare.[6]

In 1860, loyalty to the party meant that Litchfield County, with nearly equal numbers of Democrats and Republicans, was the scene of particularly heated elections. As slavery became a more contentious issue following the Missouri Crisis of 1819–20, Litchfield County's political landscape grew increasingly complicated, with slavery existing in small numbers until 1830, the rise of abolitionism and strong anti-abolitionism pockets in some corners. A 1774 colonial census enumerated 331 slaves in the county, and advertisements for runaway slaves appeared in local newspapers. While the numbers of enslaved persons in the county fell in the decades following the passage of Connecticut's gradual emancipation law in 1784, the decline was partly attributable to enslaved persons being sold to plantations in the South rather than being freed. Seven slaves remained in the town of Litchfield in 1800; slavery was completely gone in that town by 1810, but the 1830 census showed one slave remaining in both Goshen and Sharon. Yet those who stated their antislavery views risked violent responses, as happened at a meeting in Torrington in 1837 or when noted abolitionist Abby Foster Kelley visited Cornwall in 1838.[7]

Still, the abolitionist fervor in the county cannot be overlooked; it was, after all, the native soil of both John Brown and Harriet Beecher Stowe. In part due to the impact of Stowe's *Uncle Tom's Cabin*, slavery increasingly became a moral issue in the 1850s, and in Litchfield County and across the North, those who sought greater government intervention against the institution of slavery were increasingly drawn to the fledgling Republican Party.[8]

As the 1860 presidential election loomed, Litchfield County residents had much to be anxious about. There were fears that sectional squabbling could worsen an already stagnating economy. Even religion, once the hallmark of the county and its greatest contribution to the nation's history, seemed on the decline. The civic foundations of each community—institutions like town meetings, elections, juries and public school—brought continuity and comfort to county residents. Thus when the nationwide clash over slavery posed a threat to these institutions, citizens would have to decide how they would defend them.

Most Americans in 1860 learned of the changes sweeping their nation from their local newspapers. There were, in that year, three thousand different newspapers being published in the United States, more than double the number published in 1835.[9] Litchfield County was serviced by three weekly newspapers: the *Housatonic Republican* (published in Falls Village), the *Litchfield Enquirer* and the *Winsted Herald*.

Two facts are essential for understanding how Litchfield County's newspapers shaped public sentiment. First, like so many newspapers across the country, the region's three papers were strongly partisan in their politics. All three supported the Republican Party and used as their foil the Democratic *Bridgeport Daily Advertiser and Farmer*. (The notion of an impartial press in the United States arose primarily in the twentieth century.) Second, newspapers of that period openly stole from one another. It was hard work to fill three papers with news from the sleepy northwest corner of Connecticut, and the editors often copied stories, with or without attribution, from other newspapers. News from the *Enquirer*, which appeared on Thursdays, often appeared in Friday's *Herald*. And this practice didn't cease at the local level, so that news spread across the country from newspaper to newspaper.[10]

It should not be assumed, however, that because most newspapers came out only once a week that mid-nineteenth-century Americans did not crave news the other six days. They were living in the midst of an information revolution brought about by innovations in printing and the invention of the telegraph, and their desire for the latest developments was increasingly insatiable. As a result, Americans in the mid-nineteenth century were inveterate gossips. To gain the latest news, residents of Connecticut's smaller towns often pooled resources to hire couriers to ride to the bigger cities and bring bundles of newspapers back. Finally, there was a reliance on ministers to spread not only the word of God from the pulpit but also the latest news.[11] When war broke out, ministers in Litchfield County would become some of the most effective recruiting agents.

When Litchfield County's residents opened their newspapers early in 1860, they were confronted with the threat of Southern secession. Such threats were not new; one section of the country or another had been warning that it was about to break with the Union since the Alien and Sedition Acts of 1798. Thus, it is uncertain how seriously newspaper readers viewed stories like this one in the February 16, 1860 edition of the *Enquirer*:

> *We every day hear of the disaffection of the South toward the North, expressed in various ways,—in the suppression of free speech, almost of free thought, upon the subject of northern institutions and the prevailing sentiment here…describable, finally, in the thousand and one threats we hear of what the South will do in case a President is elected in a legal way, by a majority of the votes of legal citizens, in all which we find a tendency toward a final, fierce, civil dissension, unless this tendency is speedily checked.*[12]

Purposeful or not, this article situated the increasing militancy of the South as a threat to the beloved foundations of the North's civic culture. And while the *Enquirer* and most northern papers would later dismiss the seriousness of threats of secession, stories like this certainly brought home to Litchfield County readers the possibility of the dissolution of the Union and civil war.

In the spring of 1860, the biggest news in the county's three papers was the pending gubernatorial election. Prior to 1875, Connecticut's governors served one-year terms, with elections on the first Monday in April. In April 1858, William Alfred Buckingham, a successful businessman and former mayor of Norwich, was elected as the state's twenty-sixth governor. With Buckingham's victory, Republicans took control of the state's government. Buckingham won reelection in 1859.

Buckingham's 1860 reelection campaign was national news, as its early date made it a bellwether for the presidential election in November. The importance of the election was not lost on the Democrats, who nominated Thomas Seymour, a former governor, congressman and Mexican-American War hero who, as President James Buchanan's minister to Russia, was a nationally known figure.[13]

To counter Democratic enthusiasm, Republicans brought in a rising star to rally voters. Abraham Lincoln, campaigning on behalf of Republicans in New York and New Hampshire, received an urgent request to add Connecticut to his campaign swing: "You have a special call there, & a duty to perform." Lincoln made five speeches in Connecticut and repeatedly stated

Governor William A. Buckingham. *Library of Congress.*

that the issue of slavery—the "great political question of the nation"—could not be avoided. He gave voice to what Litchfield native Harriet Beecher Stowe had made clear to the country in her 1852 work, *Uncle Tom's Cabin*, that slavery was "a great moral, social and political evil." Still, Lincoln in 1860 was no radical and did not seek the total destruction of slavery; rather, he sought only to contain it.[14]

While Lincoln's message had broad appeal, in Connecticut it was especially popular with a group of young men who termed themselves the Wide Awakes. Their name likely derived from their service as bodyguards for Republican candidates campaigning in Democratic strongholds. Five members of the Wide Awakes attended Lincoln's Hartford speech and, energized by his message, escorted him by torchlight to the home of Mayor Tom Allyn afterward. Thus began a movement that would sweep the North in the next eight months.[15]

If the eyes of the nation were looking to Connecticut as a bellwether, they received a glimpse into the great political divisions that had opened over the past decade. Buckingham won reelection to a third term, but by only 541 votes. While Buckingham outpolled Seymour by a similar margin in Litchfield County, the Democrat carried the town of Litchfield. The county's most popular Republican, Sheriff Leverett Wessells, received 10 more votes than his Democratic opponent. Republicans, triumphant but perhaps worried about the razor-thin margin of Buckingham's victory, looked at the fact that ten thousand more residents voted in Connecticut's 1860 election than had the previous year and determined that energizing these voters would be a key to success in November, when Lincoln himself would be on the ballot.[16]

The firing of cannons, marking the reappearance of the Wide Awakes, awakened residents to the fact that the general election was upon them. That group had grown rapidly from the five men who accompanied Lincoln through Hartford, while also becoming more militaristic in appearance and action. The Wide Awakes marched through towns and cities carrying kerosene torches and wearing black capes and oilcloth caps to keep the fuel off them. Others noted that these capes made it easier for them to fight if necessary. Advertisements trumpeted the uniform to young Republicans for only $1.75. With meetings, drills and parades, membership in the Wide Awakes gave a sense of belonging to the young men, who also felt the excitement of civic participation. As historian John Niven pointed out, with Democratic leaders paying surrogates to cause trouble, the Wide Awakes also felt "the added thrill of mild danger."[17]

The first major county rally of Wide Awakes, described at the beginning of this chapter, was held on September 1, 1860. The language used by the *Herald* in anticipation of the event was strikingly militaristic: the Wide Awakes would "close up their ranks for the battle which is fast approaching," and they would rely upon "aid and comfort" from the "veterans and 'war horses' in the Republican ranks." The purpose of the event was clear: "the promise to do their part towards giving a rousing majority for Lincoln and [vice presidential candidate Hannibal] Hamlin in old Winchester." One week later, the Winsted Wide Awakes were preparing for another event, this one at Clarke's Hall, for which they ordered six dozen uniforms, elected thirteen officers and established an executive committee of twenty men.[18]

Similar movements were afoot in other towns. A "Wide Awake Club of earnest young Republicans" met in the county courthouse in Litchfield on September 6 "to complete further arrangements for effective organization and drill." The forty men present at the meeting set to work ordering

Litchfield, circa 1861. *Collection of the Litchfield Historical Society, Litchfield, Connecticut.*

"complete regalia" from Hartford and selected not only organizational officers—a president, three vice-presidents, a secretary and a treasurer—but also a commandant, a first lieutenant, a second lieutenant and a third lieutenant. These latter officers were to be in charge of training the men in military-style drill. By late September, seventy men from Salisbury had joined the Wide Awakes, and another group was active in Bethlehem. Soon, the various clubs began marching to other towns in the county for larger rallies. The Litchfield men marched to Goshen on October 8 for a rally featuring speeches by Congressman Orris S. Ferry and other local dignitaries. Two nights later, the Litchfield Wide Awakes rallied in their hometown, joined by men from Plymouth, who brought a brass band with them.[19]

As the election approached, the Wide Awake rallies became larger and more dramatic, especially as the results of elections in other states made a Lincoln victory seem likely. In Litchfield, the Wide Awake rally of October 11 was described as "a demonstration such as is rarely seen in Litchfield, and such as no political party has attempted for many years." A cannon was brought to town and "from sunset until after midnight, belched forth its loud thunders in honor of the glorious chain of States which had declared in thunder tones for Lincoln and Liberty."

The last speaker of the night was Stephen Deming, considered the patriarch of the Republican Party in town. Nearing eighty years old, Deming was still capable of exciting a crowd, for at the end of his speech, a motion was made for the Wide Awakes to escort Deming home. The men spilled outside and lit their torches. The Tompkins Brass Band of Waterbury moved to the front of the line as the cannon continued to roar. It was clearly a memorable night. "There is nothing, in our opinion," the *Litchfield Enquirer* reported, "quite so beautiful as a torchlight procession at night, but when it lights up a seeming forest of trees as it did on Thursday night, the witchery of the scene becomes enchantment and the graceful swaying of the gilded with light as they stood."[20]

While the classic image of the Wide Awakes is of young men wearing something akin to military garb and carrying torches, the movement in Litchfield County also involved women. If the participation of these women was less overt and less vocal than that of men, they nonetheless used the means available to them to enter the sphere of politics. The October 12 edition of the *Winsted Herald* reported that "the ladies in many places, we noticed by our exchanges, honor and encourage the Wide Awake Clubs by presenting them with handsome banners. Such a gift would tickle our boys amazingly, and they deserve it. Nuff sed [*sic*]." Despite its patronizing tone, this article makes it clear that these women had no qualms about publicizing their political leanings. At a rally in Wolcottville (Torrington) during the last week of October, a "lady of the village" dedicated a poem to that town's Wide Awakes. The author's name has been lost to history, but she clearly believed that there was a role for women in politics:

We are all wide awake here! The Ladies and All,
We are all wide awake here, rich and poor, great and small,
Some who slept a long time, have just spread their eyes—
And think in good earnest, 'tis time to rise.

Women, while not allowed to vote by law and discouraged by social custom from voicing their opinions in public, found other ways to influence voters.[21]

On November 6, 1860, ninety-four-year-old Captain Salmon Buell of Litchfield voted for Abraham Lincoln for president. He had voted for George Washington in the nation's first election. Of this the *Enquirer* proclaimed, "A long life of a freeman begun nobly and ending nobly!"

Lincoln carried the Electoral College, taking Connecticut's six electoral votes by winning 54 percent of the vote. In Litchfield County, Lincoln won

60 percent of the popular vote. The *Enquirer* celebrated: "The figures speak for themselves! The great voice of the people speaks with thunder tones! Liberty is NATIONAL and ETERNAL—slavery sectional and doomed." A closer examination of the figures leads to a more ambiguous conclusion. In the town of Litchfield, Lincoln garnered 323 votes; his three opponents polled 310 votes. Politically, the town was deeply divided.[22]

National discussions quickly turned to talk of secession, news from the South and demands that there be no compromises. Even the topic of civil war was approached in a matter-of-fact manner. The North had nothing to worry about: "The three counties of New Haven, Hartford and Fairfield have a larger white population than the entire state of South Carolina." The tone of the newspapers became more serious with each passing week in November. In South Carolina, "Secession badges are universal. Not a ship in the harbor flies the Federal flag." There were reports of resignations of southerners from federal positions and of the worsening military situation in Charleston, South Carolina. The *Enquirer* summarized the situation by stating that "a madness seems to have seized upon the Southern people and the fiery flame of Disunion appears to penetrate all the Cotton states." Still, the papers were adamant in their opposition to proposed compromises that would guarantee slavery and the perpetuation of the Fugitive Slave Act in exchange for a promise from southern states not to secede.[23]

All speculation ended with news of South Carolina's secession on December 20, which was followed in turn by six additional Southern states over the ensuing six weeks. This dramatic action did not result in apocalyptic reactions. Rather, the *Litchfield Enquirer* responded with satire. In the same December 27 issue that reported secession, the paper ran an advertisement for a runaway slave named Palmetto (symbolizing South Carolina), who had absconded from his owner, Uncle Sam. Furthermore, a lengthy piece of satire proclaimed that the Harris Plains section of Litchfield was seceding from the town because of the "refusal of the people of Litchfield to build the great Pacific Rail Road through our borders, as they promised." It is clear that the county's newspapers—perhaps reflecting the widespread attitudes of county residents—believed that the secession crisis was a matter of hysteria, a frenzy from which cooler heads would soon prevail. This is reflected in the New Year's messages delivered in the newspapers and from pulpits. The *Enquirer* reflected:

> *We cannot know what the year 1861 may have in store for us, but it is certain that through the clouds and storms which threaten us as an*

> *undivided people now at the outset of the year, before the end a light shall break upon us, the storm of strife shall cease, and after all we shall be again more firmly a united and prosperous nation than we were, even when 1860 dawned upon us….A very excellent Democrat, one of the stiff blue and true blue, said in our office the other day, that he would willingly and gladly be one of a hundred men from Litchfield to go down South and "mop those traitors clean out." He said he would willingly start to-day, shoulder his gun, and risk his life in the defense of his country, and hang every one of the secessionists.*

That the nation—or even the county—would be healed quickly was chimerical. Within weeks, an election for a seat in the U.S. House of Representatives was held, and all hints of bipartisanship vaporized. Republican incumbent Orrin Ferry kicked off his campaign by assaulting Buchanan's plan for a Constitutional Convention "so as to afford the people of slaveholding states adequate guarantees for the security of their rights!" The *Enquirer*, parroting Ferry, responded, "Oh! What a spectacle of weak-minded temporizing, of want of patriotism, of cowardly shirking of duty, or miserable sniffling is exhibited here." Democrat George Woodruff won the election and was soon after asked by the *Enquirer* if he would "support the [Lincoln] Administration in its efforts to maintain the Government"; the congressman-elect refused to answer. The election portended the political divisiveness that would be a hallmark of the county over the next year.[24]

Chapter 2

"War Fever"

The crowd grew larger and more restless with each passing hour. Those who had arrived early had a spot inside the small store next to the county jail in Litchfield that housed the town's telegraph machine. They received the news first, directly from the operator, and relayed it to their friends and neighbors—"eager knots," the *Enquirer* called them—who had spilled out into the street. Increasingly, it appeared that the event they had feared had, in fact, materialized. At 4:30 in the morning of April 12, 1861, Confederate forces in Charleston, South Carolina, fired on Fort Sumter. Word buzzed along telegraph lines, all of which remained in service between the Confederate and United States. The news reached New Haven early that Friday morning. Continuous telegraphic updates meant that Connecticut's daily newspapers printed several editions throughout the day.[1] One word was on everyone's lips: "War!"

The fact that rumors of war had turned to reality came as a relief for some. As early as February 1861, militia units were being formed in anticipation, notably a Norfolk rifle company trained by Captain Hinman.[2] Now there was no doubt that Sumter meant a rebellion. While the firing on Sumter released a hysteria of patriotism across the North, that unity evaporated quickly in Litchfield County. Over the next seventeen months—up to the time the 19th Connecticut Infantry departed for war—northwestern Connecticut would see extraordinary acts of both patriotism and dissent. Little of the dissent would be remembered, contrasting as it did with the stories of heroism and duty that the Civil War generation wanted to remember.

The opening shots of the Civil War—Fort Sumter, Charleston, South Carolina, April 12, 1861—as depicted in *Harper's Weekly*. *Library of Congress.*

Still, in the immediate wake of Sumter, the county was gripped by a patriotic fervor. Sermons emanating from county pulpits fueled this and served as centerpieces for civic gatherings across the county, taking their place alongside the singing of "My Country, 'Tis of Thee" and "The Star-Spangled Banner." Reverend George Richards, minister at Litchfield's Congregational Church, preached on "The War" on April 28. It was so popular that he was asked to present it a second time, this time for the entire town. Americans at the time—caught up in a wave of millennialism and apocalyptic beliefs—were quick to see the war as God's will. Loyalty to their nation became an extension of their loyalty to God, and they believed that prayer would bring military victory.[3]

Patriotism took more secular forms as well. Directions appeared in newspapers detailing the proper way to make an American flag, which soon appeared everywhere in the county. In April, the Sharon Young Republicans erected an eighty-five-foot-tall flagpole on the town green, and an eighty-foot-high pole appeared in Colebrook. Not to be outdone, Litchfield residents purchased a "splendid American Flag 30 x 20 feet…and a pole 120 feet high has been engaged, and will be erected during this week or next, within the central Park" of the town. "The ensign will thereafter float triumphantly from one of the highest points in the state, and over a people who would die to defend it." However, when three weeks had passed and the flagpole had not been erected, the *Enquirer* took on an angrier tone:

> *We are tired of seeing that "pole" recumbent before our window. Tuesday came and went, but...no pole raising, no enthusiastic crowd of two thousand.... When are we going to have the pole raised? It is here, the flag is here, the ground is handy, but unless some of our patriotic citizens take hold of the pole, we fear it will long lay reclining on the cold, cold ground, and will there greet our volunteers, three years hence, when they return "home from the wars." When shall we have a raising?*

The pole was finally erected in Litchfield in June. Salisbury had no such problems expressing its patriotism. The center of town was the scene of military drill and of a "great pole and flag raising." As the flag was raised, the townspeople collectively swore an oath: "With uplifted hands and uncovered brow in the presence of Almighty God, we swear eternal fidelity to that flag. We pledge ourselves to God and each other to protect and defend it, against all enemies, at all times, in all places and under all

The "Game of the Rebellion," representative of the "war fever" that swept the county in 1861. *Collection of the Litchfield Historical Society, Litchfield, Connecticut.*

circumstances, with the last dollar of our money and the last drop of our blood." In their patriotic exuberance, most believed that the war would be short. The *Enquirer* predicted at the end of May that "in three months at the farthest, the United States Government will have resumed undisputed sovereignty in all the present 'seceded' states...and the year of our Lord 1861 will have seen the termination...of the rattlesnake rebellion against the most righteous government that exists upon the face of the earth."[4]

Not only was there a surge of patriotism in the county, but the landscape took on a military appearance as well. This was evident in the traveling entertainment that was a hallmark of that era. On June 2, the Young America Troops, commanded by Captain David Baldwin, appeared in Litchfield. This was a Zouave company (so named for the French military troops fashionable at the time) that specialized in showy military drill. Decked out "in their red shirts, and with drum and colors," they "presented a most interesting and credible appearance." The appearance of military companies in the towns, as well as the drilling on town greens, helped prepare county residents for the realities of war. The extent to which a militaristic outlook permeated daily life is evident from a May 1862 public notice from Litchfield's animal warden:

> *Headquarters, Army of Occupation*
> *Litchfield Court House, May 19th, 1862*
> *A Proclamation*
>
> *General Orders No 1:*
> *Having been, by the free and sovereign people of Litchfield, elevated, promoted and installed into the important and highly responsible office of Hayward for the year ensuing, I have thought it advisable to make known to the rebels, in a public manner, the rules that I intend to inaugurate in this department of official trust and honor.*
>
> *1) All animals that are suffered to run at large in the streets in the night season will be declared contraband and be sent to Fort Wells for safe protection....All citizens are hereby called upon to aid the commanding officers in enforcing these rules.*
>
> *Henry B. Graves,*
> *Commanding the Forces of Litchfield Hill*

If this notice is tongue-in-cheek, it is equally clear that its audience would have to be familiar with both military cadence and terminology to get the joke. In the years to come, militaristic language would be used not only for reporting and recruiting but also for selling everyday items.[5]

Less humorous but equally powerful in its patriotism was an appeal in the May 2 *Enquirer* titled "What Farmers Can Do": "You who can not shoulder the musket for the defence of Freedom and Truth in this glorious struggle, do not think you are to take no part in the great contest!" One month later, a local resident again urged farmers to not only embrace their patriotic role as providers for the troops but also relish the economic opportunities with which they were now blessed:

> *Troops must be fed and the people must eat though luxuries cannot be denied. The products of the field afford the necessary sustenance. The land must be tilled more vigorously and a fruitful season invoked and turned to the best account. The demand for agricultural products cannot cease. It is never more sure of a good market and an encouraging one.*

The message received from the pulpits, community gatherings and newspaper editorials was clear: "There is something for you to *do*—each of you, here among the rocks and hills of your country."[6]

What many men wanted to do was defend the Union. The day after the Federal forces at Fort Sumter surrendered, Lincoln issued a call for seventy-five thousand volunteers to put down the rebellion. Governor Buckingham was unquestionably the key figure in Connecticut's mobilization for war, and his decisiveness in aiding the Lincoln administration was instrumental in the early Federal war effort. Even before Sumter, Buckingham anticipated war and purchased weapons, ammunition and gunpowder, competing with southern buyers for the materiel. He was personally and deeply involved in the raising and outfitting of Connecticut's troops. The governor's concern was not only for the war effort writ large, but for the welfare of individual soldiers as well. Buckingham was fond of visiting training camps across the state, where he was known to ask, "Well boys, is there anything else I can do for you?" Once, when a man asked him to hurry up the paymaster, as the soldiers had not yet been paid, Buckingham wrote a personal check to the man. The governor pushed for legislation that allowed for soldiers to send any amount of their pay back home. On one January 1862 pay day, forty-five soldiers from Norfolk sent a total of $939 to their hometown, in care of attorney Peter Curtiss.[7]

For all of Buckingham's work, however, it is important to note that Connecticut's state forces were built at the town level. Governors had the legal authority to call for volunteers for state regiments, but the men were sent from towns, cities and counties. Because of this, few men from Litchfield County were present for the war's first major land battle. Given the county's relative distance from the state's major population centers—and the corresponding lag in communications—its men were generally too late to join one of Connecticut's first three regiments. Winsted—located on the direct railroad, telegraph and turnpike line to Hartford—was an exception. Lincoln's call for troops transited the North via the telegraph, so those who lived near a telegraph station heard of his April 15 message on Tuesday, April 16. War meetings took place across the state, with meetinghouses and public squares festooned with banners, bunting and flags. Speakers and bands stirred the crowd. Men poured forward, most driven by a sense of patriotism and love of the Union, believing, in the words of historian Philip Paludan, that they "benefited personally from the bounty that the nation created." While Connecticut's initial quota in response to Lincoln's call for 75,000 men was one regiment of 780 soldiers, the state raised three regiments, totaling nearly 2,400 men, within a month.[8]

The *Winsted Herald* reported that recruiting had gotten off to a slow start in that town and that attorney William Bidwell had suggested that Winsted, Collinsville and New Hartford jointly form a company. By Saturday, April 20, volunteers had started to come forward in larger numbers. Sunday, April 21, however, was a decisive day in this first experience of recruiting. Reverend Hiram Eddy of the town's Second Congregational Church delivered a powerful sermon on Samuel, chapter 4, verse 9: "Now be men and fight!" That evening, a town meeting was held, and private donors offered a bounty of five dollars (half a week's wages for a machinist in 1861) to any man who enlisted.[9]

As many as one hundred men from Winsted and its surrounding towns—and six of the twenty leaders of the town's Wide Awake club—enlisted. Among them was Samuel B. Horne, who, according to some legends, was the first man in Connecticut to enlist. This is almost certainly not true, as Horne enlisted on April 21 and was officially mustered into the army on May 7. The records of the 1st Connecticut Infantry indicate that hundreds of men enlisted prior to Horne; most of these, however, lived in Connecticut's bigger cities: Bridgeport, Hartford, New Haven or Norwich. Regardless, Horne (who at seventeen sidestepped the requirement that soldiers be eighteen) served out this ninety-day enlistment; returned home in August; reenlisted

A postwar photograph of Reverend Hiram Eddy. *Connecticut Historical Society.*

in the 11th Connecticut in October 1861; was wounded at Antietam, Cold Harbor and Chaffin's Farm; and won the Medal of Honor for delivering an important message while severely wounded.

The scene in Winsted on Monday, April 22, was just as patriotic paintings of the era depicted the departure of men in the North's larger cities. The *Winsted Herald* reported on the

> *suspension of business, the thronged streets, the banners and the martial strains, the procession of adventurous and patriotic youth through our streets to the depot (steps, by some, perhaps never to be retraced), that prayer from the platform of the station, listened to as was never prayer listened to before by this generation, the twice a thousand faces wet with tears which the manliest sought not to hide, the good-byes, short, but too long for choking voices to fully utter, and then, as the train wound slowly around the hill, the oppressive stillness, broken by now word, but only sounds and low-toned syllables of consolation.*

Reverend Eddy was not on the train. As his "brave words have given a glorious impetus to the enlistments of this vicinity, and [as his] heart is fully brave as his tongue," Eddy had been offered command of the company. He accepted immediately with the condition that he receive the blessing of his church to vacate his contract, a request that was denied. The regiment came close to losing one of its enlisted men as well, when John McDonald of Norfolk accidentally discharged his pistol. The bullet grazed his forehead, passed through his hat and came out over his ear. McDonald declared that he was "never born to be shot." Perhaps he was correct; he served three years in the war without a wound.[10]

Other meetings similar to that in Winsted occurred across the county. Litchfield, for example, held town meetings to inspire enlistments and raise taxes "for the equipment and support" of volunteers. The measure, which was approved unanimously, also provided funds "for the support of such families in this town as may be deprived of the support of any volunteer who has or may enlist in the army." This was the first of many times the selectmen of Litchfield went to the voters to appropriate money in support of the town's soldiers. Expenditures from the town would total more than $50,000 in the war.[11]

These first volunteers were treated as heroes in their communities. The *Enquirer* captured the spirit of the times in publishing a piece by local poet William Treat titled "The Fathers, the Union, and the Flag," which Treat "respectfully dedicated to the Volunteers of Old Litchfield, Conn." In linking the service of the county's young men with those of the Revolutionary era, Treat proclaimed:

Then arm, ye sons of sixty-one,
Nor dread a Patriot's grave,
Those blessings that our Fathers won,
Our duty is to save.

Arm, sons of Litchfield's noble sires!
Where still their colors wave,
The north loyalty inspires,
My country or my Grave!

With the notion of a patriot's grave merely a rhetorical exercise at this stage of the war, poetry of this sort, no matter how maudlin, brought out more volunteers. Soon, however, the notion of a soldier's death ceased being rhetorical. Private James Burton was one of the Winsted men swept up in the first patriotic outbursts following Sumter. At the time, Burton, twenty-four years old, likely would have said he was one of the lucky ones able to secure a place in one of Connecticut's first three regiments. He mustered into the United States Army on April 23, 1861. Twenty days later, he died of diphtheria; the regiment had not yet reached Washington. The first to die from Litchfield County, his funeral, with full military honors, was presided over by Reverend Eddy. A funeral cortege preceded by four horsemen in full uniform, guns at their shoulders but with their bayonets reversed in a sign of mourning, led the procession. Eddy's eulogy was less about Burton than it was a recruiting speech:

> *To the young men of this congregation—to the companions of his youth in business, I propound the questions, Who will make his place good? Who will stand where he stood? Who will grasp the weapons, fallen from his nerveless hand, and rush forward to the conflict? As for me I am ready to stand there when my country needs me. Let us resolve to make the place good of every one of our friends who may fall in this war for God and the Father land....The patriotism which kindles the heart of the young soldier in such a cause is regeneration.*

Historians continue to debate the causes that impelled men to volunteer for military service in the Civil War. It is clear, however, that in the spring of 1861, personal messages such as this from Eddy affected a man's decision to enlist.[12]

Fifty-three men from Litchfield County—most from Winsted, Norfolk or New Hartford who served in Company K of the 2nd Connecticut Infantry—entered the service early enough to see action at the Battle of Bull Run, fought on July 21, 1861, at Manassas, Virginia. They engaged Confederate forces for hours, but by the late afternoon, the routed Union army retreated to Washington. During the course of this, three more men from the county—all from Winchester—were made prisoners of war. Among them was Reverend Eddy. On June 15, Governor Buckingham appointed Eddy the chaplain of the 2nd. This time his congregation approved his departure, as well as promised to continue paying him throughout his absence. The *Winsted Herald* termed Eddy a "Hercules in physical aspects, he is through and through the ideal and incarnation of a Christian Patriot." A little more than a month later, he was a prisoner in Richmond, held at the Liggon Tobacco Factory. Initially, the news of the minister's capture was difficult to confirm. His oratorical abilities, however, were not forgotten. The *Herald* made the request that "if Mr. Eddy is a prisoner, that he may be allowed to preach just one sermon to the rebels, and that Jeff Davis, [General] Beauregard, &c., may be compelled to listen." Finally, Mrs. Eddy received a letter from a Confederate that Mr. Eddy was alive and in good health. Still, Eddy remained a central figure in the county's war news for more than a year. In September 1861, the *Herald* reported that Eddy "is doing good works among the prisoners," but due to an escape of other POWs, Eddy was moved to Castle Pinckney in Charleston, South Carolina, with "the more dangerous prisoners." As late as January 1862, the *Winsted Herald* was still reporting Mrs. Eddy's receipt of letters from her husband as news.[13]

Litchfield County responded to the news of the disaster at Bull Run in contradictory ways. First there was a surge in the numbers of men enlisting for the Union army. Then dissenters emerged across the county, some brazenly flying Confederate flags.

The same issue of the *Winsted Herald* that brought news of the Union disaster at Bull Run carried this report: "Enlistments for the Union army never went forward so rapidly as since the sad news of Sunday burst upon the county. To Arms! Is the universal shout....We needed such a defeat—we were getting magnanimously tender of rebels." Litchfield County men responded in force, and by the fall, hundreds of men had marched off to war in the 8th, 9th (a largely Irish unit), 11th and 13th Connecticut Regiments.[14]

Municipalities were either lauded or shamed for the numbers of recruits they sent off to war. By October, the *Herald* was making comparisons among the towns. Litchfield had at least seventy men serving in the army. New Hartford had one hundred men serving, claiming that was "her full share." Cornwall, "a little town of less than 2,000 inhabitants, has sent sixty, and is to send more men to the war." Particularly noteworthy in the editor's eyes was the "patriotic community" of South Norfolk. Composed of thirty-one voters in 1860 (women and those under twenty-one could not vote), it had by October 1861 already sent sixteen men off to war. The *Enquirer* doubted "if there is any locality that has done better than this" and particularly singled out Eliphalet Barden, "as more deserving of consideration at the hands of the U.S. Government than any other man" for having four sons and three sons-in-law in the army. Comparisons aside, the overriding sentiment from the towns was one of extraordinary pride when their men marched off to war.[15]

Still, no matter how many men stepped forward to serve, it was not enough for some. Alva Stone, a forty-three-year-old carriage maker from Litchfield, enlisted in the 8th Connecticut in early October 1861. He was soon writing to his wife, Lucy, questioning why other men weren't doing the same:

> *Why don't some of those lazy young men in Litchfield fill up that Company and start it off for the War?...What about our Winsted friends? What are Asa and father doing? Is Will blowing secession yet? If so let him do it at a safe distance from the Army. Why don't #### and his crowd join the Rebel Army and be done with it—they might as well x they would then act consistently....How about Mr. Vinton? Does he speak out for the Union as he used to? Where is Geo Thompson & his Virginia Stock?*

Stone sounded a note of concern about the rash of Confederate sympathizers who had appeared across the county. But he also displayed an alarming opinion, that those with Southern relatives could not be trusted. That Stone could, from great distances, recall who in the town had enlisted and who had not suggests how closely knit the community was and how many eligible men still had not volunteered for service.[16]

With the increase in the number of recruits came the first stirrings of a complaint that would last more than a year: Litchfield County was doing its part by sending its sons to war but was not being recognized with a proportionate number of officers. The *New Haven Palladium* reported in early March that four-fifths of Connecticut's troops in the field came from the state's 2nd and 4th (which included Litchfield County) Congressional Districts, while the 1st and 3rd Congressional Districts furnished four-fifths of the officers. "This, if so," the paper proclaimed, "is hardly a 'fair shake.'" Hard numbers demonstrated the truth in this remark. By May 1, Litchfield had furnished 107 privates and only 2 officers; the county as a whole had 38 officers and 1,172 privates. Early in the war, elections were held within regiments for officers. Since no company was made up primarily of Litchfield County men, officer slots were more often won by those from larger population centers.[17]

As the number of men from the county departing for war grew, so did the expenses for its towns. In addition to the bounties, money was appropriated for supplies for the volunteers and to support their families at home. As towns were under considerable pressure to meet their quotas for volunteers, women applying for relief had to demonstrate that the town had received credit for their husbands as soldiers. This became increasingly complicated, as towns competed for soldiers by offering larger bounties. Soldiers pondering enlisting in a different town would need to weigh that extra bounty money against the inability of their dependents to receive relief funds. Historian Judith Giesberg has found that to receive relief money, a woman's "behavior was carefully scrutinized" by the board administering the funds, even cutting off funds for "not acting as a virtuous wife would do." And while the local newspapers certainly trumpeted the war as a financial windfall for Litchfield County's farmers, that was not always the case. To survive, families across the North had to hire out their children or take in boarders, activities sure to draw the attention—and potentially the judgment—of their neighbors.[18]

All the economic news was not bleak, however. The *Herald* reported in May 1862 that "it is pleasant in several points of view to see" that bonds sold "during the dark days of the republic" were at that point earning a premium of 2 percent. And, of course, the war was good for some businesses. New England had more industrial firms than the entire Confederacy, and while Litchfield County was far from Connecticut's most industrialized area, it nonetheless contained key industries. The war increased demand for Salisbury iron, needed now for cannons and their ammunition. The Hotchkiss and Sons company of Sharon—which prior to the war had made combs, pins and various tools—converted its entire operation to artillery shells. In 1860, Andrew Hotchkiss, son of the company's founder, patented a new type of exploding shell that became the focus of production. Demand grew so great that in 1863 the company moved to a larger facility—and one nearer transportation centers—in Bridgeport. The Norfolk Hoe Company sold the government one thousand hoes for trench building in South Carolina. Torrington's cloth mills, among the largest in the state, set to work making uniforms, while Gail Borden's condensed milk factory converted to making jarred fruit.[19]

Perhaps no Litchfield County business was as closely associated with the Union war effort as the Ames Iron Works of Amesville. Horatio Ames was a visionary and a salesman who corresponded directly with Abraham Lincoln to secure Federal contracts for his products. A September 1862 visitor described production of an Ames cannon that fired a fifty-six-pound shell:

> *The gun is made in the use of two furnaces which are in full blast at the same time, and in the use of a drop hammer weighing six tuns* [sic], *and a bumper of twenty tuns* [sic] *power. Beginning with a mass of iron at the breech, it is added to by a series of weldings till of the required length a work occupying from four to six days. They are able to make about four welds a day. Perfectly solid, it has to be bored, turned and polished by lathes. As nearly as we could find out, their cost is about $35,000….If the gun be as powerful as the inventor claims it to be, there is nothing of the sort to compare with it in the civilized world.*

The gun was brought to the Washington Navy Yard, where it was test fired more than one thousand times without a problem. Not content with this success, Ames developed one of the largest cannons of the Civil War, capable of hurling a 125-pound shell more than five miles. Development costs for Ames ran more than $300,000, and when the war ended before a government contract was secured, Ames was ruined.[20]

The war—with its subsequent removal of many workers from local economies—also caused manpower shortages for industry. Barnum and Richardson, the iron company headquartered in Lime Rock, was producing large numbers of artillery pieces by 1863 and would have produced more but for a shortage of workers. The same was true at Alexander Holley's Salisbury facility, and Holley himself went to England to recruit ironworkers, with little success. Manufacturing operations increasingly employed women to meet their labor needs, a reality that was even more widespread on Litchfield County's farms.

For all the emphasis on industry, farming remained a key component of the region's economy. While the average New England farm consisted of only 109 acres, an increase in mechanization and the growth of the North's transportation system were boons to farming. With the number of men in the military increasing by the day, Litchfield County's women stepped into the void. Women, historian Philip Paludan wrote, "have always been the 'invisible farmers,' comprising over half the agrarian population and performing at least half the farm labor." Now women found that patriotism existed even "in the ordinary labors of tending the farm." The Civil War increased those percentages, with more than half of Northern farms losing a man to the army. In addition to the daily routines involving cooking, washing and child-rearing, women increasingly were charged with bringing in the crops. It was typical for farm women to be awake by four o'clock in the morning, with breakfast on the table by 5:30. Once the children were off

Cover art on envelopes encouraged women to contribute to the war effort. *Collection of the Litchfield Historical Society, Litchfield, Connecticut.*

to school, the farm work began: churning butter, tending to the garden and livestock and milking the cows. All of this was made more difficult by the need for horses for the military. George Kellogg of Winsted was named an agent of the Federal government for buying horses for the cavalry. He passed through his hometown in November 1861 with a herd of "25 very nice animals." Late afternoon meant dinner preparation followed by cleaning the house and preparing for the next day. Sleep came early, perhaps by 9:00 p.m. Of course, men leaving for war simply added to the burdens of their wives and daughters.[21]

The war brought both opportunities and hardship for Litchfield County women. Some found that the work their husbands had traditionally done on the farm was no harder than their own responsibilities. This was empowering, as was the experience of other women taking jobs in manufacturing for cash wages. Large numbers of women found a way to express their support for the war effort; concern for their own sons, fathers, husbands or sweethearts; and their political views through Ladies' Aid Societies. For other women, however, the loss of a spouse—even if temporarily to the army—led to a disconnect with the broader community. The numbers of women falling into the care of hospitals, asylums, town farms or even jails rose as the war progressed.[22]

As 1862 began, Litchfield County's men were increasingly engaged with the enemy under conditions in the South that were ripe for diseases. Not surprisingly, the pages of local papers increasingly brought news of deaths to its readers. Many Connecticut soldiers accompanied General Ambrose Burnside on an expedition to North Carolina's Outer Banks. As the troops rendezvoused for the expedition in Annapolis, Maryland, Halsey Roberts and Willard Evans, both of Norfolk, died of the measles. Nineteen-year-old Francis Barber of Litchfield fell ill with dropsy and died before reaching home. Cornwall's John Mills and Watertown's George H. Baker of the 8th Connecticut and Horatio Crandell of Colbrook and the 10th Connecticut died in mid-February. Private Payne Tyrell of the 13th Connecticut, a native of Litchfield, died of typhoid and was given the final honor of having his body returned to Connecticut by a "deputation of his comrades." "He was a bright manly fellow," the *Enquirer* reported, "and his early death is greatly regretted." Of the deaths of friends and neighbors, sixteen-year-old Charles Plumb of Litchfield was moved to write, "Harris Plains is giving its full share of noble ones to death and now it has given up one who all must admit made the greatest sacrifice in enlisting. But words are mocking when we attempt to comprehend the noble lives and records, and the glorious death of our fine Harris Plains boys."[23]

A tragic—and instructive—story played out in Norfolk. Eighteen-year-old Albert Bailey of that town volunteered for service with the 11th Connecticut Infantry on November 21, 1861. While training in Hartford in early December, Bailey, according to the *Herald*,

> *paid a visit to his home…the other day, and liked it so well after a comparison with* [Hartford], *that he concluded to stay there; and that, too, with a brand new suit of hodden gray on his shoulders, and a nice little handful of bounty money in his pocket. He made some pretenses to exemption on account of tender years, but they didn't go down with the authorities at Hartford. That isn't the way they do things "in the army." A posse…went up from Winsted on Sunday last and assisted Mr. Bailey back to Hartford.*

This looked like textbook "bounty jumping"—accepting payment to join a regiment only to desert and repeat the process. The truth, reported two weeks later and with less fanfare, was more complicated: "We have since been desired to state that the lad refused to rejoin his regiment through the persuasion of his father, and not through any objection of his own." Civil War soldiers deserted with frequency over the course of the war: 13 percent of Litchfield soldiers deserted, 17 percent of New Milford soldiers, 8 percent of soldiers from Albert Bailey's hometown of Norfolk, 14 percent from Torrington and 12 percent from Winsted. Their reasons were varied. Some had seen enough of battle. Others determined that army life wasn't for them. Still others had compelling reasons to be home. Albert Bailey, termed "tender" by the newspaper, found himself receiving conflicting orders, with his father telling him to stay home and the army demanding that he report for duty. Still, he was called a "bounty jumper" and emasculated in public. Albert returned to duty, but a father's intuition can often be accurate. On April 25, 1862, the *Herald* reported that Albert had died of illness:

> *And for so great a sorrow to parents, and brothers, and sisters, how short the story! He writes,—a letter full of love of country, friends, and home. He sees death on every side, but bids the dear ones "Keep up their courage." Soon a comrade's brief missive states that Albert is sick—but not much of explanation, or of other tidings. Days of agonizing anxiety pass, and another message is received; brief, like the former, but it comes burdened with a life-time sorrow to a mother's heart, "Albert is dead." A finger-ring, taken from the pulseless hand, is thoughtfully inclosed. That is all. And this is not a solitary case, but one of ten thousand. Is there a hell deep enough for the contrivers of this wicked rebellion and the authors of such weeping and desolation.*

In the years to follow, this scene would play out hundreds of times across Litchfield County; however, few other soldiers would receive such a eulogy from the county newspapers as this young man, once deemed a deserter.[24]

Despite these deaths, the news in early 1862 was far from bleak. Beginning in February, seemingly every week the newspapers carried news of another Union victory: Forts Henry and Donelson, the taking of Nashville, the USS *Monitor*, Pea Ridge, Shiloh, Island Number Ten and Fort Pulaski. Connecticut troops were instrumental in successes on the North Carolina coast. New Orleans, the largest city in the Confederacy, fell in April, and the vital rail center of Corinth, Mississippi, was captured the next month. General George McClellan, commander of the Army of the Potomac, the

Union's largest military organization, landed on the Virginia peninsula and began marching for Richmond.

The danger of such reporting was, of course, overconfidence. On June 13, the *Herald* echoed its readers' worries that the war would end in Union victory before slavery was abolished. To this the editor noted that steps had been taken in regard to slavery: the emancipation of slaves working for rebels, the abolition of slavery in the District of Columbia and the territories, a treaty to suppress the African slave trade, the promise of the federal government to work with border states to abolish slavery in their states and the order issued to military commanders to no longer enforce the Fugitive Slave Act. Unquestionably, the most impactful sign of overconfidence—for Litchfield County and the nation—was the decision by Secretary of War Edwin Stanton to close recruiting offices. It seemed that more than enough men were at hand to crush the rebellion.

Chapter 3

"All Honor to the Ladies"

In May 1861, as hundreds of Litchfield County men prepared to head off to war, the *Litchfield Enquirer* proclaimed that the time for speeches and idle flag waving had passed. "There is a great deal of *talk*, *talk*, *talk*—a great deal of *unnecessary* talk, we mean, and profitless discussion. What we want is ACTION!" Such sentiments were common across the country, not only in the spring of 1861 but also for the eight months following the Battle of Bull Run, when "All quiet on the Potomac" became both a regular report filed from the army and the source of endless frustration for Northerners eager for decisive action against the rebellion.[1]

What was different about the *Enquirer*'s call to action was its intended audience, for the *Enquirer* declared that "[e]very woman and child ought to be employed in *doing* for our Volunteers—their personal comfort and health; or of these already cared for, for those who *are not* cared for (and there are such), who are not properly clothed or fed, or sufficiently armed." In singling out women and children to turn their patriotic sentiments into action, the *Enquirer* presaged a nationwide trend—clearly demonstrated in Litchfield County—of women on the homefront supporting men on the battlefields. Examining the ways Litchfield County women formalized their contributions through the establishment of Ladies' Aid Societies provides a glimpse into how women exercised agency to support the war effort, express their political beliefs and gain experience for postwar reform movements.[2]

Like the Wide Awakes, Ladies' Aid Societies were a phenomenon that began in Connecticut and swept the nation. These societies were part of a larger social movement in the mid-nineteenth century in which the home and work became established as separate spheres. Men who once farmed or ran small shops alongside their wives now regularly worked in offices or factories, while women increasingly found themselves alone with their children. This was only heightened by the departure of men for war. That event, in the words of historian Philip Paludan, "may have reinforced the interconnections within the world of women. The world of Louisa May Alcott's *Little Women* may have been common in many Northern communities." Increasingly, women turned to other women for companionship, friendship and support.[3]

The war—and the departure of fathers, husbands, sons and sweethearts—provided a purpose for women to gather. The first Ladies' Aid Society was established in Bridgeport, primarily of women from notable families whose husbands were in the army. From that beginning, historian Rachel Filene Sideman has estimated as many as twenty thousand Ladies' Aid Societies were organized across the country. While some women supported the war effort directly through farm or factory work, most stayed at home. Magazines and societal leaders stressed the impact that a cheerful woman could have on a

"Our Women and the War" appeared in *Harper's Weekly* while the 19th Connecticut was training at Camp Dutton. *Avalon Fund, National Gallery of Art.*

soldier's morale. Beyond that, women were urged to do what they could while remaining "within a woman's sphere." The Cult of Domesticity—or the Cult of True Womanhood—that defined gender norms in mid-nineteenth-century America held that a woman's sphere was the home, where she, through her superior virtue, was tasked with creating a moral environment in which to raise children. A man's role was to venture into the morally dangerous world in order to support his family. There was, however, a countervailing trend; women were increasingly finding work outside the home, even in politically appointed positions. For example, presidential appointments of women to post office positions rose steadily from 1855 to 1862. While enlisting in the military was certainly outside their traditional sphere, women could—and did—act to aid the men who had enlisted, and in doing so they took important steps toward broadening their roles in society.[4]

The initial need for Ladies' Aid Societies stemmed from the haphazard way in which men were sent off to war. With the federal government in the nineteenth century largely decentralized, responsibility for raising and equipping regiments passed from the federal government to the states, and needed supplies often fell through the cracks. These societies originated under a larger umbrella of benevolent organizations that formed during the Second Great Awakening in the early decades of the nineteenth century. Thus, while at one level women provided soldiers with havelocks or socks, they were also looking to save soldiers' souls with Bibles, testaments or moral tracts.[5]

In Connecticut, the Hartford Soldiers' Aid Society became what historian Matthew Warshauer has termed the "central organizer" of the movement in the state, ensuring that needed supplies were directed to Connecticut troops. The work, however, like the raising of regiments, was done at the local level. Women in Litchfield County were quick to organize themselves to support the troops, doing so informally at first. While these women worked to support loved ones, they also certainly saw their service in patriotic terms. The first reference to women providing aid to soldiers appears in the May 9, 1861 edition of the *Enquirer*: "The Ladies of the town are busy making garments for those who are to go on to the war, and 'patriotic old Litchfield' is stirred up as never before since the days of the Revolution." In providing essentials for these soldiers, Litchfield women saw themselves as the heirs to the patriot women of the town who, in 1776, helped melt down a leaden statue of King George III into musket balls. While the newspapers saw these exploits as patriotic, they were also fodder for humor, as evidenced from a report in the *Winsted Herald* one week later: "Several of the ladies

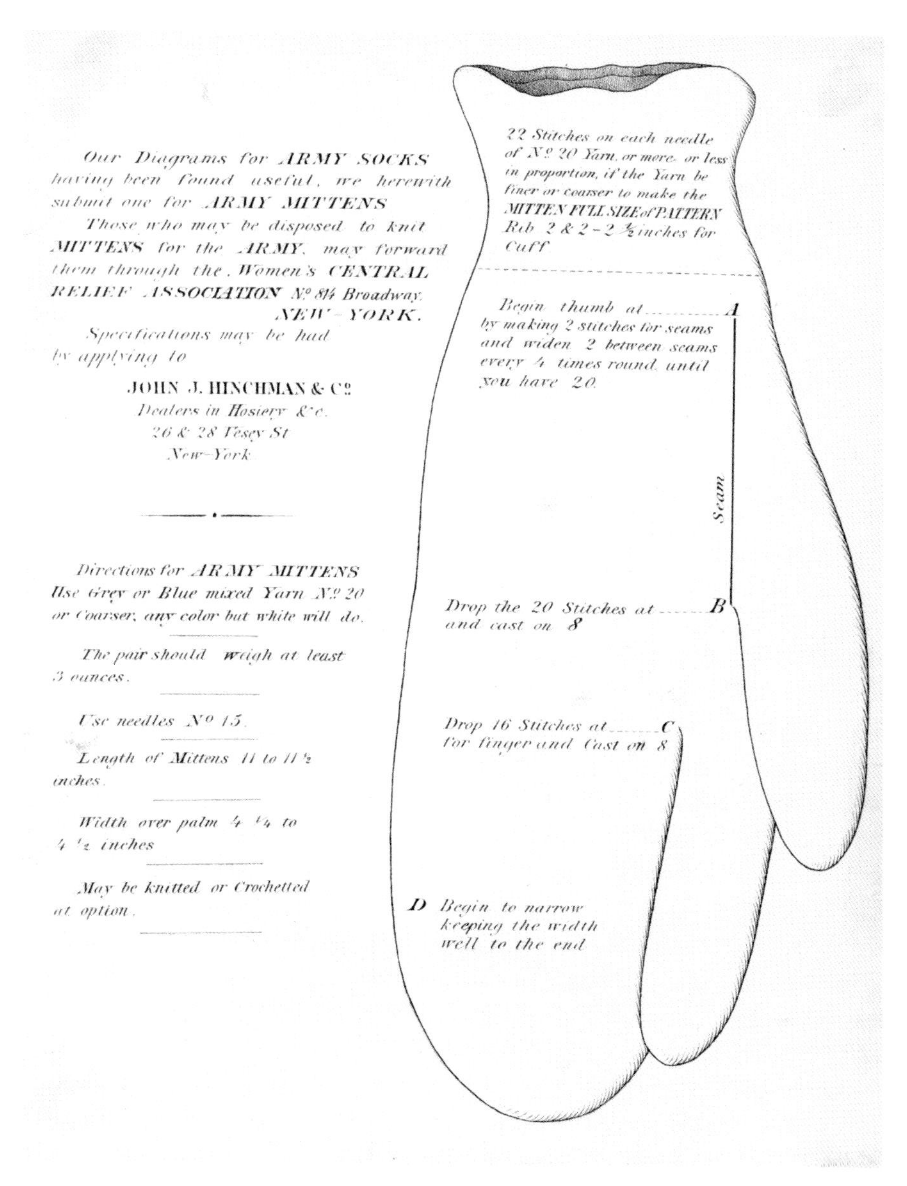

A pattern for making mittens to army specifications. *Library of Philadelphia.*

engaged in the manufacture of military equipments at Camps' Hall were last Wednesday more or less injured by the sudden explosion of a jug of ginger-pop, kindly sent in by one of their number. The wounded ones were doing well, however, at last accounts." Here is evidence of both the way men viewed these activities and the militaristic language that swept society at the war's outbreak. What is also inescapable is that men alone could not provide all the materiel needed for the war; fully equipping Connecticut's soldiers—and, more broadly, for the Union war effort to be successful—required mobilizing women.[6]

Ladies' Aid Societies spread rapidly across the county. Their scope, however, was not limited to supplying their own husbands, sons or sweethearts. The "Ladies of Norfolk," for example, made flannel shirts "for the gallant bands of Unionists" in Missouri. This, the *Enquirer* proclaimed, was an "excellent idea, and one that might well be imitated by the ladies in every town in the county, while the gentlemen might send money and muskets." Two weeks later, the same paper called on the women of the county ("Ye who have Fathers, Brothers, Husbands, Sons and Lovers who have gone forth for the fight against the traitors of their Country") to "provide for the comfort of our noble patriots." This, the *Enquirer* proclaimed, "should be esteemed an object worthy of the highest endeavor of us all." The importance of this work was clear: "[B]y united, earnest, and sustained effort we can save, not only *one*, but *thousands* of the lives of our dear countrymen, and ease the pathway to the tomb of many more." While these accounts clearly delineate between what work was appropriate for women and men, they also acknowledge that these activities were equally patriotic.[7]

This was apparent in other efforts of the Ladies' Aid Societies as well. These organizations did not limit themselves to making or gathering items for soldiers. On several occasions, women's organizations from across the county held benefits or festivals to raise funds for sick and wounded soldiers, especially those at New Haven's Knight Hospital, which opened in 1862 and treated more than twenty-five thousand wounded Union soldiers before the war's end. One such festival provided an opportunity for "all who like the cause" to "send in of their abundance and then come themselves and buy them back." On the day of the event, the *Enquirer* proclaimed, "The Hall is gaily festooned; the ladies are out in full force and beauty." Yet while it was deemed patriotic for women to organize such events, only men could handle the money. On Christmas Day 1861, the Ladies' Benevolent Association of Northfield, which had been founded in 1842 to "support the preaching of the gospel in the Congregational Church of this place," created as a subgroup the Northfield Soldiers' Aid Association. Like all ladies' aid organizations, this presented women with rare leadership opportunities. Mary Colton served as president, Fanny Camp as vice-president and Eliza Ann Wooster as secretary. While Elizabeth Catlin was elected treasurer, her work was overseen by a business committee that included two men. The April 10,

1862 issue of the *Enquirer* described the efforts of Litchfield's women to raise funds and supplies for the United States Sanitary Commission; those who wished to contribute were requested to leave their gifts with "Mr. R. Merriman." In May 1862, when "some ladies [in Winsted] wishing to aid in relieving the necessities of" African American refugees in Virginia sponsored a fundraising and clothing drive, the *Winsted Herald* called on "any wishing to assist in this enterprise" not to donate to the women, but rather to "leave their contributions at the house of Mr. L. Clarke." Although the patriotic work of women was roundly applauded, most in Litchfield County were not prepared to breach traditional gender spheres.[8]

In fact, newspaper accounts and letters home from soldiers made it clear that many hoped the war would not rearrange traditional gender norms. In the nineteenth century, the phrase "give the mitten" meant to "reject a lover." In writing to the "kind ladies" of Litchfield who had sent an enormous package of winter clothing, supplies and delicacies to the Litchfield County Guards of the 4th Connecticut, Captain Sanford Perkins of Torrington declared, "But some of the men say they hope the Ladies (especially the young) did not really intend to give them the mitten but only to last during the war, which I suppose is a comfort to that portion of the Company who have left behind a fair damsel, and are looking with pleasant anticipations to the time when they may take them 'for better or worse.'" In Kent, "all the ladies in town" were "busy knitting mittens which our brave volunteers receive without a sigh. The traditionary associations are completely reversed, and giving *the mitten* is now understood as an expression of the tenderest solicitude." With the war turning the world as they knew it upside down, Litchfield County's men expressed their hopes that these changes would not extend to their domestic life.[9]

Litchfield County's women worked throughout the war to support their soldiers and ease their separation from home by procuring both essential items and luxuries. On occasion, their work was done in response to urgent pleas for specific items. Typical of this was a nationwide appeal in early June 1861 to "Make Havelocks!" A havelock was a white cloth that covered a soldier's cap and neck, allegedly protecting him from the sun. Sunstroke, the *Enquirer* declared, "has already proved a terrible enemy. More than two hundred have even so soon bowed before it, and the hot weather has not yet set in." Having terrified Litchfield County's women about the dangers faced by their soldiers, the paper assured them that "cases like these we can prevent." What followed were specific directions for making havelocks. Twenty-two yards of white linen could be purchased for thirty cents; if women followed the

A sewing kit, typical of those used by Ladies' Aid Societies during the Civil War. *Collection of the Litchfield Historical Society, Litchfield, Connecticut.*

pattern provided by the New York Ladies' Havelock Association, this could yield fifty havelocks. "Women of Litchfield County," the *Enquirer* exclaimed, "do not let it be said that this nursery of patriotic women of the olden time is a laggard now! Let us organize in every village association that shall operate immediately. Let us emulate our sisters of other states. Let us remember our Grandmothers and follow their example. Above all, let us remember that our brothers may even now be dying because of our inactivity." Evident in this brief passage are many of the motivating factors behind the Ladies' Aid Societies. With women at the heart of the reform movements that swept the country in the first half of the nineteenth century, a call was made for Connecticut's women to continue in those efforts and to match the work of women from other states and of their neighboring towns. Additionally, there was an appeal for the women of 1861 to do what the women of 1776 did. Finally, there was the appeal to act on behalf of their own personal soldier. These appeals were wildly successful, and virtually every Northern volunteer of 1861 went South with a havelock.[10]

Calls also went out across the nation for women to gather lint for use in the army. In the days before sterilized gauze came into use, doctors and nurses employed lint to dress wounds. Even before a major battle was fought in the Civil War, the U.S. Sanitary Commission, a precursor to the American Red Cross, put out an urgent plea: "Let every woman busy herself in the preparation of lint and bandages, if she can do nothing more. No time should be lost, as they are greatly needed." As the war went on, the situation became more dire. American textile production saw a shift from linen cloth to cotton cloth in the decades before the war, but the latter's lint produced abscesses in wounds. In September 1862, the papers contained this plea: "It is said that more than two hundred deaths, among wounded soldiers brought to New York, are traceable to cotton lint." In response, accounts of the activities of the various Ladies' Aid Societies across the county mention the collection of a "quantity of [linen] lint." Katherine Bissell Bogert Roe, a teenager in Litchfield during the war, remembered "lint parties when the linen rooms were stripped of sheets and table cloths to make lint for our wounded soldiers." The need for linen lint provided the opportunity for the *Winsted Herald* to remind women of their proper sphere. "We have before us," that paper declared, "a letter purporting to come from two young ladies in Norfolk, the signers of which state that they are ready to 'shoulder their musket and march to the battlefield.' Pick lint, girls!"[11]

Reports of the lint gathering and other work of such societies lay comfortably within traditional roles of women and thus were weekly staples of the county's newspapers. Typical of these accounts is this from Bethlehem in December 1861:

> *The loyal ladies of Bethlem have been very busy of late, in working for our soldiers who have gone forth to fight the battles of our country. They have recently been forwarded to Washington, two boxes containing the following articles: 10 bed quilts, 18 blankets, 12 pairs of pillows, 9 pairs of linen sheets, 6 pairs of cotton sheets, 16 pairs of cotton pillow cases, 8 pair of linen pillow cases, 10 towels, 14 flannel shirts, 9 cotton flannel wrappers, 16 pairs canton flannel drawers, 30 pairs of mittens, 40 pairs of socks, and 450 yards of bandages, with a quantity of lint.... With this specimen of patriotism on the part of the ladies, let it no longer be said that Bethlem is a secession town.*

Here, patriotic women served as an antidote to potentially treasonous men, and in this way, Ladies' Aid Societies members demonstrated a political stance in the county. But the societies allowed women to take a more overt political role as well. In May 1861, Union general Benjamin Butler, commanding at Virginia's Fortress Monroe, refused to return to their enslaver three slaves who had come into Union lines. Butler's action was highly controversial, bringing questions about emancipation to the front burner.[12]

The formerly enslaved persons who gathered at Fortress Monroe, depicted in this Alfred Waud sketch for *Harper's Weekly*. *Library of Congress.*

Conditions could deteriorate quickly for the "contraband" in situations like these, and the Litchfield County Ladies' Aid Societies sprang to action on their behalf. "Some ladies wishing to aid in relieving the necessities of the so called contrabands at Fortress Monroe," the *Herald* reported, "will send a box of second hand clothing, well mended up shoes, bedding, &c., on the first of November. Anyone wishing to assist in this enterprise, are requested to leave their contributions at the house of Mr. L. Clarke." The next week brought another appeal on behalf of the contraband, and on November 15, the *Herald* reported the final tally of what had been collected:

> *For the Contraband: 26 pairs shoes and boots, 61 pair stockings, 25 pairs for men and boys, 16 men's coats, 10 boys' coats, 10 dresses, large and small, 14 chemises, 12 yds calico, 2 spools thread, 13 blankets and quilts, 1 bed tick, 7 felt hats, 4 caps, 25 vests, 3 cotton jackets, 7 capes and sacks, 2 shawls, 3 pairs suspenders, 12 hoods, 11 pair mittens, 2 belt ribbons, half dozen collars.*

The *Herald* added that the contribution of the town's "Negroes filled 2 pieces so that nothing more could have been added." The women overseeing this drive could have devoted their time and labor to relief efforts for Union soldiers. In assisting the contraband, these women made a statement that caring for these newly freed African Americans warranted the same attention and concern as their men in uniform.[13]

Women expressed their views on the war in other ways, too. In November 1861, "the ladies of Kent…furnished two large boxes, with many articles of comfort and luxury for the soldiers," the *Enquirer* unsurprisingly reported. The women, however, "put in with the rest some ragged socks marked for Jeff. Davis. He will need them sometime—they are so excellent for dancing—on nothing." "Dancing on nothing" was a nineteenth-century expression for a hanging, and with this gesture, the women of Kent proclaimed Davis a traitor worthy of execution. While this may sound obvious to a twenty-first-century audience, it is worth noting that while Davis was indicted for treason, the case was dismissed in 1869. To the women of Kent, the Civil War was no "brother's war"—it was an act of treason.[14]

Despite the political nature of some of their work, there is no question that the Ladies' Aid Societies existed to provide Union soldiers with both needed items—vast quantities of lint and thousands of pairs of socks and mittens—and delicacies like cakes and fruit. In doing so, the societies formed strong bonds between the soldiers in the fields and their home communities. This is reflected in an October 1861 item from the *Litchfield Enquirer*:

> *Sergeant* [Edward B.] *Smith of the 4th Regiment took back with him on Monday to his company a vast amount of comforts and luxuries for "the boys." He had Hams, Cheeses, Tubs of fresh butter, Crackers, Shirts, Stockings, pipe and cigars, amounting in all to three large dry goods boxes and one barrel full! Something over seventy pairs of good, thick, warm woolen stockings were sent. Notable mothers, sisters and grandmothers habituated to such labors have plied their needs during the past fortnight more industriously than ever, and dainty fingers which never before manipulated anything harsher than Berlin wool, have bravely toiled over the heavy blue yarn, anxious to contribute something to the comfort of their brothers in the distant camp. Ah! How cheery must be the greeting which all remembrance of the loved at home receive from our loved in the army. For this week at least our brave boys will feast and sing, and their camp and squad by night and by day will respond with the praises of old mother Litchfield!*

Soldier letters confirmed these bonds. Seth Plumb received a box from his sister Lemira. In writing to her upon its receipt, Plumb commented, "That box you sent to us was more acceptable than you can imagine. You ought to have seen us around it when it was opened. Everyone in the company thinks Litchfield is a kind of paradise." Alva Stone was returning from a soldier's funeral on December 1, 1861, when his company received an enormous box from Harris Plains. "If my box was a big thing," Stone wrote to his wife, "this was bigger weighing 420 lbs. In it was every-thing for everybody—I am very much pleased with the articles I received....There are some bright spots in the life of a soldier and if anything gives a man the heart to stand up for his home it is the consciousness that he is remembered at home. 'Who wouldn't be a soldier?'"[15]

As seen in Stone's letter, packages from home did not simply provide the men with needed articles. They raised men's spirits and, by extension, contributed to the war effort. These efforts were both impactful and long-lasting. As stated earlier, much of what was raised and collected in the county was sent to Hartford for distribution; this was true for societies from Hartford and Tolland Counties as well. The amounts collected by the Hartford Soldiers' Aid Society in just the nine months of war in 1861 are staggering:

Clothing, pieces	*19,506*
Bedding, pieces	*6,064*
Handkerchiefs, towels, &c.	*10,281*
Lint, boxes	*63*
Bandages, barrels	*41*
Old linen, packages	*49*
Old cotton, packages	*27*
Books, papers, &c.	*133*
Medicines, packages	*50*
Dried fruit, packages	*44*
Groceries, packages	*215*
Jellies, &c., preserves, jars	*250*
Wine, &c., bottles	*159*
Hospital furniture	*149*
Miscellaneous	*183*

It is no wonder that the *Litchfield Enquirer* praised such efforts by declaring, "All honor to the ladies!"[16]

Membership in the Ladies' Aid Societies gave Litchfield County women experience in leadership and opportunities to express themselves politically. Furthermore, Union victory in the Civil War rested, in part, on the dual efforts of men and women. While men grappled with Confederate armies on the battlefield, the work of women in fields and factories was necessary for the men at the front to be properly equipped and supplied. In letters to soldiers from individual women and the packages compiled by groups like the Ladies' Aid Societies, women kept up connections between soldiers and home, thereby reminding men at the front of that for which they were fighting.

The efforts continued into the postwar period. Experience with Ladies' Aid Societies and similar groups provided women with opportunities to develop essential skills, knowledge and networks to apply to other aspects of their lives. It should not be seen as a coincidence that the Connecticut Woman Suffrage Association was founded in the immediate aftermath of the war. While the efforts of women to support soldiers during the war may have been intended to fit within their prescribed domestic sphere, ultimately the way women viewed their public roles and participated in the public sphere evolved.

Chapter 4

"Peace Men"

The start of the war brought efforts in Litchfield County to set aside party differences for the good of the country. Calls for a meeting of residents of both political parties to discuss current affairs and "if expedient to nominate a Union ticket for town offices" appeared in Litchfield by August 1861. This was the first such call in the state for a Union ticket, a slate of candidates who, regardless of party, pledged to support the effort to save the Union. The *Enquirer*, which had angrily reported the election of Democrat George Woodruff to Congress, now backed off, noting that Woodruff had voted "almost uniformly patriotic and in favor of fully sustaining the government and the war." The partisan paper reported that "all parties—Republicans and the true Democrats," attended the Union Convention held in Litchfield on August 24, 1861. Delegates affirmed a series of resolutions supporting the war while condemning those who either sympathized with the Confederacy or preferred peace to a war to save the Union. Soon, "Union tickets" appeared in elections across the county. In some places, however, setting aside political differences for the sake of the Union war effort proved impossible. In Barkhamsted, for example, "the Republicans tried hard to effect a harmonious understanding with the Democrats and arrange a satisfactory ticket for which all could vote. The [Democratic Party], however, declined all overtures, and the battle was fought upon the old, dead, nauseous issues of the past." That differing views were becoming increasingly intolerable is evident in a summary of Barkhamsted's elections: "The Secesh ticket was elected."[1]

Despite the results in Barkhamsted, Union tickets did well in the fall of 1861 elections. In Winsted, it ran unopposed. Norfolk's Union candidates outpolled the Democrats by 4.5 to 1, and the coalition ticket also won in Torrington. This presaged similar movements at the state and national levels. A statewide "Union Mass Convention" held at Hartford in early January featured three speakers from Litchfield County: George Peet of Canaan, Samuel Catlin of Harwinton and G.H. Hollister of Litchfield. The convention nominated Buckingham for a fourth term, this time as a Union candidate. Following the convention in Hartford, "Morris," likely a pseudonym for a newspaper correspondent from Hartford, wrote to the *Enquirer* about Litchfield's role in the Union Convention movement: "[I]t was on your hills that the first Union Convention was held; there the present Union movement was born; you owe it to yourselves and the rest of the state that the hills speak in a voice not to be misunderstood next spring. Let treason covert as well as open be rebuked." In mentioning treason, "Morris" referred not to the Confederates but rather to their sympathizers across Connecticut, including in Litchfield County. The Union movement was significant; in 1864, Lincoln himself ran for reelection not as a Republican but on the ticket of the Union Party, with the Democrat Andrew Johnson as his vice presidential candidate. This is a story that fits nicely with the memory of the Civil War as a "good war," with bipartisanship rising from the ashes of the political wars of the 1850s. The reality of Litchfield County's political situation was far messier.[2]

Litchfield County possessed a rich and diverse opposition to the war, and elections in its towns were usually quite close. Some opposition took the form of traditional political disagreement—some opponents believed that peace was more important than the Union; still others openly supported the Confederacy. Statewide, this opposition was evident in the 1860 presidential election. While Lincoln won Connecticut with 53 percent of the vote, Stephen A. Douglas, the Northern Democrat, finished in a virtual tie with proslavery fire eater John C. Breckinridge. Nicknamed the "Georgia of New England" by abolitionist leader William Lloyd Garrison, Connecticut not only had more slaves than any other New England state in the 1700s, but its industries were also highly dependent on Southern cotton. While there was certainly a strong abolitionist element in Connecticut, there were also Southern sympathizers.[3]

At the individual level, war opponents were often those with family in the South, immigrants or supporters of slavery. In Litchfield County, those removed from the wealthy or governing classes were more likely to oppose the war. Another important aspect in establishing war opposition in Litchfield County in 1861 was the lack of a political tradition of dissent. Americans in 1860 simply did not know how to act politically during a war as large as the Civil War. The War of 1812 had taken place fifty years earlier, and the Mexican-American War was an affair of much smaller size and shorter duration.[4] In the first sixty years of the nineteenth century, about five thousand Americans were killed in combat; in the Civil War, about five thousand Americans died in a single day of fighting at Antietam Creek, Maryland, alone.

More militant than those who simply wanted peace were the so-called Copperheads, named for the poisonous snakes that live in wooded and rocky areas of the North. The number of dissenters in the North was both large and impactful. Jennifer Weber argues that the Democratic Party was so formidable an opponent to the Lincoln administration that it weakened

Copperheads, Northerners who sympathized with the South, depicted in a Republican newspaper. *Library of Congress.*

the war effort by establishing animosity at the local level, hurting recruiting efforts and politicizing the soldiers at the front.[5]

There were serious consequences for those deemed too ardent in their dissent. All that was required to arrest and imprison a citizen were two sworn statements alleging disloyalty, and estimates of those arrested for speaking out against the war range from thirteen thousand to thirty-eight thousand nationwide. Many were imprisoned without being informed of the charges or their accusers. Yet these numbers were primarily for federal arrests. Local and state records are scarcer. While Northerners and Southerners marched off to war with notions of defending freedom, free speech was guaranteed at the federal level but not yet by states.[6]

The war sparked national debates about the definition of loyalty, with many in the North shifting their primary allegiance from their state to the nation. Secretary of War Edwin Stanton believed that the "line between loyalty and disloyalty is plainly defined"—Northerners were either loyal or disloyal, patriots or traitors. Litchfield County native and theologian Horace Bushnell was more nuanced in his view, declaring that "not every disloyal person is a traitor." While Bushnell believed that loyalty during a war required defending the country and being willing to risk one's life for the Union, he did not believe that all who were disloyal—and thus unwilling to do these things—were traitors.[7]

On the eve of war, Connecticut was a shining example of the complex nature of loyalty and dissent. Dissent was fairly widespread at the individual or small group level, often fueled by rhetoric from the Democratic Party. Politically, Connecticut was a hotly contested state, and Litchfield County was part of the 4th Congressional District, which elected a Democrat as its representative in the spring of 1861. Furthermore, Connecticut had long traditions of supporting states' rights (exemplified by the 1814–15 Hartford Convention) and hostility toward African Americans. It is not surprising that significant episodes of dissent appeared in Litchfield County. In fact, dissent was so widespread that in September 1861 the *Winsted Herald* declared that the "increasing, brazen disloyalty" would be "fifty years hence…regarded as Connecticut's greatest shame."[8]

Opposition to the war came before the war itself. Prior to the Confederates firing on Fort Sumter, a patriotic meeting was called in West Winsted. An enthusiastic crowd filled Camp's Hall, expressing support for the Union and the Lincoln administration. However, Ronald Hitchcock rose to offer a resolution calling on Lincoln to withdraw Federal troops from the fort, "stop the shedding of blood, settle the difficulties honorably by further concessions, and 'revive the drooping business interests.'" A hissing crowd defeated the resolution in a near-unanimous vote. Soon after the war began, Litchfield's Esther Thompson noticed that "Copperhead pins were shamefully worn by a number of men in this town. These were a slice sawn through the center of a butternut showing beautiful outlines and internal cavities, highly polished and covered with copper filings imbedded [*sic*] in a heavy coat of varnish." Dissent existed at both the individual and organized group level.[9]

Peace flags—often simple white banners—also appeared across the county, with early versions flying in New Milford and New Preston. Most who flew these flags were not supporters of the Confederacy, but rather agreed with former Democratic gubernatorial candidate Thomas Seymour that a war was unwinnable and would simply result in needless death. "There seems to be a radical mistake on the part of many people," Seymour declared. "They appear to think the South can be conquered.... You can destroy their habitats, devastate their fields, and shed the blood of their people, but you cannot conquer them." However, as many would find out, the patriotic fervor that swept the North in the weeks after Sumter left no room for such opinions.[10]

Perhaps the county's most dramatic display of dissent occurred in Goshen in June 1861. There, Andrew Palmer, a fifty-four-year-old farmer, lived with his wife, Jane, and their eight children. Palmer owned real estate and personal property valued at more than $6,500, not an insignificant amount. By June 22, for reasons that remain unknown—except for his averring that "he had a right to put what flag he pleased on his own property"—Palmer was flying either a white peace flag or the more provocative flag of secession.[11]

Whatever flag Palmer flew drew an angry and violent response from residents across the county. As Palmer's farm on East Street was situated on high ground, his controversial flag could be seen for some distance, and Palmer may have also made verbal statements supporting the Confederacy, daring his fellow residents to do something about his deeds and words. He then stationed at least two of his sons to defend the flag. On the morning of Sunday, June 23, men leaving service at Goshen's Congregational Church called Palmer's bluff. A group was deputized to speak with Palmer at his farm. They told Palmer that he could peaceably remove the flag or it would be forced down the next day, stating that "[t]hey would not pass and repass under its polluting shadow." However, when a reconnaissance party arrived at the farm on Monday, the controversial flag still waved.[12]

Accounts vary about what happened next. An armed mob assembled, determined to forcibly remove the flag and bring Palmer to justice. Estimates

Esther Thompson. *Collection of the Litchfield Historical Society, Litchfield, Connecticut.*

on the size of the crowd range from one hundred to "an aggregate of 300 or 400 men." It is also clear that some members of the mob were armed, although it is doubtful that there were sixty-nine muskets "well loaded with powder and ball, and a small field-piece which had done duty at all the celebrations of the surrounding region from time immemorial," as the *Winsted Herald* reported. There were men from Goshen and Litchfield present; others claimed that men from Morris, Cornwall, Bethlehem, Milton, Torrington and Norfolk were also in attendance. Even the matter of who commanded the men is uncertain.[13]

Upon learning that an armed group was approaching his farm, Palmer hid the flag. The crowd demanded that he surrender the offensive banner, and when this was refused, "real war was the result," as Esther Thompson remembered. Much of this was pushing and shoving, but a musket accidentally discharged, striking one man—the *Herald* identified him as "Henry Catlin (Secesh)"—in the leg. A correspondent for that paper claimed that the crowd then made Palmer and his accomplices "prisoners of war" and demanded that one of Palmer's sons turn over the flag, threatening to hang him if he "led them astray." The mob soon possessed the offending banner and warned the family that if another flag went up in its place they would return and "raze every building on the premises to the ground." They left with Andrew Palmer in custody. He was marched to the center of town, swore loyalty to the government of the United States and was released.[14]

For the newspapers, the "marked warning" of the episode was more important than what actually happened. While maintaining that they were "no advocates for mob law," the *Litchfield Enquirer* proclaimed that the Palmer affair "tells traitors that they cannot raise the emblem and insignia of rebellion with impunity, in the free air of our Litchfield County hills." It was not enough to warn of dissent or treason, however. "Though the traitors are despicable in number, they are insidious in their plots....They must be marked. *They are marked!*" By June 1861—two months after the beginning of the war and one month before a major land battle was fought—to voice opposition to suppressing the rebellion in Litchfield County was to risk one's good name, perhaps even one's life.[15]

The threats to dissenters did not fade with the Palmer affair. Two weeks later, the *Enquirer* went even further down the rabbit hole of conspiracy by printing the names of seventeen local men it claimed had plotted to prevent Congress from meeting on July 4. That the paper cared little for libeling suspected dissenters, or printing gossip as news, was evidenced by a correction the following week when it admitted that it had no evidence for the story. Amazingly, the *Enquirer* justified its journalistic decisions in this matter by claiming that "we stated only the rumor that such was the case." Clearly, the search for dissenters was more important than getting the facts right.[16]

These threats of violence or public shaming for dissenters did little to prevent public opposition to the war. Some took the form of open displays of support for the Confederacy. Esther Thompson recounted the attempt of a "Litchfield Copperhead" to have his son baptized at the Episcopal church with the name "Jefferson Davis." Not wanting to oversee a rite in which a child was given the name of the Confederate president, "the rector remonstrated, but his objections were overruled by the shrewd arguments of his parishioner," who reminded the minister that "an Episcopal clergyman had no right to refuse the sacrament of baptism for the children of a communicant of his church." So while the minister was forced to proceed with the service, such rules did not apply to the church's musicians. William Baldwin was a member of the church's choir and an ardent supporter of the Union. When the child's name was pronounced, he "sprang to his feet, his face white as marble and perceptibly shaking from head to foot bent over the organist exclaiming in a half audible whisper, 'Give them the Star Spangled Banner! Give it to them! Give it to them!'"[17]

The Union defeat at Bull Run in July 1861 led to a surge in dissent, with a notable change, however. Gone were secessionist or Confederate flags. In their place were so-called Peace Flags, often plain white flags or, less commonly, black flags. These first appeared a few weeks before Bull Run, when Edward A. Phelps—a one-time general in the Connecticut militia—and a neighbor raised "a *black* flag on Independence Day, to signify their aversion to the glorious old banner of a once prospered and united Nation." The same week, Cornwall Doolittle, a fifty-one-year-old manufacturer from Barkhamsted, "hoist[ed] a white flag, with the inscription '*Peace and Union*.'" Antiwar meetings were held in Canaan and Sharon. In the latter town, the opposition to the war was expressed in financial terms: "*Resolved*, That the cost of this unnatural war will entail upon the people a system of taxation too intolerable to be borne."[18]

Patriotic envelope cover art depicting Confederate president Jefferson Davis going to war. Turning the envelope 270 degrees reveals how the artist thought Davis would look returning from war. *Collection of the Litchfield Historical Society, Litchfield, Connecticut.*

The largest gathering in the summer of 1861 was held at Cornwall Bridge, with five hundred people in attendance. A railcar served as a platform for speakers, and resolutions advocated a "peaceful separation" and proclaimed that "the American Union is forever destroyed." Speakers encouraged other towns to take a stand "against a further continuance of this bloody spectacle." John Cotton Smith, recently the United States minister to Bolivia, spoke and perhaps disappointed the crowd by stating that while he "deprecated the horrors of civil war," he was "loyal to the flag under which he was born and which he had seen honored upon the high seas, and in the harbors of foreign lands." Smith must have been persuasive, as the *Enquirer* reported that the final outcome of the meeting was a resolution supporting Lincoln's actions and the "integrity and stability of the Government."[19]

The level to which mobilization required citizens to put aside dissenting opinions was clearly demonstrated in Litchfield in July and August 1861. A fight broke out in Wheeler's Grocery between some "Peace Men" passing through town and a resident named Sedgwick, "who was seriously injured with a cut with a heavy weight on his forehead." Some of the "Peace Men" were arrested. Later, the *Litchfield Enquirer* even expressed fears for its own safety, as it printed rumors that "peace people and secessionists" from Milton and Woodville were planning to attack its offices. The editor of the *Enquirer* had earlier called for those suspected of holding secessionist beliefs to prove themselves loyal to the Union by flying the American flag. Following this, a "Union committee"—or what Esther Thompson called a "Vigilance Committee"—of a few dozen Litchfield men was formed to make sure that this was done. On the night of July 24, with a drummer and flag bearer at its head, the committee marched to the South Street home of George Palmer, apparently not a direct relation to the Palmer of Goshen. Thompson remembered that Palmer "dabbled in fortune telling" and was open about being a Copperhead. He further agitated his patriotic townsmen by telling one man that he "hoped his sons would die of disease" and used "profane epithets of President Lincoln." When the angry crowd reached Palmer's house, he hid in the garret, while the crowd nailed a flag to his roof. Despite repeated calls for Palmer to come out and thank the group, when no reply was made, the committee disbanded for the night.[20]

The group reconvened the following night, however, intent on visiting the Prospect Street home of Dr. E.W. Blake to "beg of him the favor of waving the stars and stripes." On their way to Blake's, the committee stopped to cheer William Deming, who proudly flew the Stars and Stripes at his home. Deming responded with a short speech, and the Union men made their way to Blake's. There "the company asked the privilege of planting the flag upon his grounds, and the further favor that he would assist them." Blake, speaking from his window, made an argument that the group found "evasive" but "entertaining"—that his "wife's relations" precluded him from flying the flag. The committee told Blake that it would be content if he would wave a flag from his window. This the dentist did, but not before first making a patriotic speech which "drew tears to the eyes of many of the listeners." The group cheered, and when Blake asked for their names, they gladly gave them. They made one more stop that night, at the home of Linus Parmalee, a sixty-two-year-old wagon maker who lived on South Street. Esther Thompson later wrote that the committee was met by Parmalee's wife, who

> *met them at her door to parry with them. She begged to swing the flag herself as her husband was asleep and should not be disturbed. This plea not availing, she spied one of the ring leaders of the band by the gate—a talented but overscrupulous young lawyer and affecting much joy at seeing him, ran down to meet him and extending her hand exclaimed, "Good evening Mr. X. I am so glad to see you! I suppose you have come to pay that little debt that you have been owing my husband so long!" This greeting was answered by a roar of laughter from the boys, who acknowledged their defeat by a speedy departure.*

Thus, Thursday night ended peacefully.[21]

Friday, however, was a different story. That morning, Dr. Blake, angered over the events of the night before and armed with the list of names he had acquired and a "stout heavy cane," attacked Henry Spencer in West Street. Attorney H.B. Graves heard the commotion from his office and rushed to Spencer's assistance. Blake struck him with a porcelain pitcher, opening a gash on Graves's head. Blake then barricaded himself in his office while an angry crowd formed outside. Unsurprisingly, the *Enquirer* reported what happened next as it would a clash between Union and Confederate forces. The dentist had erected a "skillful intrenchment. Siege was at once laid to unearth the enemy, the outworks yielded," and Blake was taken prisoner. Blake quickly "asked forgiveness of the injured, and was forgiven by at least one of them, and so was allowed to depart in peace." He was, however, "frequently and urgently advised to leave the town forthwith."[22]

Then came Saturday. George Palmer, perhaps hearing of Blake's resistance, took down the flag forcibly placed on his roof on Wednesday night. The Vigilance Committee descended on his home, where it found Palmer in the garret again, this time armed with a cooper's adze. He threatened to "kill the first man who put his head above the trap door." Three members of the committee climbed to the roof to plant the flag, while other members used a ladder to smash the door to the garret. This blow hurled Palmer and his wife to the ground, and they "were soon at the mercy of their enemies." The Vigilance Committee required both Palmers to swear allegiance to the flag, but when newspaperman Ira Addis of New Haven offered to cut down the national flag, committee member Oliver Peck tackled Addis and, assisted by Ed Vaill, strong-armed the reporter into a wagon. They brought Addis up South Street to the old town pump and forced him to kneel in a trough until "thoroughly soused." All the while they demanded he "swear allegiance to the flag, ask the forgiveness of the public, pledge his future fidelity to the union, promise perfect silence in town as to his secession opinions, and agree to write a truthful account of the whole affair and have it published in a New Haven newspaper—which pledge he faithfully kept."[23]

The next month, a flag of "unmistakable secession pattern" was hung from a gallows in front of a shop on West Street in Litchfield. On it was a placard that bore the names of residents suspected of Southern sympathies titled "Black List, No 1." The *Enquirer* ran an astonishing piece cautioning Unionist groups against destroying property but seemingly giving *carte blanche* to use violence against individuals:

> *We cannot at all approve of breaking into a man's home or store and destroying his property, even though the man may have made himself hateful, or his shop odious to the feelings of the community. If punishment is to be given, let us fall upon the man himself, and not upon his family by depriving them of a portion of the man's income.*

Squads of vigilantes, threatening home visits, heads dunked in troughs and warnings of lynchings—indeed, the residents of Litchfield had made it clear that they would not tolerate any public utterances against the Union or the prosecution of the war. Despite such measures, some dissent continued, and increasingly the people of Litchfield County looked to the government to stamp it out.[24]

In a comical but important example, a pair of "women's drawers with 'Peace' written on them" was flown as a peace flag in Northfield. Perhaps because of the immodesty of this dissent, the *Enquirer* reported, "even the secessionists here, male and female, with whom we are tolerably blessed, seemed disgusted with their armed white banner of 'peace' and the civil authority was appealed to in beseeching terms to 'take the thing down.' But our civil authority here, as in many other places, is silent…the people was the last resort." The residents of Northfield turned to vigilantism to stifle this dissent. After church services on Sunday, September 1, a Colonel Hine led a home guard detachment armed with "rails, clubs, and stones [and] made three *gallant* charges and though repulsed twice yet rallying the third time, they brought the secession monster to the ground." Who these secessionists were and how they were able to twice defeat a heavily armed force was left unsaid. What is significant is that the local governments, with but one sheriff and no additional police for the entire county, were simply not equipped to deal with matters such as this. To truly stifle dissent would require state and federal intervention.[25]

It was not long before this happened. On August 28, 1861, a large crowd gathered in Morris for what was billed as a "Peace Meeting." The main draw was Ellis B. Schnabel of Pennsylvania, a well-known critic of the war who was wanted on criminal charges in four states. A speakers' platform was set up in the center of town. A peace flag was unveiled, and Schnabel rose to speak, cheered by the crowd, many of whom were armed. Unbeknownst to Schnabel, as he prepared to speak, orders originating from Secretary of State William Henry Seward arrived, detailing county deputy sheriff Edward O. Peck to arrest Schnabel. Peck handed Schnabel a note as he descended the platform, stating that he was under arrest for treasonous speech. Schnabel

Fort Lafayette, off the coast of Brooklyn, New York, where Elias Schnabel was sent after his arrest in Morris. *Library of Congress.*

was soon imprisoned at Brooklyn's Fort Lafayette. The local organizers of the event, meanwhile, apparently dismayed by what they heard, "hauled down" the peace banner and "cut the halyards." "Never again," the *Enquirer* hoped, "shall the air of Morris be disgraced with its ill-omened vision."[26]

The arrest seemed to quiet dissent in the state. Buckingham would tell Secretary of the Navy (and Connecticut native) Gideon Welles that Schnabel's arrest was "the best news I have heard to-day. I trust and know it will have a just effect upon traitors here." P.T. Barnum, famed showman and future politician, told Lincoln that Schnabel's incarceration had made "secessionists *so scarce*, I cannot find one for exhibition in my museum."[27]

Soldiers were especially happy to see dissent stamped out. Alva Stone of Litchfield enlisted about the same time as Schnabel's arrest. Secessionists, peace advocates and Schnabel were on his mind in early letters to his wife. He asked her to give his "respect to all Union Friends" but to "Shoot the first man that blows any secession around you." Of Schnabel's arrest he commented, "I see by the paper that 'Schnabel' of 'Peace Meeting' notoriety is fighting in the rebel army in Arkansas and so he at least has found his proper place while his audience are deserting the cause of the rebels and trying to creep back into decent society. What has become of your peace men that used to congregate in your village?" For those fighting to defeat secessionists in the South, the victory over dissenters at home was welcome news.[28]

Mobilization meant more than recruiting men to enlist and outfitting them for war. It also meant bringing all aspects of society together to support the war effort. It is evident that both individuals and government officials worked to stifle expression of any sentiment other than total support for the war effort. The result was an assault on civil liberties that took the forms of physical abuse, public humiliation or imprisonment.

Still, if the intent was complete societal support for the war, that failed. In the first months of 1862, William A. Buckingham mounted his campaign for a fifth term as governor. Both the *Enquirer* and the *Herald* launched ferocious attacks on Democratic candidates for office, painting individual Democratic candidates as traitors. Not content to limit their attacks to Democratic politicians, the county papers also attacked Democratic voters. "All who refuse to take a hold and manly stand in [the Union's] support are justly liable to the imputation of being secret foes," the *Enquirer* declared. "A conditional Union man is an unconditional traitor." In a county where there were only Republican newspapers, Democratic voters had no other local alternatives for news; in these pages, they read that if they voted for their party of choice, they were nothing more than traitorous heathens.[29]

Yet these attacks also demonstrate that for all the work done to stamp out dissent and opposing viewpoints in Litchfield County in 1861, partisan politics did not stop. Even amid the threats of violence and imprisonment and the coming recruiting drives, party bickering—and the two-party system—lived on amid the hills of northwestern Connecticut.

Chapter 5

"We Know Our Duty"

The skies above Colebrook blazed with green and purple swirls that first week of August 1862. "So great was the brilliancy of the northern heavens for a time," the *Enquirer* reported, "that our villagers attributed it to the burning of some building in that direction." It was not a fire but rather the aurora borealis that captivated residents, but in its brilliant patterns they saw an omen about a different type of conflagration. Editor Clarke at the *Herald* said it best: "Wonder if those lurid skies had anything to do with the drafting order for 300,000 men, issued at about same day and date!"[1]

Looking back on it, even those dubious of omens could not be blamed for setting aside their skepticism. Those northern lights coincided with the most tumultuous period of the Civil War for Litchfield County. Between July and October 1862, nearly 2,000 men—one half of the county's total who served in the Civil War—enlisted, trained and marched off to war together in the 19th Connecticut. That number very nearly doubled the approximately 1,100 men who had enlisted from Litchfield County in the preceding fifteen months of war. Why were so many men needed at this point? What mechanisms were used to begin the process of raising them? How did federal, state and local officials work to encourage enlistments? The answers to these questions provide key understandings of how mobilization worked at the community level in the Civil War.[2]

The first half of 1862 seemingly brought only good news about the war to Litchfield County. By June, the end of the war seemed near; victory was certain. Perhaps nothing made Northern expectations of imminent victory clearer than the April 3, 1862 decision by Secretary of War Edwin Stanton to close recruiting offices in the North. Then, the Confederate army under a new commander, Robert E. Lee, launched a series of attacks against Union forces outside Richmond. These actions, known as the Seven Days Battles, saw the Union army retreat while suffering serious casualties. As summer set in, disease struck Union camps. Union forces were losing twenty thousand men per month, and fears grew that Lee would invade the North. Whereas weeks before the end of the war seemed at hand, now only one thing was certain: the Northern army lacked sufficient manpower.[3]

The need for men became clear soon after the closing of the recruiting offices. On May 19, Assistant Adjutant General Lorenzo Thomas telegraphed Buckingham, urging the governor to "Raise one regiment immediately." This would be the 14th Connecticut Infantry, and to command the regiment, Buckingham appointed a man with strong Litchfield County associations, Dwight Morris. Raising the regiment, however, was a slow go. The patriotic language of the previous year still appeared in the newspapers. The *Herald*, for example, declared that "our National enemies are still strong in their determination to destroy the Union....[T]he Army needs reinforcements....Connecticut should be true to her early record of patriotic devotion to liberty and public order."[4]

In focusing on issues of patriotism, the *Herald*—and the state and national authorities—failed to recognize other reasons that prevented men from enlisting. Foremost among these were the financial burdens that enlistment placed on the families of enlistees. This was demonstrated in the case of a Bridgeport militia squadron that put on "so creditable a display" in firing off an artillery display to celebrate Buckingham's recent electoral victory that it was recruited for full-time service in the army. The men accepted at first but soon turned to finding substitutes, as "it is not by any means an easy thing for staid business and family men, with... debts that should be paid, to pull up and start off for the war at twelve hours' notice." Adding to the difficulty of finding enlistees was the labor market. Wages were high with so many men already off to war, and others had contracts that required their employer's permission to enlist. That finances were hindering enlistments became clear to the War Department, which in late June announced that each accepted recruit would receive a premium of two dollars and that every recruit who enlisted for three years would receive his first month's pay in advance. Further dampening interest in enlisting were the casualty reports that filled Northern newspapers; the Union army lost more than twenty-five thousand men in Virginia's Shenandoah Valley and Peninsula Campaigns alone.[5]

Concerns about officers also affected the raising of troops. Residents of the county had previously expressed concerns about a lack of officers from their towns. The appointment of Morris as the colonel of the 14th Connecticut did little to quell these; although born in Litchfield, he was a resident of Bridgeport. With about five thousand men from Connecticut in the army, there were only a handful of Litchfield County officers. The lack of promotions led to conspiracy theories. Charles Andrews was a young attorney (and future governor of the state) living in Kent in 1862. In his diary, Andrews recounted how his friend Ben wished to enlist but "is getting ambitious and wants a commission. I wish I was so situated that I could get him one. A little money to grease the wheels makes things move much easier."[6]

The orders to form the 14th Connecticut were part of a broader national effort to raise fifty thousand additional men. The lukewarm initial results of that effort and the suddenly urgent need for manpower in the wake of Union defeat in the Seven Days Battles necessitated a different approach to recruiting. However, Lincoln feared that a decision to reverse Stanton's April closing of the recruiting offices would result in a "general panic and stampede." Political massaging was necessary to stem the crisis. Secretary of State William Henry Seward served as the administration's point man in the crisis. On June 30, he met with New York governor Edwin Morgan and Pennsylvania governor Andrew Curtin at the Astor House in New York City. There, the three men planned that governors of the Northern states would ask Lincoln to issue a call for additional troops. Ultimately, eighteen governors signed a letter to be sent to the president; some delivered the letter to Lincoln personally.

Lincoln responded to the letters of the governors with a July 1 proclamation declaring:

> *Gentlemen: Fully concurring in the wisdom of the views expressed to me in so patriotic a manner by you in the communication of the 28th day of June, I have decided to call into the service an additional force of 300,000 men.*

Abraham Lincoln, photographed by Alexander Gardner in October 1862. *Library of Congress.*

I suggest and recommend that the troops should be chiefly of infantry....I trust that they may be enrolled without delay, so as to bring this unnecessary and injurious civil war to a speedy and satisfactory conclusion.[7]

Raising these troops would be done, at least initially, at the state and local level. In Connecticut, it started at the top, with a proclamation from Governor Buckingham. Issued on July 3, it was direct in its statement of the crisis and the duty facing patriotic Connecticut men:

Citizens of Connecticut—You are again called upon to rally to the support of the government. In the name of our common country, I call upon you to enroll your names for the immediate formation of six or more regiments of infantry to be used in suppressing the Rebellion....The Rebellion, contending with the desperation of a hopeless and wicked cause, must be met with equal energy. Close your manufactories and workshops, turn aside from your farms and your business, leave for a while your families and homes, meet face to face the enemies of your liberties!

If Union victory were a sure thing, men could be excused for staying home, but with the fate of the republic in the balance, Buckingham believed that the Union ranks would swell with new recruits.[8]

Both Lincoln's and Buckingham's calls were terse and devoid of the flowery language employed to induce recruits in April 1861. Perhaps the two politicians understood that the real work needed to execute the proclamations would be done on the ground. In Connecticut, that work began on July 11 with orders issued by Joseph D. Williams, the state's adjutant general. Williams was born in Lebanon, Connecticut, in 1818 and attended the public schools in Hartford. At eighteen, he enlisted in the East Hartford Artillery Company. Following Williams's stint in the Connecticut General Assembly, in 1855 Governor W.T. Minor tapped him to serve as the state's twelfth adjutant general. In this capacity, he became the commander of Connecticut's military forces; his primary duties involved overseeing the raising of regiments, their initial training and their transfer to federal control. Williams was an unsung hero of Connecticut's war effort, working tirelessly for the Union cause until, exhausted, he resigned in 1863.[9]

Buckingham and Williams first decided that Connecticut's entire quota of 7,145 men would be composed of infantry (ultimately the 2nd Connecticut

Light Artillery was also raised at this time). To encourage volunteers to recruit their friends and neighbors, commissions as second lieutenants were dangled in front of anyone who enrolled thirty or more men. First lieutenants and captains would be elected by a company. While the colonel and lieutenant colonel would be appointed by the governor, each new regiment's major would be appointed from the captains of a regiment. Given the criticism that only cronies of the governor could hope to become officers in Connecticut regiments, such orders were likely to spur enlistments by enterprising men. Despite the great need for men, limits were put on who could enlist. Only those between the ages of eighteen and forty-five were legally allowed to join, and only those "in physical strength and vigor will be received."[10]

The federal government was well aware that securing recruits could be a challenge and thus offered financial incentives. State volunteers would receive the same rate of pay as if they were members of the Regular Army. In addition, upon signing up, recruits would immediately receive a bounty of $2. More significantly, when soldiers mustered into federal service, they would receive $25 of a $100 bounty for enlistment.[11]

Williams next laid out how the new soldiers would be organized. Hoping to raise at least six regiments of infantry, he directed that each regiment be composed of ten companies, with each company containing:

1 captain
1 first lieutenant
1 second lieutenant
4 sergeants
8 corporals
2 musicians
1 wagoner
Between 64 and 82 privates.

With the three field officers (colonel, lieutenant colonel and major), a lieutenant serving as adjutant (the colonel's administrative assistant), a surgeon, two assistant surgeons and a lieutenant serving as quartermaster, this would give a regiment between 823 and 1,008 men.

To overcome the factors that made raising the 14th Connecticut so challenging, Buckingham and Williams employed both creative and practical solutions. For the first time, they established a recruiting infrastructure across the state. The state was divided into recruiting districts, each coordinated by a war committee centered in a major town. The governor empowered these committees to determine each district's share of the statewide quota. Buckingham also agreed to follow the recommendations of the district war committees when it came to the appointment of officers, a measure especially hailed by those in Litchfield County.[12]

Each of Buckingham's districts became the center for the recruiting of one of the regiments called for by the War Department's quota. The 15th Connecticut was organized at New Haven, the 16th at Hartford, the 17th at Bridgeport, the 18th at Norwich and the 19th at Litchfield. The 20th Connecticut was to be recruited from Hartford, Middlesex and New Haven Counties. The 21st Connecticut was formed from the eastern part of the state, and its efforts were centered in Norwich.[13]

War committees coordinated the recruiting efforts of each municipality in the state, aided in the calculation of their district's quota and recommended officers for the new regiments. Buckingham assumed that local representatives had a better sense of who might make effective leaders than those at the state level. The committees were largely staffed by civic-minded businessmen well suited to handle the financial responsibilities of the work. As the system raised 8,036 men in forty-five days—nearly 1,000 more than the state's quota—they were clearly successful.

Ultimately, the biggest factor in the state reaching its quota was the offer of bounty money to enlistees. The state legislature quickly approved a bill providing $90 of state money to each man who joined one of the new Connecticut regiments, in addition to the $100 federal bounty. While the state had not previously offered a bounty, some Connecticut towns had in 1861.[14]

On July 14, Adjutant General Williams urged that no time be wasted in holding town meetings to "set forth to the people the exigencies of the present hour, to pledge your private means to assist volunteers and their families, and especially to appoint a town committee whose duty it shall be to raise money, encourage enlistments, and nominate persons of energetic habits and patriotic impulses to act as recruiting efforts." It was, perhaps, in their appointment of recruiting officers and in the recommendation of bounties that these committees did their most important work. Williams urged the committees to select recruiting officers who "will be competent to receive commissions." The expectation was that once they had enlisted a requisite number of men—forty to be a second lieutenant, sixty to be a first lieutenant and eighty-three to be a captain—the recruiting officers would receive a commission in the new regiment, subject to approval by the governor.[15]

For all the essential work these town committees did in response to Lincoln's call, little is known about their composition or procedures. Using Woodbury as an example, some understanding of their functioning can be gleaned. Immediately after Williams's July 14 circular, legislators from Woodbury and neighboring towns—Willis A. Strong and Dr. Charles Webb of Woodbury, Almon Downs of Southbury, Henry Peck of Bethlehem and Truman Warren of Watertown—called for a meeting of residents of these adjacent towns to "adopt a plan of concerted action for raising men and money in this district." Attendance at the July 17 meeting was "very large" and "enthusiastic." A nominating committee put forth candidates for the town's war committee. While the nominating committee met, the rest of the audience listened to patriotic speeches and songs. Webb and four attorneys—William Cothren, James Huntington, Nathaniel Smith and Reuben Allen—were recommended. These men were unanimously approved, and the newly constituted war committee was charged with the correspondence, recruiting and fundraising needed to meet the town's quota for the new regiments. A town meeting was scheduled for July 24 to approve any new taxes "to support the families of such volunteers from the town," and the meeting was adjourned. Most towns in the county held similar meetings between July 15 and August 2 to ratify the work of their war committees.[16]

On July 11, the *Winsted Herald* reported that "the most spirited meetings are being held all over the country to promote new enlistments. The North is awaking [*sic*] as it has never done before." However, the crowds at these rallies and town meetings were often composed of older, prominent men from the communities, not necessarily prospective soldiers. Beyond the flags, bunting and patriotic music, some saw signs that recruiting could be difficult. The *Enquirer* ran an editorial on July 31:

> *It is the most discouraging aspect of the present state of affairs, that so many, whose feelings and motives are right on the Great Question of Saving Our Country, and yet doing so little or are doing absolutely nothing, personally, for the promotion of the cause, by securing men for the ranks. Our people attend meetings, they vote large bounties to volunteers with the most generous impulses, but in the personal labor of actually sending off recruits they are all too deficient.*

The blame, according to the *Enquirer*, rested not only with men of military age:

> *There is not a man, hardly a woman or child, who reads these lines, but that may materially aid the work, and in a way in which they can do more for the cause than by any other. You who are physically, or by reason of age or sex, or by some unaccountable circumstance, are debarred from enlisting yourself, can by a little personal exertion, influence one or two others to enlist in your stead....It is easy for us to vote for bounties for volunteers, it is easy to cry out "Go, boys, go!" but who of us go ourselves, or influence others personally to go.—We haven't learned yet what it is to make sacrifices, most of us haven't, and until we do we shall never conquer, unless we do, we do not deserve to conquer.*

Across the North, the parades and rallies paled in comparison to those of the spring of 1861. There had been many opportunities for those who wished to volunteer to do so. Casualty lists and the realities of soldier life had dampened enthusiasm for enlistments.[17]

Some believed that the challenge of securing volunteers was so great that success could come only through a draft. Nobody wanted a draft. Some feared that it would lead to riots or violence. Others thought it reflected poorly on a community's patriotism. In some areas of the country, the wives of volunteers were treated better than the wives of draftees. Of a draft, the *Enquirer* pleaded, "*Let it not* come to this. Let us be up and doing while the day lasts. Let us show our sister states that Connecticut will not be the first to falter. Let us, in Litchfield County, show our state, we know our duty and will willingly perform it." Fears of a draft escalated with the passage of a new Militia Act on July 17. This was not intended to actually coerce men into the service. Rather, it was hoped that the possibility of a draft might provide a carrot-and-stick approach. Fear of a draft would persuade men to volunteer; the bounties being offered by federal, state and local governments to volunteers made this more lucrative. That same day, the *Enquirer* outlined the $338 in benefits (exclusive of monthly pay) that a married father of two or more could earn by enlisting from federal and state inducements. While bounties soon became "the standard method of obtaining troops," they were not without the risks of overburdening taxpayers and repurposing volunteers' motivations from "love of country" to "love of money."[18]

Buckingham's decision to organize recruiting around seven districts did not mean that the new regiments would be composed solely of men from specific geographic areas. While the preceding fourteen regiments that had been formed in Connecticut drew considerably from a particular city or county, each had men from across the state. However, with serious questions swirling about whether the new regiments would be filled, Buckingham was urged to consider recruiting each of the new units locally. In this manner, men would march off to war with friends and neighbors, under the command of officers they likely knew. "Let us have a Litchfield County Regiment if possible," the *Enquirer* entreated, "officered and manned from this County. Now, while the iron's hot, Strike!" The result, the *Herald* responded, would be "that Litchfield County shall have a regiment to be proud of."[19]

Also instrumental in Buckingham's recruiting plan was to have men led by local officers whose names were put forward by the town war committees. Concurrent with calls to raise a county regiment, names were proffered to be the unit's commander. The *Herald* proposed General Moses Cooke of Goshen, but this was only a nod to the esteem of Cooke in the county. Cooke was too old and in poor health. The actual choice was obvious. A week after putting forth Cooke's name, the *Herald* responded with a more serious candidate, Leverett W. Wessells, "our present popular and capable sheriff." Wessells was born in Litchfield on July 28, 1819, to Dr. Asabel and Grace Wessells. Educated in his hometown, he struggled with a lung disorder that necessitated his moving to Florida, where his brother, Henry, was a lieutenant in the U.S. Army. (Henry Wessells would later serve as a Union general in the Civil War.) Leverett returned to Litchfield after two years and studied medicine under Dr. John Wolcott, but poor health forced him to give up his studies. Instead, he was appointed deputy sheriff of the county and, in 1849, was named Litchfield's postmaster. In 1854, he was elected high sheriff of Litchfield County and was repeatedly reelected. Wessells was well liked and had worked in positions that allowed him to interact with many county residents. He was a leader of men and possessed good organizational abilities. He was a fine choice to lead the regiment. His illness, however, would flare up almost immediately upon his assuming a military career, and Wessells's tenure at the head of the Litchfield County Regiment would not last long.[20]

Colonel Leverett Wessells. *Collection of the Litchfield Historical Society, Litchfield, Connecticut.*

Wessells's shortcomings were known at the time. "He is not," the *Herald* admitted, "'brought up in the school of the soldier,' but he has seen not a little of military life in his connection with the army in Florida." His strengths, however, outshone this: "By commissioning him, the Governor will not confer so much honor upon him as he will advance the interests of the cause, and best promote enlistments in every town in this county where Sheriff Wessells is so largely known and highly esteemed." The *Enquirer* and the *Herald* both recognized Wessells's appeal as a recruiter. "Wherever Mr. Wessells is known he is respected and loved, and we believe the patriotic youth of the county will rally to his standard more enthusiastically than to any other man." What Wessells lacked in knowledge of drill and tactics he made up for in his ability to bring in recruits. That was the essential element in the summer of 1862. After all, a good lieutenant colonel could handle the military aspects of the regiment until the colonel was up to speed.[21]

In the month following Lincoln's call for 300,000 volunteers, war meetings swept Litchfield County. Nearly every town had one, and a large county-wide meeting was held in Litchfield on July 22. Many of these meetings followed a similar pattern involving patriotic speeches by political figures, religious leaders and military veterans. Songs, often "The Star-Spangled Banner," were sung, and three cheers were offered for Old Glory. Resolutions expressing the town's commitment to the war effort were unanimously adopted, and wealthy residents frequently offered private bounties. The main attraction, however, featured young men of the town coming forward to enlist.[22]

Winsted appears to have held the first meeting in the county, on Tuesday, July 15, at Camp's Hall in the West Winsted section of town. A reporter described it as a "rousing" event, "perhaps the largest and most enthusiastic…ever held in the county" despite its having been called on short notice. One account states that more people listened from outside than could fit inside the building. The main speaker was Buckingham himself, and following his address, an anonymous donor "pledged to give $1,000 to the first company that shall be raised in Winsted within 15 days." The *Herald* suggested, "To those who would like a finger in that $1,000…now is their time to subscribe." At the end of the meeting, an enlistment paper was started "and names are rapidly attached to it." Those in attendance had "no fears that old Litchfield County will not come up to the highest requirements of duty and the occasion."[23]

Salisbury held its meeting on the nineteenth, at which five men pledged a private bounty of $100 for each of the first forty-five men from the town who enlisted. Falls Village and Goshen held meetings on the twenty-first. The former featured an election of a town war committee, "eloquent appeals to the patriotism of our citizens" by civic leaders and Reverend James Deane of North Canaan, whose address was particularly powerful. He announced that he would "close his church, put the key in his pocket, and his congregation go with him" to war. With the help of a $100 bounty from the town, Falls Village filled its quota that night. Goshen also pledged a $100 bounty to each volunteer and voted that a tax be levied on town residents to raise $4,600 to give to enlistees.[24]

The main event that summer was the county-wide meeting held at the Litchfield Courthouse on Wednesday, July 22. Every town in the county was represented except for North Canaan and Harwinton, which held their own town meetings that day. Seth P. Beers, an eighty-one-year-old Litchfield attorney (he had attended Tapping Reeve's Litchfield Law School) and prominent Democratic politician, was elected to preside over the meeting. No estimates on the size of the crowd were given, although the *Enquirer* proclaimed that "we should doubt if such a convention, so large in its representative number…so hearty and sympathetic the ardor of its members…ever assembled before in this county." Beers opened the meeting with an impassioned speech. Born three and a half months before the British surrender at Yorktown secured American independence, Beers invoked the spirit of '76, recounting "the zeal manifested among these same old hills in the revolutionary days….Let us meet [the rebels], not as *drafts*, for drafted men make poor soldiers, but as *volunteers*—every man volunteering if necessary. Were he 60 or 70 years younger he would shoulder the old Queen's Arm [a musket] himself and see what he could accomplish towards clearing the James River of Jeff Davis, Beauregard, and the Devil."[25]

Unlike the town meetings, which can best be described as rallies, this was a business meeting. When Beers finished, seven resolutions were put before the assembled crowd. The first—passed unanimously—was to raise an entire

Local and County News.

Litchfield Co. Aroused!
GRAND MEETING OF HER CITIZENS!
A LITCHFIELD CO. REG'T ORDERED!
THE SPIRIT OF '76 REVIVED!
OLD LITCHFIELD COUNTY WILL DO HER DUTY!

The *Litchfield Enquirer*'s July 24, 1862 edition reported on the county meeting held to encourage a Litchfield County regiment. *Library of Congress.*

regiment of three-year volunteers from Litchfield County. The second, passed "amid great cheering," recommended to Governor Buckingham that Leverett W. Wessells of Litchfield "is a fit and suitable person to receive a colonel's commission in the Litchfield County Regiment." The other resolutions laid the groundwork for fully raising the regiment. They called for the regiment to be rendezvoused in Litchfield County, for the training camp to be in the town of Litchfield, for the towns to offer a $100 bounty and for town meetings to be held to approve this bounty. Finally, the convention invited the "sons of Litchfield County, wherever they may wander…home to enlist in a regiment to be composed of their comrades, friends, and brothers." Over the next month, Litchfield County town officials would accuse one another of enlisting men from other towns in the county, yet they had no qualms about encouraging men from other counties to enlist in the Litchfield County regiment.[26]

The meeting adjourned with shouts of "Work! Work! Work! Every one of us!" or "Now the talking is over let us have the work!" Not all were excited by the meeting. Charles Andrews, the young attorney from Kent, recorded in his diary, "The convention was a big fizzle. What in thunder the organization meant to do by it is more than I can guess. I came home feeling as though a huge joke had been practiced on the whole county." Unfortunately, Andrews left no further elaboration.[27]

The county convention over, the town meetings resumed, albeit with a more businesslike tone. Woodbury's on July 24 still had patriotic speeches but set about the business at hand quickly. A vote was taken on the bounty and a committee formed to contact the men from town currently in the service to determine their "location and wants" and to "see that they were cared for to the end of the war." The *Enquirer* reported that there was one dissenting voice, that of Dr. G.G. Atwood. The paper wanted his name handed "down to posterity." (One week later, an enraged Atwood wrote to the *Enquirer*, insisting the paper's "malicious onslaught" against him was untrue, that he opposed the draft and bounties because he felt that patriotism alone should be the motivation for men to save the Union.) Litchfield's town meeting on Friday, July 25, was a strictly business affair, with a resolution adopted unanimously to offer $100 bounties and to empower the selectmen to borrow money if needed to pay for them. The most notable aspect of the meeting was that the presiding officer, Judge O.S. Seymour, and the individual who offered the resolution, George C. Woodruff, were prominent Democrats.[28]

Most towns passed their resolutions calling for bounties unanimously—Barkhamsted, Norfolk, Sharon, Torrington and Warren did so in the last week of July or first week of August. The votes were closer in some towns. In Bethlehem, opponents of bounties argued that they would turn men into mercenaries paid to kill Southerners. Still, the resolution passed by a 35 to 25 margin. Morris, scene of the peace rally where Schnabel had been arrested a year earlier, approved the bounty by a vote of 62 to 50; of this, the *Enquirer* declared, "As Morris has something of the reputation of a 'Secesh' town, this vote is deserving of an honorable mention." It is also worth noting that the votes in Bethlehem and Morris demonstrate that for all of the enthusiasm for the war effort that summer, there remained pockets of bitter opposition. Cornwall supported its bounty resolution unanimously, but passing the bounty was one thing—raising the 42 men the town set as its goal was another, especially with 53 of the town's 190 men of military age already in the army. "Men of Cornwall, shall it be done?" one speaker queried. "Cast away the thought that it cannot; be resolved that it shall." The speaker then tried another tack. "Women of Cornwall, hurry along your husbands, sons and brothers to the field. The exigencies of the hour demand the sacrifice; let it be made." Women may not have been trusted with the vote, but they were seen as superb recruiters for the army.[29]

There was one final grand rally that summer. It was held in New Milford on Friday evening, August 1. Rain forced it to be held indoors, at the Congregational Church. The meeting marked a high point in the bipartisan efforts to raise the regiment, for the two main speakers were Governor Buckingham and his 1862 Democratic opponent, James Loomis. As the two men entered the church, a cannon was fired to welcome them. Loomis spoke first, calling for political unity and volunteers.

Buckingham was emotional when he followed his rival to the podium, thanking Loomis profusely for his work and assuring the crowd that "my heart beats in unison with his." Buckingham spoke for an hour, providing the audience with a detailed overview of the current state of the war effort but urging the townspeople not to despair: "If [Buckingham] did not believe in our triumph and the restoration of our government, he would never meet with his countrymen on an occasion like this." When Buckingham finished, George S. Williams, an attorney educated at Yale and Trinity College, declared that he would ask "no one to go further than he would go himself" and announced that not only was he willing to enlist to serve his country, but he was also willing "to die in its defence." With this, the crowd sang "America," and the rally ended. A town meeting immediately followed, offering a $100 bounty to enlistees.

There remained but one bit of business before the real work of filling the regiment began. That was the appointment of recruiting officers, the men who, in the words of veteran and regimental historian Theodore F. Vaill, "opened offices and canvassed mountain and valley, field factory, shop, highway and hedge for recruits." This was difficult work, but these were plum positions. The men were well compensated, and successful work as a recruiting officer often led to an officer's commission. Appointment of recruiting officers was a task Adjutant General Williams assigned the town war committees in his July 14 circular to town selectmen. The towns responded by naming prominent citizens or men with appeal to a certain demographic. A.B. Shumway of Litchfield, for example, worked for the *Enquirer*, which gave him broad connections in the town. James Q. Rice of Goshen was the headmaster of a school in that town, giving him a network of former students to tap as potential recruits. Irish-born Michael Kelly from Sharon worked to enlist members of that town's significant immigrant population. The eloquent George S. Williams served as a recruiting officer from New Milford. Still, not all were happy with the selections. In writing home upon hearing about the recruiting officers, Alva Stone of Litchfield, who was serving with the 8th Connecticut Infantry, cut to the heart of the matter: "A man who has never been in the army would know but little what men are wanted here—or how sorely we need them right away."[30]

Chapter 6

"We Want as Many Men to Do It as They Have Got"

In the last week of July 1862, the swelling numbers of men who enlisted in what, to this point, was only a hypothetical Litchfield County regiment received proof that their military service was indeed real when word arrived that their regiment would be known as the 19th Connecticut Infantry.

Additional signs appeared that the raising of the regiment was entering a new phase. By late July, the pages of local newspapers were filled with rumors about who would fill the officer positions within the regiment. That Leverett Wessells would serve as colonel was a foregone conclusion. Of the competition to secure commissions for other leadership positions in the regiment, the *Winsted Herald* reported, "There are at least a full regiment of applicants for these and minor offices, and the Litchfield hotels and bars are enjoying as rich a harvest from their visits thither as if it were 'court week.'" The competition for these positions was fierce, for not only was prestige on the line, but town pride as well. The perceived slight of Litchfield County men for officer slots in the early Connecticut regiments was one of the factors that led to the demand for geographically based regiments. Towns were determined to get their men into significant roles. Additionally, there was a dramatic difference in pay between enlisted men and officers. In the fall of 1862, Union army privates received a base salary of $13 per month. Lieutenants were paid $105.50 per month.[1]

The selection of officers was of such widespread interest that men already in the army wrote home about candidates for positions in the 19th. Alva Stone of Litchfield, serving with the 8th Connecticut in North Carolina, wrote that

The officers of the 19th Connecticut Infantry. *Collection of the Litchfield Historical Society, Litchfield, Connecticut.*

"the name of WESSELS strikes us favorably and we shall rejoice to hear of his appointment to a Colonelcy—His name will be a 'tower of strength' to the County....[B]etween you and me I do wish that some other name than XXXXXX might be brot [*sic*] forward to command a Company for Litchfield for there is more in the right kind of man to start with than some imagine." Stone also spoke of the turbulent political waters that needed to be navigated by aspiring officers, intimating that wealth was a key to a commission: "It does take a pile of money to start business as a Captain of a new Company and a man must keep up his end with his brother officers or they will be down on him." Stone also expressed his "hopes that Lieut [Luman] Wadhams would be out again with a commission—but am almost afraid he comes under the ban of the Government." Wadhams had recently served as Stone's lieutenant in Company E of the 8th but resigned due to illness and a dispute over rank. Stone worried that the politics of the army would keep the widely admired Wadhams from a deserving position.[2]

Charles J. Deming of Litchfield, who had been serving in Company I of the First Connecticut Heavy Artillery, was appointed a first lieutenant and regimental adjutant, the colonel's administrative assistant. The *Herald* reported on August 8 that he "has the reputation of a clever fellow." Deming described himself as "not a talking man but a fighting man." Bradley D. Lee of Barkhamsted was also commissioned a lieutenant and named the regimental quartermaster, responsible for the procurement of food, clothing and equipment for the men. That was certainly a daunting task, and the August 8 edition of the *Enquirer* reported that Lee "is already on the ground" well ahead of the rest of the regiment. He would have his work cut out for him but would be assisted by Franklin J. Candee of Plymouth, who was appointed the regimental commissary sergeant. As such, he would distribute rations to the men, sell goods and food to the officers and oversee the preparation of meals.[3]

The physical and spiritual health of the men were also provided for in raising the regiment. The 19th would go off to war with a full medical complement and a chaplain. That the community parted with these essential men speaks to the commitment made in mobilizing for the war. Henry Plumb of New Milford, who had studied medicine at Yale, would serve as the regiment surgeon throughout the war. Joining Plumb were assistant surgeon Jeremiah Phelps, a thirty-eight-year-old Norfolk native who practiced in Wolcottville, and John W. Lawton of Naugatuck, another Yale-trained physician. Phelps never left the state; commissioned on September 11, 1862, he resigned four days later, sparking one acquaintance to comment, "Apparently he was less

Surgeon Henry Plumb. *Collection of the Litchfield Historical Society, Litchfield, Connecticut.*

Lieutenant Colonel Elisha Kellogg. *Collection of the Litchfield Historical Society, Litchfield, Connecticut.*

enthusiastic about soldiering." The ability to resign a commission was yet another benefit an officer held over an enlisted man.[4]

There was serious competition over who would serve as the regimental chaplain. Commissioned chaplains were paid $100 per month plus rations for himself and his horse. There was initially enthusiasm for Reverend Hiram Eddy to return to the field as chaplain of the county regiment, but his prior experience as a prisoner of war dampened these calls. Ultimately, when the 19th marched off to war, it did so under the spiritual guidance of Reverend Jonathan Wainwright, who followed a remarkable path to that role. A Connecticut native and University of Vermont graduate, Wainwright led an Episcopal parish in Wilmington, North Carolina, until the summer of 1861. Then, when he refused to offer a prayer for the president of the Confederate States, instead insisting on a prayer for Lincoln, he was forced to resign. Making his way through the lines of the armies, he settled in Torrington, but not before, as the *Litchfield Enquirer* reported, he "told the people when he left that he should visit their country again before the war ended in a different capacity, and with more powerful appliances to back up his exhortations to them to hold fast to law and government."[5]

Wessells, while widely popular, presented two challenges: an experienced military man would be needed to oversee the training of the men, and the colonel's poor health likely meant that he would not remain with the regiment long. Thus, the search for his lieutenant colonel was especially important. The *Herald* put forward three candidates:

Abram Kellogg of New Hartford, a former captain of the 2nd Connecticut; Alan Brady of Torrington, who had served as the lieutenant colonel of the 3rd Connecticut; and Major Sanford Perkins, also of Torrington, the major of the 14th Connecticut. Governor Buckingham, however, had another candidate in mind: Elisha S. Kellogg, originally of Glastonbury, a major of the 1st Connecticut Heavy Artillery. The number of men being reassigned from the 1st Heavy to serve in the fledgling 19th caused the 1st's commander, Colonel Robert Tyler, to explode and demand "to know if the Governor of Connecticut is going to make a 'd----d yeast pot' of his regiment, to raise officers for the new regiment now forming." Others tried to assuage him by pointing out that the "fact that so many officers are taken from the Conn. First shows the high appreciation in which that Regiment is held."[6]

While Kellogg would not arrive in Litchfield until mid-August, one veteran would remember, "The regiment was from the beginning Kellogg's," while a regimental history proclaimed, "There is not a scene, day, nor a memory from Camp Dutton to [the war's end] that can be wholly divested of Kellogg." Kellogg, thirty-eight years old, was an adventurer. A former member of the British merchant marines, he raced to California for the gold rush and was working in a machine shop in Derby, Connecticut, when the war began. Kellogg, described by a comrade as a "gold-hunter and wanderer," would soon imprint himself on the hearts of these men.[7]

With the regiment's personnel rounding out, its organizers turned their attention to finding a location for its camp where the volunteers from across the county would assemble, receive their initial training and become members of the U.S. Army. Town pride—and some legitimate logistical concerns—entered into the discussion of a site. While the county meeting recommended the camp be located in Litchfield, the *Winsted Herald* and *Housatonic Republican* newspapers raised concerns. "Half a dozen other places might have been selected within the County with more advantages," the *Republican* declared. For both papers, the central concern was transportation, especially Litchfield's lack of a railroad. The nearest station to Litchfield was in East Litchfield—seven miles away—and the elevation gain between the station and the center of town made the transportation of the supplies necessary to equip a regiment of one thousand men especially challenging. "Cut off from railroads and cheap and easy transit," the *Republican* pronounced, Litchfield "surely has not many recommendations as a rendezvous." The *Republican* favored nearby North Canaan as a site, especially since two railroad lines converged there. The *Herald* was more specific in its recommendation, arguing that the camp could be sited in Litchfield, but just over the line from Wolcotville so that "the rendezvous should be contiguous to a railroad."[8]

Selecting the site of an army camp required considering factors besides transportation. Those problems could be overcome, but a water supply was nonnegotiable. Litchfield's status as the county seat and the fact that it held the geographic center of the county made the town a logical setting for the camp. Once that decision was made, the search was on for a site that could provide fresh water for one thousand men over an extended period of time. It was found on the "beautiful sloping field" of Cyrus Catlin's farm on South Chestnut Hill, a mile southeast of the center of town. The Bantam River flowed along the base of the hill, providing water for bathing, and more importantly, there were three wells nearby. Boosters were exuberant, with the *Enquirer* declaring it to be "the very best ground that could be selected in the town, and probably the best in the state."[9]

However, opposition to locating the camp in Litchfield was not limited to those from other towns. On July 21, Alva Stone wrote to his wife in Litchfield from his post in North Carolina, "The Enquirer seems to want to have the Regt quartered in your village—if this were done Pop Corn merchants would grow fat out of the soldiers—and it might be all very fine for your to have a 'training' every day so as to have something to look at—but I assure a worse thing for the morals of the community could not possibly happen—You have no idea of the rough men that are collected together in the formation of a Regiment of Soldiers." Stone was certainly correct in one regard: residents of the county would turn out in droves to see their sons, sweethearts and neighbors be trained for war.[10]

Much of July saw excited reports of the response of county men to the calls of the president and governor. "We have cheering reports from the various parts of the County," the *Enquirer* announced on August 1, "and confidently expect 300 men will be put in camp the first week." War fever swept young and old. Several recruits were said to be only "waiting for the consent of their parents, which ultimately will be given." Meanwhile, Rollin Beecher, "a man extensively known and highly respected in this community…intends to take his place in the face of his country's enemies" despite the fact that at fifty-two, he was seven years too old to serve in the Union army.[11]

By the end of the first week of August, Winsted reported fifty volunteers, Salisbury forty volunteers, Plymouth and Woodbury thirty and Watertown fifteen. Canaan, Barkhamsted, North Canaan, Sharon and Torrington were on track to meet their quotas. Town leaders in Litchfield boasted, "We shall take our full town quota in the Regiment into camp as soon as it is formed." "Harwinton…has just sent 30 of her best boys into the Litchfield County Regiment," the *Enquirer* reported. "Three cheers for old Harwinton!" Newspaper readers followed the tallies of enlistments with the same rapt attention that a future generation would read baseball box scores.[12]

Still, the newspapers were unafraid to question the patriotism of entire towns if enlistments lagged. At the end of July, the *Winsted Herald* expressed its fear "that the more southern towns of the county are not yet so fully aroused as the northern" and reminded its readers that "the first duty of every man…[is] to do whatever he can to encourage and forward those enlistments." There was no room for mitigating circumstances—men were either heroes or traitors. This sentiment was made clear in a letter from Alva Stone of the 8th Connecticut: "Is Gilbud sure of missing a draft in case one is made?…How about XXXX? Where is the stinking secesh XXXX? What says XXXXX about coming? And are those lazy XXXXXX boys going to feed themselves among the recruits as they did last year? Will XXXX fail to make all the money he can?"[13]

Despite the praise heaped on those who enlisted—and the potential for those who didn't to be labeled traitors—it soon became clear to officials that the regiment would struggle to fill its ranks. Failure to raise a full regiment meant that Litchfield County men would be used to fill out the other regiments from across the state. Having made the case that the state could raise regiments by appealing to geographic pride, county leaders now risked bringing embarrassment on northwestern Connecticut.

It is unclear if serious consideration was given to the reason why enlistments lagged behind the expectations of county leaders. Certainly some towns—Cornwall and Warren, for example—had already sent far more than their share of men off to war. Also, the newspapers carried stories sure to make men question enlisting. Many were certainly aware of the travails of the 13th Connecticut, which saw twelve of its members die of disease before the unit had even departed its New Haven training camp. While the 19th Connecticut was being raised, reports arrived that the 5th Connecticut had been struck hard by Confederates under Stonewall Jackson at Cedar Mountain, Virginia. In a relatively brief fight, the 5th suffered thirty-seven men killed, seventy-five wounded and fifty-eight missing and captured. Casualties were listed in the papers, and those pondering enlistments likely saw familiar names. Did these news stories, juxtaposing the realities of war alongside the calls for duty and patriotism, contribute to the slowing number of volunteers?

Nonetheless, the shortfall in recruits was overcome, and a full regiment was raised. To understand how this happened, it is necessary to discuss the factors that motivated men to serve in the war. Historians have debated these motivations for decades, and a wave of new studies has appeared over the past twenty-five years. James McPherson, among the most highly regarded of all Civil War historians, has argued that the primary motivating factor for recruits was a sense of duty, which was often employed to "persuade reluctant parents or wives to sanction their decision to enlist." McPherson added that few soldiers were motivated by the issue of slavery or a sense of adventure.[14]

Chandra Manning, however, in her book *What This Cruel War Was Over*, emphasized that emancipation became a central motivation for the Union soldier. Key to this transformation were the initial encounters between those Northerners already in the service and enslaved persons. In June 1862, Seth Plumb—a fellow Litchfield resident and comrade of Alva Stone's in the 8th Connecticut—wrote from North Carolina to friends in his hometown, informing them that

> *we don't know anything about slavery at the North. I believe it is the worst crime ever dreamt of yet, and will keep the nation in fire and blood till it is crushed. You don't know anything about the malignity of the slaveholders. They have always had their way and it more than kills them to lose their n*[------] *and be ruled by the Yankees. I think many of them will leave their country when we get them whipped.*

Nearly three months later, with the men of the 19th in training camp, Plumb again wrote home, describing an exodus of African Americans fleeing slavery in Fredericksburg, Virginia:

> *The blacks flocked out with us by the hundreds. In the throng were ox carts piled full of little ones, and old women, women carrying their babies in their arms, and nearly all had bundles on their heads. Till the last bridge was set afire, they kept coming, old and young of all shades and in every*

> *description of dress....* [H]*undreds of little children had to walk to the Creek. One old slave with a flock of little ones said, "I* CAN *stand it to live a slave, but these my childrens."*

Clearly these sights—sights rarely experienced by a New Englander—had an impact on Plumb. Firsthand experience with slavery changed minds; it is certainly feasible that hearing these accounts from friends and neighbors could have motivated men to enlist.[15]

If the process of encouraging enlistments depended on rallying hesitant enlistees with calls to honor, duty and abolitionism, religious mobilization was also required. At the heart of the national effort to do this was Litchfield native Henry Ward Beecher, famed minister and abolitionist. Addressing those who may have harbored concerns that the war's violence would be offensive to God, Beecher declared, "God hates lukewarm patriotism as much as lukewarm religion and we hate it too. We do not believe in hermaphrodite patriots." Civil War armies pulled men from all sections of society, as Stone's warnings to his sister about the morality of recruits in training camps demonstrated. Still, if newspapers sought to play on expectations of honor and to highlight the political issues at stake for potential enlistees, ministers, as will be seen, used their pulpits to assuage any religious concerns.[16]

In appealing to religious impulses, Litchfield County officials played a trump card: the newly freed Reverend Hiram Eddy. Released through a prisoner exchange on July 26, Eddy's return to Winsted on Wednesday, July 31, was a total surprise, as a thunderstorm had knocked down the telegraph lines. There were no friends, family or welcoming committee for what the *Herald* termed Eddy's "unheralded and unexpected arrival." The next morning, a procession of Winsted's recruits led Eddy to his church, where he proclaimed, "I am for the Union ten thousand times more than ever before—my hairs have whitened during my years of captivity, but for every white hair I have scored a black mark against this rebellion." Eddy then went to work recruiting volunteers across the county. Typical of his efforts was a rally held in Winsted on August 5, where Eddy was the featured speaker but was joined on the dais by a group of local officials, including "two or three ministers. Five or six names were added to the list of volunteers." Dudley Landon Vaill, in his history of the regiment, called Eddy "a powerful advocate to the cause; night after night he spoke in different towns, urging the call to service fervently and with effect," and he placed the minister's photograph at the front of his book.[17]

Cultural, political and religious apprehensions could be put to rest with words and emotional appeals. Economic worries were harder to mitigate. The preceding fifteen months had provided plenty of opportunities for men to volunteer based on their patriotic, political or religious impulses, yet hundreds of thousands of Northern men remained on the sidelines. What prevented their enlisting? Certainly there were those who opposed the war and others who feared service. Economic factors, however, cannot be overlooked. Depression had gripped the nation in 1857, and by 1860, one third of the North owned 95 percent of the wealth. Further economic woes ensued with a recession that struck New England in 1860–61. Concerns about how secession would affect trade between North and South fueled an industrial slowdown and bank failures. Historian William Marvel has found that the statistically poorest group of volunteers were those who enlisted in April 1861; the war was a boon to the unemployed. As Marvel wrote, "Legions of men without work or money found employment with President Lincoln's call for militia." But what of those who held jobs but lived in or just above poverty? They were likely reluctant to give up those jobs for the low monthly wage of an army private; officials needed to overcome these concerns to fill the rolls of the 19th Connecticut.[18]

Overcoming the financial concerns of would-be volunteers would be tremendously expensive, with the cost borne by the federal, state and local governments. This money was spent on bounties, financial inducements paid to enlistees. Wealthy individuals in certain towns had offered private bounties even in the war's earliest days. The bounties offered in the summer of 1862 were on a vastly greater scale. Canaan provides a glimpse of what the bounty system looked like for a typical Litchfield County volunteer in the 19th Connecticut. The federal government offered a $100 bounty; because Connecticut lacked real county government, the onus fell on towns to offer bounties at the local level. This Canaan did, fulfilling the recommendation of the county meeting that towns offer $100 per soldier. The Connecticut state bounty was $90, payable in installments of $30 per year of service. Also, a recruit received $2 of his first month's salary immediately upon enlistment. Since federal and local bounties were typically paid in two installments, recruits could expect to receive about $132 upon enlistment. With pay for a private at $13 per month, after a year in the service, the recruit would make $316, with another $130 in bounty money owed him upon completion of his term of enlistment. By way of comparison, median wealth in Connecticut was $500 in 1860. Marvel has analyzed the finances of twenty men from North Canaan who enlisted in the summer of 1862. He determined the family wealth for eighteen of the enlistees and found that a whopping 83 percent fell below the state's median wealth. Fully twelve of the men did not own property at all. For the state as a whole, 79 percent of the three-year volunteers fell below the median income level.[19]

While the bounty system went a long way to removing the economic concerns of potential recruits, it was not the only financial inducement offered to Litchfield County men. The departure of the first recruits from Massachusetts in April 1861 was followed by a significant increase in the number of women in almshouses. An estimated 30 percent of Union volunteers were married. Departing for the front not only created more work for women, but it also left them in financial danger. These concerns led states like Connecticut to offer payments to the wives and children of soldiers. In Connecticut, these payments were made quarterly, with a wife receiving

PENSIONS,

BOUNTY AND PAY

PROCURED FOR DISCHARGED SOLDIERS AND **RELATIVES** OF DECEASED OFFICERS AND SOLDIERS

—BY—

HENRY ROGERS,

Attorney at Law and Government Claim and Pension Agent.

OFFICE, 7 *Leffingwell Building*, 153 *Church St.*,

Corner of Court Street, NEW HAVEN, CONN.

Hereafter charges for procuring certificates of Bounty and Pay will be made as follows,

Viz. upon $100 *Bounty* 5 *percent or* $5, *upon pay for a sum of less than* $50 — $5, *over* $50 — 10 *percent.*

Letters of inquiry answered.

REFERENCES BY PERMISSION,

Hon. Henry Dutton, Judge of the Supreme Court.
Hon. Thomas B. Osborne.
P. A. Jewett, Surgeon U. S. A.
George H. Watrous, Esq.

Cash bounties and promises of aid to families were motivating factors in securing enlistments. *Collection of the Litchfield Historical Society, Litchfield, Connecticut.*

$18 and each child $6, up to a maximum of two children. Towns disbursed funds and kept careful records, as they were reimbursed by the state. The process began in November 1861. Alva Stone of Litchfield noted that when he reported to Hartford to formally enlist in the fall of 1861, "we all gave our place of residence—whether I was married or single and I supposed the thing was settled so you could draw pay—at least I was told so then."[20]

Payments to families were also used to hold soldiers to their duty. Payments stopped when a soldier was discharged at the end of his service or if he was found to be from a town different from that in which he enlisted. Payments were also stopped if a soldier deserted, regardless of whether or not he returned to his wife and children. Families continued to receive payments if a soldier died. Sylvanus Clark of Litchfield, for example, enlisted in the 8th Connecticut in September 1861 and died of disease on March 14, 1862. His widow, Ellen, continued to receive $18 per quarter until these payments were replaced by a postwar pension. Thus, an important message was sent to recruits. Do your duty and your family will receive financial assistance. Desert and you will not only bring dishonor on yourself and your family, but they could also face financial ruin.[21]

The first quarterly records to include Litchfield men who enlisted in the 19th Connecticut are those from November 1862. All totaled, the town was making payments to sixty-three families (twenty-one to a wife only) for a total of $1,369.83, an average of $21.74 to each family. Of those, thirty-six were the families of men who had enlisted in the 19th. The amounts of their payments were prorated to the date of their acceptance into the U.S. Army, which for most was September 11, 1862. Of the thirty-six, sixteen were for $18 to wives only, seven were to families with one child and thirteen were to families with two or more children. Norman Perkins enlisted despite being the father of six children. Two other men from Litchfield volunteered even though they had four children each. William Parmalee presents a particularly tragic human face to this process. When he enlisted in September 1862 as the father of one child, he anticipated his wife drawing $24 per quarter in assistance. It is doubtful that he knew she was pregnant. Their second child was born in February 1863, and she received the maximum payment of $30 per quarter. Mrs. Parmalee was receiving that amount when her husband was killed at Cold Harbor on June 1, 1864.[22]

Bounties should not be viewed only as a means by which the least fortunate men could be brought into the service. It would be wrong to think that these men were mercenaries. It seems clear that they would not have fought for the Confederacy had its bounties been higher. Rather, the bounty men of

1862 were likely also motivated to enlist by patriotism, a sense of duty and, perhaps, abolitionist beliefs; the presence of bounties and aid to families made it economically feasible for them to serve their country.

Similarly, it would be a mistake to argue that bounties served only to entice the poorest Northerners to join up. The newspapers reported creative uses of bounty money, hoping, perhaps, to spur volunteers from among the more entrepreneurial minded. For example, at the time of the final push to fill the 19th, the *Herald* ran a story from Truro, Massachusetts, a Cape Cod town whose entire quota in the summer of 1862 was four. Those four slots were snapped up by brothers who "received a bounty of $325 each—total $1,300, they clubbed the funds, and purchased a farm for the old folks, whom they leave in possession while they go to the war." Stories of this type may have influenced men to accept a bounty. For some, bounties represented a form of financial safeguard for their family; for others, they represented economic opportunity.[23]

Many feared that the system would produce "bounty jumpers," men who claimed their bounty money, deserted and then enlisted with another regiment. The *Herald* warned of this possibility as early as July 27 in an article titled "CAUTION TO TOWNS," the use of capital letters amplifying the urgency: "Towns in their anxiety to furnish their quota of troops must be careful that they do not pay their bounty money without the equivalent. The only safe course for them to pursue is to delay paying the bounty until the man is mustered into the service by the proper *United States* official." This was, more or less, the system Litchfield County's towns used, but it was not foolproof. There were at least two volunteers of the 19th who deserted within three or four days of receiving their initial bounty money. Deputies and special agents were employed across the North in the summer of 1862 to track down deserters. In Connecticut, those who apprehended deserters could receive "the sum of five dollars, and five cents mileage from the place of arrest to the place of delivery—provided the award and the mileage does not exceed ten dollars." Estimates claim that there were as many as 100,000 Union soldiers absent without leave by December 1862.[24]

Perhaps of more immediate concern to towns than the possibility of bounty jumpers were the rivalries the cash outlays created. While the July 22 county meeting recommended each town offer a $100 bounty, the bidding for recruits by towns in some cases escalated rapidly. Towns soon veered from the recommendation of the county meeting and offered larger bounties. Watertown, for example, offered $250. Other towns found themselves in trouble because they were late to the game in offering

Seth Plumb. *Collection of the Litchfield Historical Society, Litchfield, Connecticut.*

bounties. New Hartford watched its potential recruits go to other towns to enlist. Five men from Falls Village had already crossed the border and enlisted in the 10th Massachusetts in 1861, likely because that state offered more aid to families; potential recruits continued this shopping around in the summer of 1862. There was real concern in the northwestern towns of the county, where men could easily cross into Massachusetts or New York. In mid-September, the *Herald* addressed these concerns by appealing to state pride, calling those who joined a New York regiment "great fools. The Connecticut regiments are better paid, better equipped, and will be better cared for than the New York….We beg of all Connecticut men who enter the army, to enlist under the banner of their own State." Volunteers, however, benefited from rising bounties. New Hartford held an emergency town meeting on August 6 and voted to award volunteers a $125 bounty. Neighboring Barkhamsted, with its bounty at $100, suddenly had difficulty meeting its quota.[25]

The high bounties offered that summer also sparked resentment among those men already in the service, an understandable response since most of those men had marched off to war without large cash inducements. Seth Plumb understood the need to entice men to volunteer but couched his opposition to bounties in worry about the type of volunteer they might produce:

> *Those rebels can be whipped, but we want as many men to do it as they have got, and I think now we are likely to have them. Offering two and three hundred dollars a head for volunteers to go and help their brothers in the field who are outnumbered looks as if patriotism was rather scarce, and must be bought into men. I think we are able to hold our own with what men we have got, but where are the men that were going to rush into the field if they were really needed?…Sometimes I think we are not worthy to triumph.*

More direct in expressing his resentment of the bounties was Private Henry W. Loomis, a Watertown resident serving in the 1st Connecticut

Heavy Artillery. Writing to William Cothren, an influential and wealthy citizen of Woodbury, from Fort Scott, Virginia, Loomis stated that there were two things that

> *rather displease us. First—the enormous bounties paid to the new regiments, either to buy them, or stir up their patriotism....Second—that these same new regiments, after having been dragged to the field by love of money or fear of a draft, should be styled the cream of the State, the best men who have left the State, and other appellations equally flattering to them. Now, we cannot see why these new men should receive a higher rate of compensation for their services, than we who have been out through all the campaigns.*

In their letters, Plumb and Loomis struggle to balance their frustrations with the fact that reinforcements were desperately needed by the Union army. If that desperation led Northern communities to entice new recruits while causing resentment in those men who had earlier volunteered for nothing more than their sense of patriotism or duty, it was a risk that needed to be taken.[26]

Recruiting posters for the 19th Connecticut further highlight the motivations of those who enlisted. In the summer of 1862, broadsides appeared in the town of Litchfield proclaiming, "Litchfield Awake. Volunteers to Arms!!" This line, however, was the poster's only attempt to stir local or national pride. Devoid of images, the poster relied on words and—perhaps more importantly—numbers to recruit volunteers: "Save your Bounty." "Volunteers choose their own Officers. Drafted men have no choice, they go where sent. Drafted men receive only $13 a month, they get no Bounty, Families get nothing." The broadside then listed all the financial incentives available to volunteers, from bounties to aid to families to monthly pay, and announced that a volunteer would make $506, while a drafted man would receive only $117. An advertisement in the *Litchfield Enquirer* reminded volunteers that this was "the time to enlist in your Home Regiment" but also stated that bounties and advance pay would total $200 and warned that the town's bounty expired on September 1.[27]

Evidence suggests that recruiting officers created their own posters or advertisements. Another poster from July 1862—this one running over the

Litchfield Awake.

Volunteers to Arms!!

Enlist *NOW* and save your Bounty.

Only a few days before the *DRAFT*.

The Governor declares it must be made.

Volunteers choose their own Officers.

Drafted men have no choice, they go where sent.

Drafted men receive only $13 a month, they get no Bounty, Families get nothing.

Volunteers for 3 years, or the War, receive

United States Pay, per year,	$156,00
" Bounty,	100,00
Town of Litchfield Bounty,	100,00
State Bounty, per year,	30,00
" " for wife,	72,00
" " for two children,	48,00
Total,	**$506,00**

Volunteers for nine months receive

United States Pay,	$117,00.	State Bounty,	$22,50
State Bounty for wife,	54,00.	" for two children,	36,00

Town of Litchfield Bounty, - - $100,00

Total for nine months, $329,50.

A Drafted Man gets only $117,00.

A recruiting poster for the 19th Connecticut. Note the emphasis on bounties. *Collection of the Litchfield Historical Society, Litchfield, Connecticut.*

name of William Bissell, with headquarters at Litchfield's Mansion House hotel, announced to "MEN OF LITCHFIELD COUNTY" that "THE COUNTRY DEMANDS OUR SERVICES." There could be no mistaking its employment of the language of duty and manhood, declaring, "Our brothers in the field call to us for succor. Of the promptitude and valor now displayed depend not only their lives, but the life of the nation." Its text concluded by urging potential volunteers to "hasten, like men, to the rescue." Yet the bottom half of the poster details the economic incentives offered to new recruits, itemizing the town, state and federal bounties; monthly pay; and "allowances" for wives and children. This totaled $533 for a volunteer's first year in the service at a time when the average carpenter made $500 a year, the average day laborer $345 and the average farm hand $180 plus board. It is clear that those officials responsible for raising the regiment had determined that appeals to economics were the surest way to secure the needed recruits.[28]

Officials were likely correct in their approach. Kent's Charles Andrews recorded, "Volunteering is quite successful here our quota is filled and we might get men enough[,] more if there had been no limit to the bounty." This was soon remedied when a town meeting extended the offer of a bounty to all who enlisted before August 20 and to others after that date at the discretion of the selectmen. Whereas reports from mid- to late July lamented the slow nature of recruiting, quotas were met and a full regiment raised from within Litchfield County marched off to war. There can be no question that the bounties were instrumental in achieving that. Nor can it be denied that this came at a steep cost. Over the course of the war, the federal, state and local governments expended an incredible $585 million in bounties.[29]

At the turn of the twentieth century, Dudley Landon Vaill, son of a veteran of the 19th Connecticut, wrote that the unit comprised men "who recognized soberly the duty that was presenting itself in this emergency, and men of a very different stamp from those drawn into the ranks in the later years of the war by enormous bounties." It is understandable that this is how Vaill wanted to remember his father's motivations for enlisting, and later recruits did receive larger bounties. However, it is inaccurate to suggest the recruits of the summer of '62 were not influenced by financial incentives. The evidence is not just overwhelming; it is, in many cases, heart rending. Receipts detail how recruits from Salisbury that summer wished to disburse their bounty money. These indicate that the literacy rate among these men was significantly lower than that of the regiment—or American society—as a whole. Many of the receipts direct W.R.

Whittlesey, a treasurer of the Salisbury Bank, to allocate recruits' bounty money to pay off debts. Some, like Amos Wooden, requested their money be turned over to the Gibbs family; Goodrich Gibbs was a blacksmith who made or repaired tools for farmers and laborers. Wesley Gibbs and Elijah Briggs were among those who directed Whittlesey to use their bounty money to pay off debts; they would both go on to win the Medal of Honor. Being a bounty man did not make one a poor soldier. Jacob Warner, who was illiterate, asked Whittlesey to place $150 of his bounty money in the bank for the use of his wife. Such disbursements, however, were not limited to Salisbury men. Homer Curtiss from Warren enlisted in Company H of the 19th. In a September 13 letter to his mother, he was quite specific as to how he wanted his bounty money used: "I sent $26 by Lucy yesterday and I send $30 today by Frank. There will not be much of surplus after paying $6 for the picture and $48 to Swift + Hine [a general store in Warren] but whatever there is use as you would like." Curtiss and his family were certainly not impoverished—they had more than $8,000 in real estate and property—yet he still owed a considerable amount of money to the store. Even those who did not enlist specifically for financial reasons benefited from the economic boon of enlisting in the summer of 1862.[30]

Chapter 7

"I...Got My Man"

Alva Stone thought little of the bounties and continued to cling to the hope that love of country would swell the ranks. On August 2, he wrote, "It does seem to me that recruiting officers need not... run around to every man and beg of him to enlist—it ought to be enough to know that the Country is in danger—to bring out the man spontaneously...if I only had the voice large enough I would wake up the State of Connecticut once if she slept forever after I am getting cross and must stop to cool off." However, the recruiting efforts of the county not only relied on newspapers, posters and town meetings to spread the word of the need for men and the benefits of enlisting but also on personally visiting as many men as possible.[1]

Each town in Litchfield County appointed recruiting officers who were formally sworn into the military to perform this duty. Service as a recruiting officer was often a step toward an officer's rank. As Theodore Vaill later wrote, "The offer of a commission to anyone who should enlist forty men proved a great incentive to effort, and every young man who contemplated enlisting was straightaway beset with a persistent horde of rival drummers—each armed with a persuasive tongue and marvelous list of inducements." The governor maintained the right to approve all commissions and recruiting officers needed to satisfy minimal military requirements.[2]

Alexander B. Shumway of Litchfield provides a good example of a typical recruiting officer. Born in North Adams, Massachusetts, in 1836, Shumway dropped out of school when his father died. He went to work for the *North Adams Transcript* and then the *Pittsfield Eagle*. Moving to

Connecticut in 1856, he worked for the staunchly Democratic *Bridgeport Farmer* and then moved to Litchfield with his wife, Fanny, in 1859, taking a job as the foreman and later editor of the pro-Republican *Enquirer*. Likely appointed a recruiting officer due to his connections through the paper, Shumway was soon "busy recruiting....He has already enlisted several men and expects to enlist many more before the regiment goes into camp." The experiences of recruiting officers like Shumway, Michael Kelly of Sharon, David Soule of New Milford, James Q. Rice of Goshen, Edward Roberts of East Canaan and James Deane of North Canaan offer glimpses into both the travails they faced and the essential roles they played in filling the ranks of the 19th Connecticut. Their appointments appear to have been related to their connections to particular demographic groups, institutions such as churches or schools, or their politics—several were prominent Wide Awakes. Recruiting officers faced significant obstacles in their work, including political opposition, protective mothers and the economic circumstances of individual families. Yet for the most part they succeeded due to interpersonal skills, their status in the community and sheer persistence.[3]

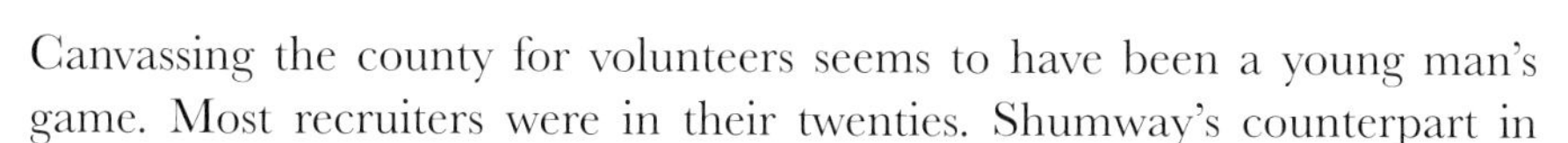

Canvassing the county for volunteers seems to have been a young man's game. Most recruiters were in their twenties. Shumway's counterpart in Litchfield, William Bissell, was, at forty-two, an exception, as was forty-year-old Rice. For their efforts, recruiting officers were reimbursed by the federal government for food, lodging and transportation up to the time they mustered into the United States service. In some cases, recruiting officers were offered bounties. Bissell and Shumway, for example, were both voted $100 bounties by the town of Litchfield.[4]

William Bissell. *Collection of the Litchfield Historical Society, Litchfield, Connecticut.*

Michael Kelly was a twenty-four-year-old resident of Sharon in the summer of 1862. Born in Roscommon County, Ireland, he immigrated to the United States, where he studied for the priesthood at the Amenia Seminary. Leaving the seminary, he took a job casting ammunition for cannons at the Hotchkiss & Sons factory. Wages

Michael Kelly. *U.S. Army History and Education Center.*

at the factory were high, but Kelly left for the army the day after Lincoln's July 1, 1862 proclamation. Hotchkiss himself expressed his sorrow at Kelly's leaving, urging him to consider that men were needed to make armaments as much as for soldiers, but ultimately wished his employee well. Kelly hoped to be a recruiting officer, and while nativism may have swept the state in the 1850s, with the war raging Irish soldiers were needed for quotas to be met. On July 3, Kelly's appointment as a first sergeant was approved by Governor Buckingham.[5]

Kelly had already been hard at work. He spent all of July 1 riding or walking through Sharon. He enlisted seven men, a considerable achievement for a day's work, and received promises of enlistment from many others. Kelly then traveled to Litchfield with three selectmen from Sharon to "arrange in full for the raising of the [County Regiment] per order of the Governor." The next day, he noted that "the 4 ½ mail brings me a commission from Gov Buckingham as a recruiting officer." This meant serious business. "Now for work," Kelly recorded, "& to work we got at once."[6]

While July 5 brought Kelly five more recruits, he also had run-ins with several women in town. It was nativism that caused the first confrontation, as the women

> *did* [not] *wish a husband, son to go* [to] *war. Some of them showed awful madness, but the more I was abused, the harder I worked &c. I don't understand why county women would oppose me so rough & be nice to the Yankee officer. It is because I was born in Green Erin. One woman chased me with a large knife; another daubed in the face with cow manure while talking with her husband in the front yard. Foolish women, I feel sorry for them, their husbands and sons will go anyway.*

July 6 saw nine recruits, the wife of one of whom "hit [Kelly] an awful blow with a broom," but Kelly "got out of her yard before she had a chance to hit me a second." (The woman was Margaret Curley; her husband was wounded at Cold Harbor, had a leg amputated and was discharged for disability in March 1865.) Kelly grew to accept such attacks as occupational hazards and even found humor in them. On July 7, "persuading [a Mr. Sweeney] to join the great army to save the Union," a woman "came rushing at me like a tiger and daubed me with barnyard stuff. I had to go to Mr. Gay's to wash up. Had them all laughing while telling them of my adventures." Kelly most frequently encountered problems from women. Were these wives or mothers who feared for the safety of husbands or sons? Were they worried about how they would survive economically without the men around? While the Ladies' Aid Societies were largely composed of upper- and upper-middle-class women who were unequivocal supporters of the war, Kelly's experiences hint at a class divide.

Kelly repeatedly encountered Southern sympathizers. He wrote on July 7 of having "met many copperheads today" but also blamed their political allegiance on "Yankees who ought to know better than talk the way they do, as they are the cause of the uneducated ones so fierce against…the Union." Ten days later, he wrote of "an awful encounter. A man, or Copperhead, by name of Freeman, abused me bad because I induced one of his men to enlist. He threatened violence and would not let his man leave the field. I retreated & left my horse in care of a loyal man and took the three men I had back to Freeman's field and got my man. Tories and Copperheads everywhere. I was called every name." Clearly dissent was alive and well and was having a direct impact on the recruiting effort, but Kelly ultimately enlisted thirty-three men.[7]

Twenty years old in the summer of 1862, Edward Roberts was a schoolteacher in East Canaan. He began recruiting later than Kelly and ultimately enlisted at least nine men. One of these men, however, was part of a remarkable story. On July 31, Roberts enlisted Andrew McGrath of Canaan. That same day, Andrew's brother Edward enlisted; if he did so with Roberts, the recruiting officer didn't record it. The two brothers set off for training camp together. There, on August 20, another brother, John, joined them. Then, on September 5—only days before the regiment left for the war—Patrick McGrath, the boys' father, also enlisted. What were his motivations? Was he swept up in the martial excitement that gripped the county in early September? Was the bounty money too good to pass up? Or did fatherly instinct compel him to protect his sons? Patrick served throughout the war, but on that fateful day at Cold Harbor, John fell mortally wounded in the same line of battle as his father and brothers.[8]

David Soule's path to being a recruiting officer followed a different route. Soule was working as a carpenter in New Milford in the summer of 1862.

On July 6, he met Daniel Marsh and Garwood Merwin on the sidewalk after dinner. The group was soon joined by Henry Noble and Henry Hoyt. The talk naturally turned to the enlistment drive for the 19th Connecticut, and Soule blurted out, "Boys, if you will go with me into Mr. George C. Noble's office, I will enlist if you will." They all agreed, and there were five new enlistees for what became Company H. Soule and Marsh then began to recruit others for the company. Beginning before noon the next day, the two traveled to upper Merryall and immediately enlisted six more men. Soule reported that over the next five days, he and Marsh secured about sixty men, which combined with the men raised by Frederick Berry of Kent and Walter Burnham of Washington formed the basis for Company H. Soule proved to be so good at recruiting that the town fathers urged him to stay on in that role.[9]

Top: David Soule. *Connecticut State Library.*

Bottom: James Q. Rice. *Collection of the Litchfield Historical Society, Litchfield, Connecticut.*

James Q. Rice served as the recruiting officer in Goshen. Born in Sullivan County, New York, and a graduate of Wesleyan, he had hoped to practice law, but poor eyesight prevented him from completing his studies. Instead, Rice operated a successful academy in Goshen and was, like Skinner, active in the Wide Awake movement. Rice was well known in the county; Alva Stone wrote home from North Carolina that he was sure Rice would "call out a host of men." Tapping into his network of former students, Rice was highly successful as a recruiter, enlisting 45 men over the course of a month. Combined with men from Torrington, raised in part by M.H. Sanford, the two towns raised 102 men for the 19th.[10]

Also noteworthy were the roles—both official and unofficial—played by members of the clergy in raising the regiment. On August 1, the *Winsted Herald* reported that "the Rev. Mr. Deane will open a recruiting office [in North Canaan] as soon as the requisite papers can be secured." James Deane was born in Utica, New York, in 1836 but moved to Salisbury when very young. He attended academies in Sharon and Middletown and graduated from Williams College in 1857. Deane intended to study law but instead enrolled in the Auburn Theological Seminary back in central New York. An ardent abolitionist, he became the minister of the East Canaan Congregational Church on the eve of war. He was married with six children when he took to the road to recruit what became Company F of the 19th.[11]

While Reverend Deane was enlisting troops in a formal capacity, other clergymen—like Reverend Stephen Fenn of the Congregational Church in Cornwall—were doing so informally. On July 22, Fenn wrote to his brother, "A week ago last Sun I preached on the rebellion and especially on the fact that something needed to be done and told them about the way to do it and closed up with Old America, 'My Country Tis of Thee.' Well the audience got pretty thoroughly alive by that…old people were in tears and some of the young ones began to clap and shout." Scenes like this played out across the county, with church services becoming de facto recruiting rallies. In this way, the churches raised up Christian soldiers. In Warren, Reverend Francis Lobdell preached a sermon on Sunday, August 3, "the aim of which was to stimulate young men to enlist." He may have inadvertently created a firestorm when he said that "of all the ladies with whom he had canvassed on the subject of the war, not more than half a dozen had been even willing to have their relatives enlist, and had thrown every possible obstacle in their way." The *Enquirer* rejected the argument, saying that while "[t]his may be true in a few instances, it *cannot* be true of ladies generally. They are certainly more patriotic than the men." Fenn wrote of a similar episode in a letter to his brother on September 9: "One of my parish, a good [woman] but a little Southern in her sympathies, whose boy (a good fellow and one of my boys) has enlisted—came to me yesterday on church grounds and charged me with sending her son into the army—that after hearing me preach that sermon he come home [and] chose to go—well what could I say? I could only soothe her by telling her I was glad he had done it." If Fenn here expressed a hint of pride in turning young men into soldiers for the Lord, these episodes show an inability of these ministers to empathize with how wives and mothers may have viewed the recruiting of their husbands and sons. Ministers did much to proclaim to potential volunteers that serving their country was fulfilling a duty to God; they did little, at least from the pulpit, to offer comfort to the wives and mothers or those being encouraged to enlist.[12]

As the initial wave of patriotic fervor waned, recruiting became increasingly difficult in the county. There were many reasons for this. The approach of the harvest season, for example, led the father of Goshen's Fred Lucas to refuse—temporarily—Fred's request to join. Other towns, especially the county's smaller hamlets like Cornwall and Warren, had already exceeded the number they were expected to give to earlier recruiting drives and reported having "few men to spare." Both casualty lists and news stories about the Confederate treatment of prisoners of war may have discouraged enlistments. The shortcomings were not only felt by recruiting officers but also by the men serving in the field. Alva Stone wrote home on August 8, expressing his concern that "[n]ow at the end of a month, some are 'talking of enlisting'—others fishing for an officer—and still others are blessing their stars that they have by a month or two of time escaped a draft. Go on Gentlemen—keep [d]allying—I blush to say that the State of Connecticut should have to resort to a draft in order to raise her quota of men."[13]

A draft was exactly what the State of Connecticut ultimately had to employ. In the midst of what must have been an exciting and anxious time—of county and town meetings, recruiting officers traversing the region, rivalries spurred on by bounties and fears about the war efforts—the Lincoln administration made the situation far more complicated and challenging. Faced with continued Union struggles in the war, Lincoln issued a second call for 300,000 troops, this time to serve for nine months. Connecticut had mechanisms in place to conscript citizens into their militia units, and subsequent federal laws allowed for those units to be nationalized.[14]

Litchfield County towns were immediately affected by Lincoln's second call. Virtually overnight, towns—already scrambling to meet quotas for the first call—needed to enlist twice as many troops and had only eleven days to do it before a draft. No one wanted the draft. Even the war's biggest supporters feared that a draft would lead to violence or be seen as a sign of flagging morale. In Litchfield, a September 2 town meeting increased the bounty to $200 to entice volunteers. Other towns followed suit with actions that, if understandable, also heightened the rivalries between them for recruits. However, the coming of the draft also sparked an impetus for men to enlist, especially in the three-year regiments. The *Herald* succinctly stated the reason: "*Drafted soldiers get no bounties.*" Meanwhile, the *Housatonic*

Republican presented what was at stake in plain mathematical terms. The paper reported that a three-year volunteer from North Canaan stood to make $558, "but if drafting is resorted to that amount will be reduced to only $156."[15]

The draft also raised the possibility of additional deserters or men fleeing conscription. Enrollment officers in the county hired special agents to hunt down these men. This latter threat was real, as a Hartford newspaper proclaimed, "Anyone who has information of the departure of any man to Canada to avoid the draft will serve his country [by] reporting the name of the renegade to the War Committee of this city." Estimates suggest that forty thousand to fifty thousand men evaded the draft nationwide in the summer of 1862. This estimate, if accurate, would represent about one-sixth of the men called for in Lincoln's draft.[16]

That the number of draft evaders was not larger was attributable to two other exemptions to the draft. The first was through a medical exemption, which men realized was the cheapest way to avoid service if they qualified. Enormous numbers of men sought a certificate of medical exemption. The other legal means of avoiding the draft was by hiring a substitute. There were those who hired substitutes purely out of patriotic stirrings; Abraham Lincoln himself, too old and otherwise occupied to be drafted, hired a substitute. Beyond rare cases like this, the *Hartford Courant* reported that there were three types of men who hired substitutes: those who felt that they were indispensable to their own businesses, those who were afraid of military service but rich enough to hire a substitute and those whose "patriotism is good, first rate, as long as they are not drafted." The draft caused the prices for substitutes to skyrocket, with some Connecticut men paying $2,000 for another to take their place. Agents for Connecticut men who wished to hire a substitute were soon working the crowds in New York City.[17]

Litchfield County offered a cautionary tale about the use of substitutes to meet quotas for the draft. Robert Vosberg, a Barkhamsted resident, moved to Hartford in the summer of 1862 and opened a recruiting office. He succeeded in enlisting a number of men and was in line for a lieutenant's commission. This, however, was refused by Buckingham, and Vosberg sold the paperwork on the recruits to another recruiting officer and accepted $450 to serve as a substitute. He then, upon being sworn into the service, collected another $250 in bounty money. Flush with the equivalent of more than a year's income for the average American, Vosberg deserted, bound for Canada. He nearly made it but was apprehended near the border and confined to the Old Capitol Prison in Washington for the rest of the war.[18]

One did not have to go to big cities like Hartford or New York to find a cottage industry in finding substitutes. It was reported that in Wolcottville, "Messrs. Down & Church have driven a clever business this past week in procuring substitutes for parties in our larger cities who have been drafted."[19]

The newspapers played their part in using fear of the draft as a recruiting tool for the 19th. "Six more days before the draft!" the *Litchfield Enquirer* proclaimed. "Let us all make it our whole business for the next six days to see that each of our towns has its quota enlisted, and, if possible, send them into our own LITCHFIELD COUNTY REGIMENT!"[20]

On August 6, Colonel Wessells sent out the following order:

> *Headquarters 19th Reg C.V.*
> *Litchfield, August 6, 1862*
>
> *All Recruiting Officers for the Regiment will, without delay, report to the Head-quarters, personally or by letter, their names and Post Office address, with the number of men already enlisted, and hold themselves in readiness to bring their squads into camp at this place, immediately upon my requisition.*[21]

All that remained was to turn the men into soldiers.

Chapter 8

"The Army of Exempts"

In the summer of 1862, President Lincoln's two separate calls for a total of 600,000 new volunteers for the Union army left Litchfield County officials scrambling to meet their quota of nearly two thousand men. Recruiting officers knocked on doors and held patriotic rallies. Military officers procured the supplies and equipment needed to establish a training camp in Litchfield. Town leaders hurried to secure funding for bounties, cash incentives designed to entice men to volunteer. Military conscription seemed increasingly likely. However, a medical exemption was one way for men to avoid this draft, and in August of that year, hundreds of men lined up outside the offices of the county's medical examiners with hopes of obtaining a medical certificate. This set the stage for a morality play, with the volunteers as the heroes set against a villain.[1]

Dr. Josiah Beckwith seemed an unlikely candidate to be that villain. Beckwith was born in Stanford, New York, in 1803. He graduated from Union College before studying medicine, receiving a degree in 1829. Moving to Litchfield, he married Jane Seymour, a daughter of the recently deceased merchant Moses Seymour Jr. The newlyweds moved into the Seymour home, and Dr. Beckwith ran his medical practice and pharmacy out of the home, quickly rising in prominence. Within two years of receiving his medical degree, Dr. Beckwith had his name put forth as a candidate for governor of Connecticut.

Dr. Josiah Beckwith. *Collection of the Litchfield Historical Society, Litchfield, Connecticut.*

He served as president of the state's Board of Medical Examiners and had several business interests in town. A son, Josiah Jr., was appointed to the United States Naval Academy.[2]

In some ways, the scandal that surrounded Dr. Beckwith in the summer of 1862 resulted from outdated army medical practices. At the start of the war, the federal government left it entirely up to the states to license physicians and mandate necessary components of their training. All men who entered the Union army had to undergo a medical examination. Folklore holds that the only medical requirement to serve in a Civil War army was that a recruit needed two teeth—one over the other—to tear the ends off cartridges while loading a rifle. While this was not true—and men were rejected from the ranks of volunteers—the anecdote reveals the truth that such examinations were less than thorough. Men were urgently needed, and the enrollment boards were under extreme pressure to get as many men in the field as quickly as possible. Additionally, enrollment board surgeons were paid between $100 and $130 per month, an amount insufficient to get many experienced or skilled doctors to leave their practices for an assignment not at the front lines.[3]

The coming of the draft, however, created special circumstances. Prior to August 1862, those with health concerns could simply opt not to volunteer. The regulations governing the draft required men to demonstrate that they were medically unfit for military service, defined by the government as having "great deformity of body or limb; permanent lameness; loss of eye." The subjectivity inherent in the first of these conditions led Adjutant General Joseph D. Williams, chief administrative officer of Connecticut's troops, to mandate that the state's surgeon general appoint examining surgeons for each recruiting district. They were empowered to examine men and, if medically necessary, provide certificates of exemption. Certificates were technically only recommendations, and the power to declare men ineligible for conscription rested with the selectmen of the individual towns. In practice, however, towns passed over drafted men who produced exemptions, pulling another name instead.[4]

Concern over the likelihood of a draft fueled interest in exemptions. In the first week of August, Connecticut's surgeon general, Dr. Henry Allen Grant, named three doctors to examine prospective soldiers in Litchfield County: Beckwith in Litchfield, Sidney H. Lyman in Washington and James Welch in Winsted. Potential draftees were warned that they were subject to "heavy penalties" if they accepted an exemption certificate from any other doctor. The cost of an examination, whether a certificate was granted or not, was twenty-five cents. The *Litchfield Enquirer* identified the three medical examiners, explained the process and sarcastically hoped "much comfort may it do" those seeking a certificate. The *Winsted Herald*, however, was quick to see the potential danger of the examinations to the recruiting effort. Identifying the county's three examining surgeons for its readers, editor T.M. Clarke expressed his desire that

> *they will "be just and fear not" in the discharge of it. Hitherto the slightest pretext has procured an exemption; and it has been a not infrequent thing*

> *for physicians to go round their particular friends and leave certificates of exemption without even an application. The fact is, that most men who can perform their ordinary business can do military duty, and should do it. To such, let no certificates be issued. If, when drafted, they are actually unfit for service, the regimental surgeon will soon enough discharge them. There is no danger that the three gentlemen named above will be too sparing of their certificates—we only fear that they will be too free with them.*

If Clarke was wrong in supposing that regimental surgeons would be thorough enough to exclude those unfit to serve, he was correct that up to that point it had been easy to get an exemption. Of course, to that point there had been no conscription—an exemption was not needed to avoid the service.[5]

Still, Clarke was right to worry. Immediately after the announcement of the names of the county's examining surgeons, their offices were overrun by those seeking exemptions. "From all we hear and see," the *Winsted Herald* proclaimed about the examiners, "they have an abundance of business now." Reporting on its hometown, the *Herald* noted Dr. Welch was "besieged in his office by the swarms of applicants for certificates of exemption from military service. The Doctor makes thorough business of his examinations, and does not recognize his own certificates of former years." When one potential conscript presented Welch with a stack of eighteen prior certificates, the doctor asked, "You are well enough to work?" The applicant replied that he was, and Welch replied, "Then you are well enough to fight." This reply made Welch something of a hero, with a variant of this reply—usually phrased as "If you can work a little, you can fight a little"—appearing in newspapers across the state.[6]

If Welch's proclamations became a patriotic rallying cry, events taking place in Litchfield quickly brought scorn and accusations against Josiah Beckwith. The crowds in Litchfield were even bigger than those in Winsted. "We have observed Litchfield," the *Herald* reported, "to be lively with not precisely the lame, the halt and the blind—but so far as we can see, stout, able-bodied men, anxiously enquiring the way to the Doctor's dispensary. Even as early as four o'clock in the morning they have besieged the doctor's door, and late at night the glimmer of the night lamp betrays the examiner still engaged in his patient and laborious examinations." In the coming days, Dr. Beckwith became a controversial figure, but no one ever accused him of not working long hours.[7]

He was accused of accepting payment in exchange for certificates, of playing party politics, of using his position as a medical examiner to make a statement about the war, of "caring more for these [men] than for the nation others were struggling to save" and, more ominously, of cooperating with those having "secession proclivities." A common sentiment about Beckwith's practices was expressed by W.A. Croffut and John M. Morris, who wrote in their 1868 book *The Military and Civil History of Connecticut During the War of 1861–65*, "Stout young fellows bent over canes, and feigned excruciating rheumatism, or moaned agonizing internal and invisible maladies. Every day someone received the twenty-five cents exemption, flung away his staff, and walked off with a firm step."[8]

Dr. Beckwith kept records of the men he examined between August 7 and August 12. An analysis reveals some general trends about Beckwith's operations. At an approximate average age of thirty-two years old, the men who sought exemptions were older than the men who made up the 19th Connecticut, training that month at a camp a mile and a half from Beckwith's home. This fact is unsurprising when dealing with alleged physical infirmities. Furthermore, few of the men who came to see Beckwith had only one recorded malady. More common were diagnoses like those of Richard Morrall of Plymouth, who was found to be deaf, missing his thumbs and suffering from poor circulation, or a thirty-nine-year-old man from Harwinton whom Beckwith found to be struggling from "great depression," a fractured sternum and kidney disease. A third general observation is that Beckwith's account books strongly suggest that men from the county's more distant towns traveled together to see the doctor. On August 11, for example, Beckwith saw five consecutive men from Roxbury, seven from Plymouth and five from Washington.[9]

What is most remarkable about the records kept by Beckwith is the sheer number of men who sought exemptions. Beckwith saw 321 men on August 7 alone; this was, perhaps, his first day as a medical examiner. It is an indication of the cursory nature of these examinations that if each examination took five minutes, it would have required nearly twenty-seven hours to see all of these men. Beckwith recorded a malady and issued a medical certificate for 307 of the 321 men examined that day. On August 8, 141 men were given a certificate. Beckwith issued 183 more certificates on August 9. On August 12, 54 men were seen, a lower number for reasons that will be explained; 41 of those men received a certificate. In total, Beckwith issued 672 medical certificates—91 percent of the men he examined—between August 7 and August 12, 1862.[10]

A sampling of eighty-four exemption certificates issued for men in Woodbury gives insight into the conditions Beckwith diagnosed. Twelve exemptions, one in seven, were for hernias. As many of the men who served in the Civil War would find out, hernias were common among laborers in that era when manual labor was more common. For these men, service in the army was out of the question. About 10 percent of those granted certificates were diagnosed with "general weakness," a vague term that certainly may have contributed to questions about Beckwith's practices. About 8 percent were diagnosed as either having lung disorders or being deaf. The remainder of the men from Woodbury presented an assortment of varied illnesses with heart problems, piles (hemorrhoids), rheumatism, swollen lymph nodes, foot problems, varicose veins, blindness, fractures, liver problems and knee problems contributing to multiple exemptions. There were three additional drafts after August 1862, yet not one of the eighty-four men from Woodbury who received a certificate in August 1862—most from Beckwith—served in the Union army. This argues against the charges of Beckwith's corruption.[11]

Citizens took matters into their own hands with those they deemed cowards. Most notable among them was John Hubbard, a prominent Litchfield attorney. Born in Salisbury in 1804, Hubbard was admitted to the bar in 1828 and practiced in Lakeville. He served in the state senate and as a prosecutor before moving to the county seat and opening a legal practice in 1855. In the summer of 1862, Hubbard was the Republican candidate for Congress. His actions may have been politically motivated, but each day Beckwith examined applicants for certificates, Hubbard traveled from his home on South Street to the town green, where the line to see the doctor formed. There, Hubbard mocked and badgered the applicants, making sure that the men were aware of "the need and peril of the nation, and set for the meanness of shirking duty to the flag and country." Croffut and Morris maintained that Hubbard and Seymour were successful in their efforts and that "almost every day, a number thoroughly ashamed of their despicable intentions banished

John H. Hubbard. *Library of Congress.*

pretended ills, stood erect in manhood, and enlisted for three years of the war." Perhaps this is true; it certainly makes for a good story. There are, however, no specific names mentioned.[12]

The newspapers were the most vicious in assaulting Beckwith and those with exemptions. The *Housatonic Republican* was unsparing in its criticism. Its venom was not directed at Beckwith but at the "army of exempts—the Bombastes Furiosos, who have shouted and bawled 'Preserve the Union'—the chaps who have suddenly discovered that they are afflicted with all sorts of ills—more than ordinarily fall upon humanity—the fellows who have hitherto been the boasters and braggarts, whose power, and strength, and work be their natural praise." The attack became harsher and tinged with sarcasm:

> *These are the much to be pitied unfortunates, who now breathe more freely than they have for a week past—because they've got certificates! The facial portions of these sufferers have resumed their wanted symmetry—because they have got certificates! Their legs appear to have regained their former power of locomotion—because of certificates! Backbones have become stiffened, sundry coughs have abated, lame legs, arms, backs, etc., have been cured miraculously within seven days—because of certificates!...We have found out who are the lame and the halt, we have learned more of human nature, though, what we have learned is discreditable to humanity, and we have had considerable fun over the skeddadling to Litchfield for exemption certificates.*

The *Republican* hedged its bets by admitting that "some of these persons, no doubt, are legally exempt." In presenting the story of the medical exemptions, the *Republican* focused on those seeking certificates rather than on Beckwith. However, the paper was wrong in saying that *some* of the men were legally exempt; in securing their certificates, they were *all* legally exempt once the selectmen rubber-stamped their paperwork.[13]

The *Litchfield Enquirer* suggested those who had secured medical exemptions be dealt with through public mockery, calling for the formation of an "INVALID GUARD for mutual protection." The paper proposed organizing the unit by medical condition, with a company for the "lame, and the halt, and the blind," another for "the short of wind, and the short of sight, and the short of leg" and a third for "the asthmatic, and the gouty, and the consumptive." Further emasculating was the paper's call to "let a little child, or an old woman in breeches, lead them."[14]

Most vociferous in its condemnation of Beckwith or the applicants was the *Winsted Herald*. Six articles on the topic appeared in the August 15 issue alone, including one that dubiously announced the "gratitude" with which most residents of the area had greeted the news of the draft, as it meant "the rebellion, insolent with victory, was to feel the might of the awakened North." This was at risk, however, and in assessing blame the *Herald* pointed its finger squarely at Beckwith and those it alleged were posing as infirm, all of whom it considered to be Confederate sympathizers. "Then, however, came the day of exemptions," editor T.M. Clarke wrote, "cripples and disloyal came first, but so little judgment (or honesty) was shown that all alike got certificates." Desire for certificates proved contagious: "The loyal man seeing his disloyal neighbor thus exempted, presently becomes dissatisfied and hies away to the surgeon. He, too, has cut a finger while paring apples or been frost or flea bitten at some point in his history, and he too gets a certificate. Each excuses his own shame by reference to his neighbor's." The *Herald* left little doubt about where the blame lay. It was "originally in the law, secondly in the surgeons. It is within bounds to say that not one half of the certificates which have been granted should have been granted; while some surgeons (as Dr. Beckwith, for instance, at Litchfield) have seemed to proceed upon the principle that they were authorized to issue a certificate to every man who would pay twenty-five cents for it, without regard to physical considerations."[15]

Then the *Herald*, deciding that neither the law nor the surgeons could be trusted, determined that its readers would be the best judge of the veracity of the medical conditions diagnosed through the examinations. It printed the names of the men who had presented certificates of exemption to Winchester's selectmen through August 14. In this way, newspaper readers learned about the medical conditions of fifty-two residents of their town, including that John Brooks had lost his testes, that C.B. Webb suffered from fistula *in ano* and that John Woodruff had tender testicles. There was no way for the paper to have known this in August 1862, but of the fifty-two men whose names were printed, only two may possibly have served in the Union army later in the war. The *Herald* listed John Leo as exempt because of a deformed ankle; a John Leonard of Winchester volunteered for the war effort in November 1864. C.A. Bristol was granted a certificate for deafness; Charles A. Bristol volunteered from Winchester in December 1863, joined the 2nd Connecticut Heavy Artillery and was promoted to corporal in the war's final days. That less than 4 percent of men with certificates from August 1862 served—and those by choice—and the fact that men needed

LIST OF
CERTIFIED COWARDS IN WOODBURY!
AS PER SURGEON'S CERTIFIACATES.

NAMES. DIRE DISEASES.

ATWOOD, MORRIS—Sprain in hip—inactive Militia.
" FRANKLIN—Fractured limb—still difficult to march from pain and swelling.
" MARTIN VAN BUREN—General weakness—tendency to lung disease.
" RODERICK—Hernia, (single rupture,) Piles, &c.
" LEMAN G.—Disease of limb—growing deaf in one ear.
" LEWIS H.—Injury of leg, with scrofulous swellings about the system.
" PRESTON—Hydrocele—loss of a toe and thumb.
" WHEELER—Heart disease, hernia, effusion into knee joint.
" GARWOOD H.—*Retired* "physician—stricture in urethra and intestines," **(This certificate obtained to save 75 cents, on military tax, a physician being exempt from draft, and the surgeon's fee being 25 cents.)**
" ALBERT D.—Enlarged and diseased scrotum, of *long standing.*
ALLEN, HENRY—Deafness, ulceration of ear, scrofulous disease.
" GEORGE P.—Weak wrist joint, and disease of skin. *(Selectman, who acted on validity of certificates.)*
AMES, R. SMITH—Projection of bone in hip joint.
BURTON, NATHAN—Weak legs and joints, with feeble lungs.
" JESSE B.—Injured foot and ankle, destroying feeling and contraction.
" WILLIAM—General weakness, unfit for service.
" JOHN W.—An injury to the *brain* and knee-pan, from fall.
BACON, SIMEON W.—Rupture.
" TIMOTHY C.—Chronic rheumatism, impaired hip joint, lameness, &c.
BISHOP, EDWIN M.—Varicose leg.
BLAKESLEE, GILBERT—Hernia.
BRADLEY, EDWARD E.—Bad ankle joint, disease of big toe, inactive militia.
BETTS, JOHN—PULMONARY DISEASE.
BOULTON, FREDERICK—"Stiffened shoulder, conjestion of lungs, tendency to consumption." **Note—walks five miles daily to his labor, does over work in factory, can hold two** *Fifty-sixes* at arms length.
BEARDSLEY, STANLEY E.—PROBATE CLERK OF ROXBURY—" *Natural delicacy of constitution.*"
CLARK, WILLIAM J.—Rheumatism of shoulder joint, difficulty to move or walk to business. (Oh !)
CANFIELD, JOHN B.—Disease of heart, congestion of lungs.
CASTLE, SAMUEL D.—Diseased lungs, with hœmorrhage.
DRAKELEY, GEORGE—Hernia.
DAWSON, FRANCIS—Blind in right eye.
FOWLER, WILLIAM—Permanent lameness and rheumatism.
" JOHN J.—Defect in sight and hearing, and chronic rheumatism.
GIBSON, ASAHEL B.—General weakness. *Inability to perform duties of a pedler.*
" FRED. W.—Great nervousness, and extreme debility, and unable to labor.
" CHARLES J.—Broken leg, permanently weak and diseased.
GORDON, WILLIAM A.—Injury of arm, spine and lungs.
HAYES, EPHRAIM J.—Bloody discharge from lungs, and fractured arm.
HOYT, JOHN R.—Injury to arm and leg, bleeding t[illegible] in rectum.
HURD, ALBERT S.—Hernia.
HYLAN, JOHN—Varicose veins above knee joint.
HOLLISTER, FRANKLIN—Disease of hip.
ISBELL, CHARLES—Hernia.
JUDSON, RODERICK—Saltrheum, surface raw, unable to labor half of the time.
" T. FRANKLIN—Weak and feeble constitution, general debility.
" THOMAS F.—Permanent weakness of right knee, incipient hernia.
" HERMON W.—Total deafness in one ear, piles, general debility.
KELLY, FRED. H.—Stiff ankle.
LEWIS, GEORGE B.—Injury to knee joint, excused from active service, but to be enrolled in the inactive militia.
MINOR, CHARLES D.—Asthmatic breathings, weak lungs, tendency to consumption.
" JOHN H.—Loss of one lung, heart disease.
MITCHELL, ASAHEL W.—" *Partial deafness,* (can hear the word *sixpence,*) *weakness of the breast,* GENERAL DEBILITY !
McGEE, JOHN—Disease of the organs of generation.
NETTLETON, SCOVILL—Feeble constitution, liver disease.
NICHOLS, EDWARD F.—Defective vision.
" JOHN S.—Spasmodic asthma, obstructed breathing.
NORTON, OMAR E.—Blind in right eye, and injury to ankle.
OSBORN, AARON—Lost three fingers and use of foot.
" DANIEL—Hernia.
" NEWEL—Feeble, weak, inactive militia.
PECK, SANFORD—Double hernia.
" JOHN J.—Fractured limb producing lameness; piles, &c.
" ROBERT—An *incurable disease* of the *skin,* severely aggravated by exercise. **(Town Clerk)**
" S. FERRIS—*Confirmed dyspepsia; bebility ! !*
PROCTOR, NATHANIEL L.—*Congestion of lungs and throat, with bleeding.*
PARKER, ORLA M.—Enlarged veins and limbs, general numbness, and piles.
" JERVIS—Injury from a fall.
ROBERTS, EDWIN—Stiff and deformed elbow, and scrofulous.
STEELE, ALBERT M.—Defect of sight.
SOMERS, DANIEL C.—Chronic inflammation; disease of kidneys.
" GEO. M.—Asthma; stiffness of shoulder, and congestion of lungs.
SCOTT, SAMUEL B.—Bleeding piles—injury of head and side.
SMITH, FRED. A.—Hernia.
" HORATIO N.—Deafness.
SEELYE, WALKER S.—*Congestion of liver.*
SHELTON, WM. M. P.—Scrofulous ulcers; limb smaller and weaker than the other.
TERRILL, NATHAN S.—Disease of throat and air passages.
" LAUREN—Hernia; liver complaint; weak and infirm constitution.
TYLER, JAMES—Hernia.
" WM. M.—*Double Hernia.*
TUTTLE, WM. G.—Hernia; piles; and spinal disease.
WARD, JOHN T.—Liver disease; piles; and general debility.
WALKER, WM. B.—Hernia.
" FRED. A.—Bleeding from bowels; heart affected.
WAY, WALTER E.—Debility from hemorrhage.

A singular fact is connected with the above list. The largest part of them are among our most able-bodied men, and probably wished to save, above all other things, their *one dollar tax.* They could haue been exempted just as well after a draft as before if their reason was valid, except for this ***important consideration,*** there will be no able-bodied men left in town if a large majority of the above are taken for *specimens of invalids.* Very many of the above certificates were obtained of Surgeon Beckwith, of Litchfield, (since turned out of office,) under the personal application of *doctor* G. H. Atwood, ***Commissary of Certificates,*** for pecuniary rewards, levied, as is believed, according to the ***desperateness*** of the case. The inactive militia has repudiated this conduct, "*with groanings which cannot be uttered*" but once.

"List of Certified Cowards in Woodbury!" *Museum of Connecticut History.*

a new exemption for each draft, suggests that the medical examinations the *Herald* thought might doom the war effort were accurate.[16]

Sarcasm and ridicule were nothing new in nineteenth-century American newspapers, but they were usually reserved for public figures. In seeking to avoid the draft, even for what may have been perfectly legitimate reasons, men opened themselves up to the possibility of public scorn. The press reaction to the exemptions was predictable from partisan newspapers. More revealing of public attitudes, perhaps, was the reaction of town officials. Woodbury, for example, made the medical certificates presented to its selectmen public, and the details of them appeared in a published broadside of unknown authorship titled "List of Certified Cowards in Woodbury! As Per Surgeon's Certificates." No attempt was made to distinguish between those who may have been looking to avoid the draft and those with genuine medical concerns. Furthermore, while the medical condition listed for each man is nearly word for word from Dr. Beckwith's report, the sarcastic tone added by the broadside's author(s) made clear its intent to shame those listed.[17]

The broadside also took aim at Beckwith with a new charge: that the doctor was granting exemptions in exchange for "pecuniary rewards, levied, as is believed, according to the *desperateness* of the case." While the broadside offered no evidence for this charge, it did name an alleged accomplice of Beckwith's, Dr. Garwood H. Atwood. According to the broadside, Atwood filed applications with Beckwith for many of the eighty-four men from Woodbury who were exempted. There was no evidence for this claim either, but it does offer an explanation of how Beckwith granted so many exemptions in a relatively short period of time. Also potentially damning is the fact that ten Atwoods, including Dr. Atwood himself, appeared on the list of Woodbury men with exemptions. Atwood not only was listed as suffering from a "structure in urethra and intestines," but also in calling attention to the fact that Atwood chose to pay the twenty-five cents for an exemption certificate instead of the one-dollar military tax that would also have saved him, as a doctor, from serving, he was also labeled as cheap.[18]

The Woodbury broadside was quick to identify the town's political leaders who sought exemptions, including George P. Allen, a selectman "who acted on the validity of certificates" and was diagnosed with a weak wrist joint and disease of the skin," and Robert Peck, the town clerk, who had "an incurable disease of the skin; severely aggravated by exercise." In singling out the maladies of those exempted from the draft, the author(s) of the broadside took direct aim at the manliness of these individuals. Stanley Beardsley, a probate clerk, suffered from a "natural delicacy of constitution." William J. Clark was marked for "rheumatism of shoulder joint, difficulty to move or walk to business. (Oh!)" Albert Atwood's diagnosis of an "enlarged and diseased scrotum" was said to have been "*of long standing*." The broadside reminded readers that Frederick Boulton, who was diagnosed with a "stiff shoulder, congestion of lungs, [and] tendency to consumption," was known to "walk five miles daily to his labor, does over work in factory, [and] can hold two *fifty-sixes* at arm's length."[19]

A report from New Milford emphasized the degree to which those seeking certificates risked being labeled cowards. The article excoriated those deemed to be shirking their duty. "We have one class of men, however, that we would gladly do without. We mean the 'Regiment of Certified Cowards.'" If the accusation of cowardice was common by this time, so was the solution: "Some are disabled, possibly, but if so, why don't they stand the draft like men, and be rejected by the regimental surgeon." The *Litchfield Enquirer* then made the stakes very clear to those who sought exemptions, couching its language in the gender norms of the time: "There are a few strong, athletic six footers here, apparently well able to serve their country, who have thrown away their honor and their manhood, for fears of the dangers and privations of doing their duty. Though our hearts tremble and our cheeks pale at the thought of dear ones in this terrible war, we *scorn such cowardice*, and women as we are [told] would rather husbands and brothers were dead than dishonored." Unsurprisingly, the *Litchfield Enquirer* did not provide an opportunity for these women to confirm this statement, but the message was clear: there was no place in the community for a man who sought to avoid the draft through medical exemption. The willingness, not just of partisan newspapers but also of public officials, to level accusations of cowardice speaks to the urgency of the mobilization effort. In seeking men to fill the ranks, community leaders smeared reputations and vilified individuals, many of whom had legitimate medical issues.[20]

Soldiers in the field and in the 19th Connecticut's training camp were enraged by the legions seeking exemptions. A despondent Seth Plumb of the 8th Connecticut wrote home from Virginia, "It is sad to think that the best men in the county should be the last to support its laws by offering themselves." Alva Stone, Plumb's comrade in the 8th Connecticut, saw problems in the initial implementation of the medical exemption system, writing home on August 16, "So the Med. Ex. Committee could not be formed without the most superannuated old Cob in the County must head the list—Ha Ha Ha." As to the individuals who sought exemptions, however,

Stone had mixed feelings. He believed that those seeking exemptions would make poor soldiers.[21]

Theodore Vaill, who while the drama surrounding Beckwith was playing out was a mile or so away at the training camp, colorfully remembered the issue in his regimental history of the 19th:

> *There is a difference in men. The Nineteenth contained hundreds who… would almost rather have died than stay at home; while only a few days before, Litchfield had witnessed the irruption* [sic] *of a vast horde of heroes who would rather have died than go. Great, strapping men, who before the war had always boasted of their bodily puissance, and who were never suspected, before or since, of having any other disease than a rush of pusillanimity to the heart, came limping and hobbling into town, and with a touch of earnestness inquired for the office of Dr. Beckwith, who was dealing out certificates of exemption from military duty to the mob of cowards that day and night besieged his doors.*

Vaill, not present to see the crowd outside Beckwith's door, parroted the reports of the newspapers. In doing so, he helped to cement the dichotomy of heroes and shirkers in the county's collective memory.[22]

If the papers savaged Beckwith for the exemptions he issued, they also praised men who acted against those with certificates. For example, the *Winsted Herald* reported that Clarke Roberts, a wealthy farmer in Colebrook, "Employs a good many hands about his harvesting, and uniformly on their application for work inquires whether they have certificates." A man with a certificate was paid $0.75 a day; a man without was paid $1.25. Chastising the medically exempt was not the exclusive domain of the papers or public officials; individuals could do their part to encourage men to do their duty.[23]

Stopping individual examiners, however, was another matter. On Saturday, August 9, amid examining hundreds of applicants for exemptions, Dr. Beckwith was summoned to Hartford to account for his actions in response to the rumors that had reached the capital. Beckwith returned to Litchfield, but by five o'clock Tuesday morning, the streets of town "wore the appearance of a gala day, so great was the rush for certificates." John Hubbard, joined by prominent New Haven attorney and newspaper editor James Babcock, spoke to the masses, with Hubbard begging "his friends

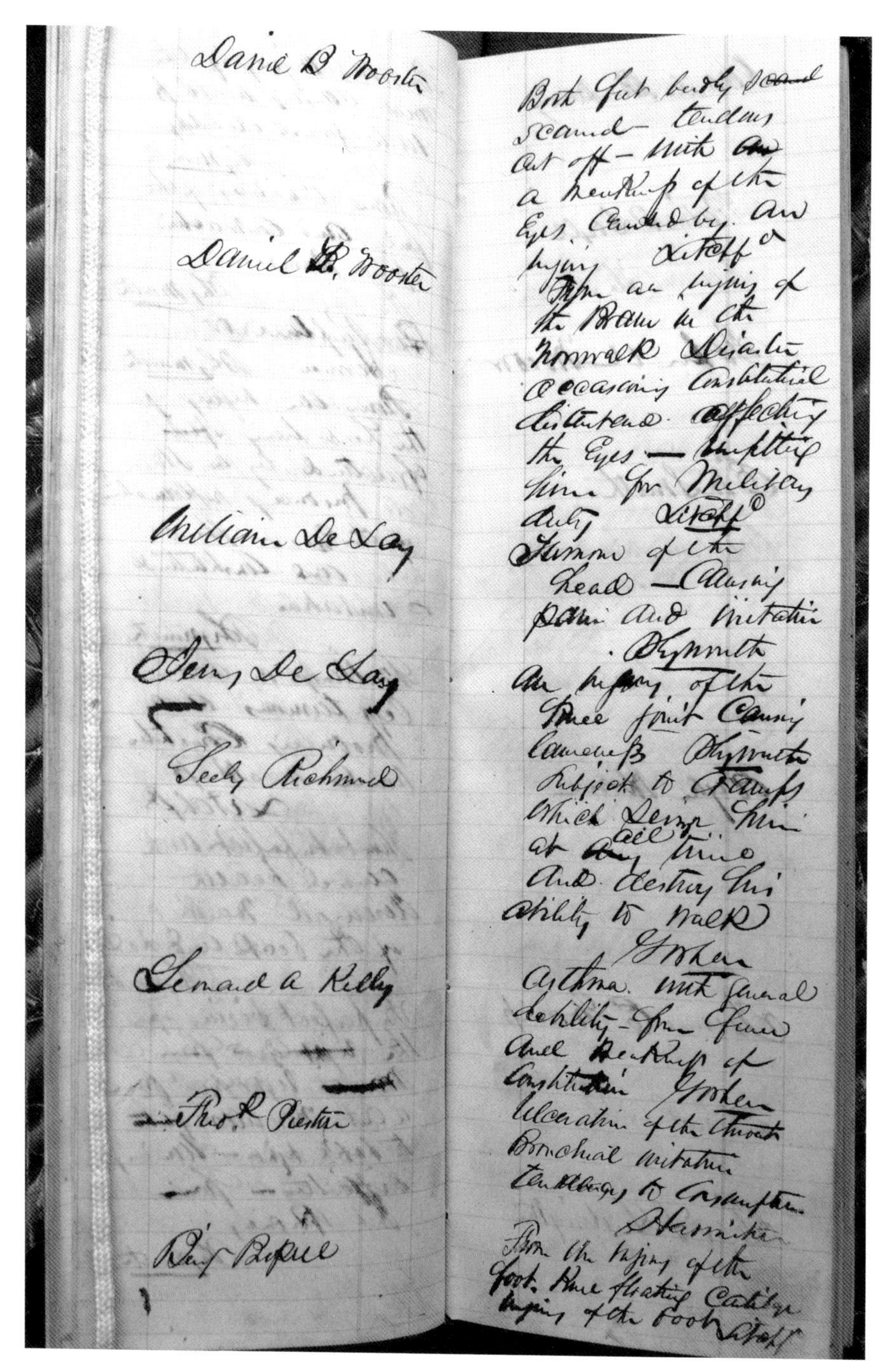
Daniel B. Wooster
Daniel B. Wooster
William De Lay
Henry De Lay
Seely Richmond
Leonard A. Kelly
Thos. R. Preston
Benj. Russell

Both feet badly scald
scared — tendons
cut off — with a
a weakness of the
Eyes. Caused by an
injury Litchfd
From an injury of
the Brain in the
Norwalk Disaster
occasioning constitutional
disturbance affecting
the Eyes — unfitting
him for military
duty Litchfd
Tumor of the
head — causing
pain and irritation
Plymouth
An injury of the
knee joint causing
lameness Plymouth
Subject to cramps
which seize him
at all times
and destroy his
ability to walk
Goshen
Asthma with general
debility — from feeble
and weakness of
constitution Goshen
Ulceration of the throat
Bronchial irritation
tendency to consumption
Harwinton
From the injury of the
foot. Have floating cartilage
injury of the foot Litchfd

A page from Dr. Beckwith's account book identifying the men examined and their ailments. *Collection of the Litchfield Historical Society, Litchfield, Connecticut.*

to go home and not give the world the impression that the entire county is composed of invalids and cowards." Beckwith opened his doors for business, but a telegram that morning shut down his operations. Surgeon General Grant had suspended his commission as a medical examiner.[24]

In the days that followed, Beckwith sat down to defend himself in writing. In a piece published in the *Enquirer*, Beckwith began by stating that he never sought the position of medical examiner and proclaimed that "if we have erred in the discharge of our duty, it has not been done intentionally." His defense hinged on the claim that he had belatedly received General Orders No. 2, which spelled out the conditions under which men could be exempted; with "no guide," he was compelled to modify "the requirements of the disabilities for exemption." Furthermore, Beckwith insisted that his certificates were "merely recommendatory for exemption, specifying the disability, and leaving the grade of it to be determined by the order of the General Order of the Surgeon General." This Beckwith had applied and waited for; he claimed to have received it only the day before he appeared in Hartford to defend himself. In the interim, he had sent recommendations to the selectmen of the county's towns on how to proceed on the certificates with uniformity.[25]

Beckwith also defended the right of every man to "an impartial examination by surgeons appointed for that purpose." He reviewed his credentials and maintained that "the manner in which the examinations were conducted [was]...rigid and scientific—performed by myself personally, stripping the applicant enough to disclose his disability, subjecting the limbs and joints to rigid scrutiny, and a disease of the chest and other organs to the several tests necessary to ascertain their condition." Beckwith insisted that reports from other doctors were accepted only with accompanying affidavits and that certain conditions, like deafness, required two witnesses for a certificate to be issued. He refuted the arguments of the editors who insisted that men should be brought into the service first and only exempted by army doctors. This, Beckwith wrote, would have "loaded the enrollment with a large number of disabled men, who, on being drafted into the Federal service, would have been rejected and continued drafts, necessarily occupying much time and made at great expense to the state."[26]

This was a powerful and potentially convincing defense. However, Beckwith failed to adequately address why so many men from all over the county flocked to his office. He argued that it was due to his central location but did not explain why men from Winsted and Washington, home to the other medical examiners, traveled to Litchfield. Nor did he explain how he could be so thorough in the narrow window of time for the exams. However, in his concluding paragraph, Beckwith veered from a defense based on medical practices to assert that Union major general George B. McClellan's recent disaster on the Virginia peninsula was the result of medical examiners issuing too few certificates of exemption: "The 30,000 men who carried with them the diseases into the service which have proved fatal in the swamps of the Chickahominy would have fallen more gloriously in the carnage of battle before the city of Richmond, and that if he had possessed a force of 5,000 more effective men instead of the number who failed from physical disability...he might have been in possession of Richmond." With McClellan becoming a polarizing figure, this statement—coupled with the eye test of those in Litchfield who saw the line stretching from Beckwith's door and the assaults of the newspapers and town selectmen—doomed Beckwith. He would be regarded by many as antiwar or corrupt at best, a traitor at worst.[27]

The attacks on those who sought exemptions are notable for several reasons. First is the failure to recognize due process. Those who received certificates had followed the law and submitted themselves to examinations by a commissioned surgeon. While the papers did acknowledge that some men may have had legitimate cases, there were no attempts to excuse these specific men from the criticism. Second, that criticism was purposefully couched in language designed to emasculate those with certificates. Finally, what is truly remarkable about the assaults on these alleged cowards is what is missing. For a month and a half in August and September 1862, the three newspapers in the county were full of articles about what they deemed a corrupt process of medical examinations and the cowards who sought exemptions. However, the papers were virtually silent on those who were hiring substitutes to avoid the draft. Over the course of the war, nearly 95 percent of white-collar and commercial draftees bought their way out of the draft, either through hiring a substitute or paying a $300 commutation fee. Not until August 1863 did the *Litchfield Enquirer* print the names of men who had paid the fee or hired a substitute; even then this was done without the mocking or sarcasm that had been hurled at those who sought medical exemptions. Furthermore, some Litchfield County towns extended bounties to men who hired substitutes. It was not until the war's end, in the midst of a county-wide celebration of returning soldiers, that there was open mockery of those who had hired substitutes, yet even then they did not mention specific names. It appears that the message was that one could avoid ostracization if he had the hundreds or even thousands of dollars necessary to hire a substitute. To only be able to afford the twenty-five cents for a medical examination was to risk losing one's good name.[28]

Chapter 9

"You Men of the Nineteenth Want to Be Soldiers"

When, exactly, the 19th Connecticut would form was a mystery. Volunteers expected to be called in to camp the week of August 4. This, however, had to be delayed, since "so many camps were called for at once, the supply of equipage in the hands of the Quartermaster General was exhausted." Regimental Quartermaster Bradley Lee was on the ground in Litchfield, desperately trying to secure what was needed, and with government supplies running low, regimental organizers turned to the public for assistance. Advertisements appeared in newspapers, including one in the August 1 edition of the *Enquirer* seeking contractors to provide rations, that gives a modern reader the sense of what the soldiers ate in camp:

> *The complete ration to consist of three-fourths to a pound of Pork or Bacon, and one fourth pound of Fresh or Salt Beef; twenty two ounces of Bread or Flour; one pound of potatoes three times a week; and at the rate of one hundred rations of eight quarts of beans, or ten pounds of Rice or Hominy—ten pounds of green Coffee, or eight pounds of roasted or ground Coffee; fifteen pounds of Sugar; one gallon of Vinegar; one and one-fourth pound of Adamantine Candles; four pounds of soap; two quarts of salt; and twice per week, one gallon of Molasses.*
>
> *Fresh beef to be furnished as often as the Commanding Officer may request; and all the articles to be of the first quality.*

This amount of supplies, by necessity, had to be transported by rail, and this posed a problem for the 19th Connecticut. From the East Litchfield Station to the campsite was more than five miles along winding roads, gaining nearly five hundred feet of elevation on the way to the camp. Rufus Smith, a thirty-nine-year-old operator of a livery stable in Litchfield, received the contract to "transport all merchandise" from the East Litchfield Station to the camp. For this he earned one and a quarter cents per pound of supplies. Smith agreed as well to provide scantlings of hemlock or chestnut for construction at the camp and firewood for the soldiers' use at either $4.00 per cord for maple or $5.75 per cord for chestnut. Finally, Smith supplied rye and oats at $7.00 per barrel. If the war offered opportunities for men to make money through bounties, it also offered financial opportunities for intrepid contractors.[1]

Stores took advantage of the shortages. Newspapers were filled with offers not only for objects that soldiers might need but also for everyday objects, advertised with militaristic language. Typical was an advertisement for Bishop & Sedgwick's, a Litchfield store selling dry goods, household materials and groceries. "Attention Battalion!" its advertisement barked. "Forward March to Bishop & Sedgwick's Where you can find all kinds of Army Goods! Swords, Pistols, Sashes, Belts, Knapsacks, Havelocks, Rubber Pillows and Blankets, Canteens, and lots of small goods for the soldiers. Call and see them. Bullet Proof Vests, Blue and Gray Flannels, Army Shirts. Come quickly, as they are going fast, at Bishop & Sedgwick's."[2]

Work occurred at the camp even without military supplies. Officers soon appeared on the scene. Adjutant Deming arrived from the 1st Connecticut Heavy Artillery to assist Wessells in organizing the new regiment. Tents, structures and fences needed for the camp were erected. The open fields of Cyrus Catlin's farm buzzed with activity as Litchfield's volunteers erected the Sibley tents that would be the soldiers' homes for the next month. Instructing the Litchfield boys on the fundamentals of tent construction was Luman Wadhams, in his third stint with the Union army. Born in Goshen in 1834, he lived in Waterbury and worked as

Captain Luman Wadhams. *Connecticut Historical Society.*

a machinist when the war broke out. Five foot ten, with hazel eyes and a sandy complexion, he had served as a sergeant in the 1st Connecticut and was a veteran of Bull Run. In the fall of 1861, he and his younger brother Edward enlisted in the 8th Connecticut, in which Luman served as a second lieutenant. His experience was valued, as his new comrade Seth Plumb reported that "Lieutenant Wadhams made the best shot in the regiment. This is news to use." Wadhams, however, soon resigned and came home. Despite proposing marriage to Louisa Baldwin of Litchfield, he became restless in civilian life, and when the 19th was being raised, "hearing that his old friends and neighbors were generally enlisting, Wadhams felt *that his time* had again come." He enlisted on August 8. Luman, with his new comrades, erected sixty tents on the hill, enough to house six hundred men.[3]

With no supplies and little equipment, Wessells delayed calling in the recruits. The war, however, continued, and as Confederates moved north from the Virginia peninsula, the urgency in getting the recruits to the army increased. As early as July 28, Adjutant General Williams ordered Wessells to assemble his volunteers immediately. Finally, on August 13, recruiting officers in the county's towns received the following order:

> *Headquarters, 19th Reg't C.V.*
> *Litchfield, Aug. 13, 1862*
>
> *All officers recruiting for this regiment will bring their squads into Camp at this place on Tuesday the 19th, or without delay thereafter and report to these Headquarters.*
>
> *L.W. Wessells,*
> *Col. 19th Reg't C.V.*

The wheels were in motion; the men of Litchfield County were getting closer to war.[4]

Departing for camp was more memorable for some than for others. The men from Litchfield, approximately 110 strong, simply assembled at the camp on Tuesday, August 19, and set to work. Many of the county's other towns, however, had elaborate sendoffs for their men as they departed for war. In East Canaan, the men assembled "under the big elm near Alderman

Ives's house." Edward Roberts reminisced about that day a half century later. Addressing his comments to his former comrades, he wrote, "You remember you bid goodbye to your home; your dear ones. How your backpacks were loaded with what your mother thought you would need, which to have carried would have broken you down." Amid the excitement and nervousness, Roberts had one very clear memory of that day. At the Ives home, several patriotic speeches were made, a common theme of the sendoffs. The words were long forgotten when Roberts put pen to paper, but the veteran remembered that speaker A.A. Wright "tied red, white, and blue ribbons in the button-holes of each comrade going to the front. The writer carried his throughout the war and returned it to the donor. While they were the same ribbons they were all one color, faded to a dingy white." The speeches over, the men "fell in line, in teams, drawn by one, two, or four horses, as could be provided, and started on our trip with flags and banners for our rendezvous at Litchfield."[5]

Michael Kelly and the men from Sharon were up early on the twenty-first. The orders from Wessells had arrived the day before at town hall, and the call to assemble echoed across the hills and valleys. "We all hustle now," Kelly recorded in his diary, "putting our effects away & in care of our people so that if we live to come back, we can have them…and bidding relations, friends, and neighbors, Goodby. It was 9½ AM before the many vehicles of all kinds started, owing to the ministers of the different churches, Methodists, Presbyterians, Episcopalians, lecturing us and giving each a testament."[6]

The men from Cornwall, Kent, Salisbury, Sharon, Falls Village and Canaan all passed through Goshen on their way to Litchfield. James Q. Rice, Goshen's recruiting officer, had his men assembled early near the meeting house. From that vantage point, they cheered the arrival of their future comrades. As the men arrived, the women of Goshen hosted a picnic for the volunteers. Between the men headed to war and those accompanying them to Litchfield, an estimated 350 people passed through Goshen.

Men also came from the towns south of Litchfield. Homer Curtiss of Warren left for Litchfield on the twenty-first. The next day, he wrote to his mother from the camp. He described how he left home at 7:30 a.m. and headed for the town center, with girls lining the road. "Everything was ready," he reported, "and we started off in style, as I hope you will hear." It took an hour to march to New Preston, where they had to wait two hours for the men from New Milford and Kent. "Finally," Curtiss declared, "we all got underway and in a cloud of dust such as I have been a stranger to heretofore."[7]

In New Milford, like in other towns, a convoy of wagons and carriages assembled to escort the volunteers to camp. On the town green, boxes of rations had been piled up for them, and these were loaded into wagons. A large crowd assembled to see the men off, and the *Litchfield Enquirer* reported that "tears and blessings mingled with the more substantial offerings to the brave fellows." In line with the gender expectations of the time, a group called the New Milford Girls averred that "we will wait for our beaux till the soldiers come home." Absent from the ranks of the New Milford boys was David Soule, who was asked by town leaders to remain in his role as a recruiting officer to help New Milford meet its quota of the nine-month men. He could not watch the departure, afraid that he would be deemed a coward for staying behind. He later wrote, "I did not make myself conspicuous, as I did not care to meet the boys who had enlisted and hear their remarks."[8]

The men, no matter the town from which they hailed, shared the experience of being greeted in Litchfield. Most of the companies brought large groups of well-wishers and even bands with them. Litchfield's Ladies' Aid Society hosted a welcoming reception featuring sandwiches and hot coffee. Litchfield's hotels and bars also did a brisk business, and the festivities must have been successful, for Homer Curtiss reported volunteers from his hometown of Warren becoming sick from eating too much at the welcoming celebration.[9]

Sandwiches and coffee were nice, but they would not put down the rebellion. Michael Kelly reported that the march from Sharon to Litchfield took thirteen and a half hours but still had a mile to march to reach camp. And so the recruits trudged on to the camp, organizing by town to form companies: ninety-five men from Winsted and Norfolk; a group from New Hartford, Barkhamsted and Colebrook; and Rice's men from Goshen and Torrington. A large contingent arrived, drawn from New Milford, Bridgewater, Roxbury, Washington and Warren. Twenty-two men had volunteered from Warren, nearly three times its quota. Salisbury and Canaan's volunteers marched in just ahead of the men from Plymouth, Harwinton and Watertown, "and so on, eight companies in all....All looked well and...a more nobler more athletic and more intelligent set of men never passed under review before." The assemblage of these men at the camp was the culmination of nearly sixteen months of mobilization for war.[10]

By day's end on the twenty-first, eight of the nine companies of volunteers were in camp; only Woodbury's men were missing. Many of the men thought only of sleep, but not all enjoyed a rest. Homer Curtiss wrote home that after departing the welcoming reception,

> *we got over to ground to where we were disembarked and marked to the* G[eneral] H[eadquarters] *and from there to the camp and from there to our present location, 3 or 4 miles in all. After our arrival we did nothing but get our baggage together and shift for ourselves in the way of beds—I was detailed by Lieut Burnham to choose my mate and guard the baggage of Washington and Warren.*

The men from New Milford were told that there was no room for them and "passed a rather strenuous night" at an old mill halfway between the center of Litchfield and the camp. Most of the volunteers were assigned to tents, and there they dropped their belongings. Despite their exhaustion, the men gathered around campfires and got to know their new comrades. As the companies were organized by town, the volunteers were likely familiar with one another, but it was certainly a process for these men to go from saying hello as they passed in the street to entrusting one another with their lives. What began around a campfire on a hillside in Litchfield would be tested hundreds of miles away at Virginia locales none of them had heard of—Cold Harbor, Winchester and Petersburg. Those who returned to Litchfield County, however, would never forget that their journey began here, at the place they were calling Camp Dutton.[11]

It was not called Camp Dutton in the earliest reports. It began life as Camp Wolcott, named for Oliver Wolcott Sr., a signer of the Declaration of Independence. Camp Wolcott would have been a fitting name for a training camp for men setting off to save the Union. Tragedy, however, intervened.

Henry Melzar Dutton, whose namesake father had served as governor of Connecticut, was born in Bridgeport in 1838. He graduated from Yale in 1857, taught at an academy in the New Haven area and then enrolled at Yale Law School. After being admitted to the bar, he opened a law practice in Litchfield. Soon after the rebellion's outbreak, Dutton volunteered as a private in the 5th Connecticut. He rose to be the first lieutenant in Company C. The 5th participated in the Shenandoah Valley Campaign against Stonewall Jackson in the spring of 1862, where Dutton was commended for gallant conduct, and was part of the force struck by Jackson at Cedar

Lieutenant Henry Dutton of the 5th Connecticut. *Collection of the Litchfield Historical Society, Litchfield, Connecticut.*

Mountain. In the heart of the fighting, Captain George Corliss of Company C fell, and Dutton took command. Seizing the flag, he led the unit in a charge across a wheat field, "directly into the jaws of death, as cool and collected as if he and they were on dress parade." Pounded by Confederate artillery, the 5th fell back to its original position. Dutton never made it, struck down by a Confederate volley as he attempted to bring his men to safety.[12]

The *Enquirer* quickly incorporated Dutton's death into the recruiting effort for the 19th: "Surely his life, so pure and manly, his devotion to his country, so ardent and sacred, his noble martyrdom, so sad yet so triumphant, will nerve anew every heart and brain that go hence from our communities to fill his place and the broken ranks of his comrades." Colonel Wessells issued an order naming the training site "Camp Dutton" as a "mark of appreciation all must feel for his services in the field."[13]

How did Camp Dutton appear to those who arrived on August 21? The men from Company A who set up the tents and laid out the camp did so with designated "streets" for each company and another for field and staff officers. This was typical of training camps at that point of the war. There are no known images of Camp Dutton during the war, but depictions of other camps from that summer show rows of tents situated back to back, so that their flaps opened onto the company street. (In one letter, Curtiss described the location of his tent as "back row.") Individual tents for officers of a certain rank sat at the head of the street. A flag flew above a tall pole at the camp's entrance, with a guard detail on duty at its base. Prominent was a parade ground, often located between the entrance and the tents, sometimes in the center of the camp, with five streets on either side. Soldiers' accounts reveal that the tents of the 19th were sited near the crest of Chestnut Hill, while the parade ground was on the west slope of the hill, visible, in those days, from the eastern edge of Bantam, more than two miles away. Cool breezes alleviated the summer heat, and in addition to the three springs for drinking water, the Bantam River at the western edge of the camp allowed for bathing.[14]

David Soule was not absent from the camp for long. Buckingham had promised him an officer's commission if he "succeeded in obtaining volunteers to stave off the draft." He spent one day printing circulars but was overcome by the feeling that his place was with the 19th and "went home to Long Mountain, and early next morning packed my satchel and told my people I was going down to the village and take the stage for Camp Dutton, Litchfield, and join my company, as I did not want to be called a shirk." Soule was on the 1:00 p.m. stage to Litchfield. Arriving at the camp at sundown, he proceeded to Company H Street, where he was greeted with cheers and "exclamations of 'I told you so! Dave Soule is no coward or shirk!'"[15]

The whereabouts of the Woodbury men remained a mystery. The women of the town had hosted an enormous farewell dinner featuring three adjoining tables of food, with "many bushels more held in reserve." Many remembered that such a "fine collation was never served up in old Woodbury." But the men never left; perhaps Wessells's order to report to camp never arrived. When there was no sign of them by the end of Saturday the twenty-third, the colonel was forced to act. It was about fifteen miles from Camp Dutton to Woodbury, and Wessells arrived by 8:00 a.m. on Sunday morning, suggesting the urgency of the occasion. Word was dispatched throughout the town for the volunteers to assemble at William Cothren's house with all haste, and the men were ready within four hours. The warning gave the women of the town time to plan a second farewell collation. It was a scene never to be forgotten. Cothren remembered "the shrill sound of the fife and rattle of the drum, as the sounds re-echoed over the silent hills, the tears of husbands, wives, children now separating to meet they know not when." "Tender, affectionate, and cheering words" were offered by Reverend Robinson of the town, and "the volunteers climbed into carriages provided for the occasion. Many friends and neighbors joined the procession on foot and escorted the men to Litchfield."[16]

Who were these men? An analysis of the regiment's enlistment papers helps paint a picture of the average recruit in the 19th Connecticut. He was twenty-seven years old, a little more than a year older than the mean age of a Union soldier in the war. The average recruit was five feet, seven and a half inches tall. The regiment was almost equally divided between married men and bachelors, an increase over the war's early days when bachelors were more likely to serve. About 10 percent of the men were foreign born, and many of these men had a particular skill; for example, English- and French-born cutlers found work in the knife shop in Northfield. The county's long-standing support of public education meant that 95 percent of its men who marched off to war in the summer of 1862 were literate. About 48 percent of the men were farmers, 10 percent were mechanics and 8 percent were laborers. While the men were statistically representative of their home county in many of the categories mentioned here, they were different in one significant way: they possessed less wealth than the average man of the county. This suggests that the financial inducements offered that summer allowed men to volunteer who had wanted to act on their patriotic impulses earlier but were unable to for economic reasons, or that other men simply found the opportunity too great to pass up.[17]

At least twenty-five men who volunteered for the 19th had previously served in the Union army. Seven had been discharged from previous service, most often for disability. William Cogswell had enlisted with the 5th Connecticut and had been captured at Harrisonburg in Virginia's Shenandoah Valley. Exchanged and discharged shortly afterward, he reenlisted three months later in the 19th. Alfred Benedict fought with the 3rd Connecticut, a three-month regiment, at Bull Run, where he was wounded and captured. Sent to a Confederate prisoner of war camp, his three months of service became fourteen. Finally exchanged and discharged in June 1862, he enrolled with the 19th Connecticut two months later, showing either an extreme dedication to the cause or a heart filled with revenge. Several of those who had previously served, like Luman Wadhams and Charles Deming, became officers in the 19th.

Of all the recruits in the 19th who had previously served in the military, none had a more unusual backstory than George Hempstead. Born in Bath, New York, in 1838, his family moved to Litchfield when he was a child. With a knack for business, Hempstead moved to Macon, Georgia, before the war to work in a mercantile operation. He joined the local militia company and, caught up in the excitement of the war's outbreak, found himself in a Georgia infantry regiment. Ultimately, Hempstead concluded that he was on the wrong side of the war. In a remarkable coincidence, there was a man from New Hampshire in the Georgia regiment who had reached the same conclusion. In July 1861, the two Yankees in gray obtained passes to fish in the James River. They hired a young African American boatman and plied the waters along the Virginia coast, all the while edging toward the Chesapeake Bay. They sailed past Confederate pickets and ran a white

Augustus Fenn. *U.S. Army History and Education Center.*

shirt from a pole to catch the attention of Northern sailors. Brought aboard a Union vessel, they were escorted to Fortress Monroe and interrogated by Major General Benjamin Butler. The men not only convinced Butler of their true sympathies but also provided him with the positions and strength of the Confederate forces he was facing. Hempstead soon returned to Litchfield, "where he was welcomed by his mother, sisters, and friends as one brought back from the dead." He worked in Hartford for about a year but returned to Litchfield when the appeal for 300,000 men was made in July 1862. There, Hempstead became one of the first men to volunteer. The regiment would rely on those with prior experience, like Hempstead, to prepare the novices for the challenges that lay ahead.[18]

Those who had previously served, however, were but a tiny fraction of the unit. More representative of the group was Augustus Fenn of Plymouth. Said by some to be the first man to volunteer for the regiment, Fenn was, at eighteen, an unusually young lieutenant. His commission angered some of the veterans who had reenlisted in the 19th, wondering how they were eclipsed by someone with no experience.[19]

Fred Lucas of Goshen turned twenty-one while at Camp Dutton. The eldest child of Daniel Lucas, he worked alongside his father on the family farm in the summer and taught school in Goshen in the winter. He longed to enlist in the Union army, but his father insisted that he could not be spared from the farm. Finally, when James Q. Rice, Fred's former teacher, began recruiting a Goshen company, the younger Lucas could no longer stand it. He became a soldier.[20]

So did John Iffland. He worked at the Lewis Garrett farm in Litchfield. An immigrant from Germany, the twenty-seven-year-old Iffland dreamed of a farm for himself and his wife, Emily, and believed that the bounty money represented his best chance to get it. An anguished family urged him not to enlist, but his dream was too strong. Edwin Perkins, who lived just east of Iffland, left behind his wife, Amelia, one-year-old daughter Cora and infant son Edwin to go to Camp Dutton. He was joined there by his forty-year-old uncle, Norman Perkins. Norman had six children, the eldest of whom was eleven. The youngest, a son named Almon, was born the day before his father enlisted. When Henry Scoville of East Litchfield departed for Dutton, he left behind a wife who was six months pregnant. Norman Barber, twenty-three, left behind his wife, Susan, and their one-year-old son, Willis. It is easy to get lost in the numbers when considering the units that made up the army. Each of these units, however, was made up of real people; while some marched off to war filled with excitement, many had decidedly mixed feelings.[21]

Men came to Camp Dutton from many different backgrounds. Theodore Vaill was born in East Lyme thirty years earlier, the son of Reverend Herman Vaill, who moved to Litchfield when Theodore was young. He was educated at Frederick Gunn's School in Washington and at Union College, where bouts of illness interrupted his studies. Dwight C. Kilbourn was born in Litchfield in 1837 and educated in the town's public schools. He was reading law with Origen Seymour and Henry Graves when the war broke out. Francis Young enlisted from Salisbury but had been a medical student at Yale when Sumter was fired on. Albert Nettleton worked making musical instruments at the Fluteville Flute Company; he would serve as a regimental musician in the 19th. Charles Brinell enlisted in Company H but would become the colonel's personal waiter.[22]

Men of many different ages joined the 19th as well. Several members were under eighteen and by law needed their parents' permission to enlist. One of them, Elijah Briggs of Salisbury, would be awarded the Medal of Honor for capturing a Confederate battle flag at Petersburg in April 1865. Henry Ayers of Torrington was only fourteen when he arrived at Camp Dutton. Men came forward from the other end of the spectrum as well. Two volunteers from Woodbury, Amos Lucas and Ira Thomas, were both sixty-one years old. Each indicated on his enlistment papers that he was forty-four years old, a year shy of the cutoff. Thomas, however, was listed in the 1860 census as being fifty-nine years old. For Thomas, a farmer five feet, nine inches tall with gray hair and a light complexion, legend holds that he dyed his hair and whiskers to fool recruiting officers. Age mattered little: young and old made fine soldiers, or failed, in military service.[23]

These were the men who volunteered to fight for the Union in the summer of 1862, part of "Father's Abraham's" 300,000 more. The 19th was composed of young and old, rich and poor, educated and illiterate. Some fought for the Union, others to free the slaves and others for the money. Different backgrounds, however, no longer mattered. Four weeks at Camp Dutton melded the men into a cohesive unit; they set aside their individuality for the good of the regiment. Individualism gave way to unquestionably accepting orders. They came to Camp Dutton as civilians and left as soldiers.

Each company, formed from volunteers from a town or two, was assigned a letter. "When I say we in future," Curtiss wrote, "it will probably mean our company, Co H 19th C.V." Men ceased to be from their hometowns, instead associating themselves with their company. While these usually broke down along town lines, the companies were symbols of the men's devotion to their cause. The men who marched to Camp Dutton in groups from their hometowns were formed into companies as follows:

A—Litchfield
B—Salisbury, with some from Kent
C—Goshen and Torrington
D—Plymouth
E—Winsted
F—New Hartford
G—Cornwall and Sharon
H—New Milford, Washington, and Warren
I—Woodbury and Watertown

By August 24, nine companies comprising 815 men had reported to Camp Dutton. Civil War regiments, however, were made up of ten companies. That, along with a final push to fill the unit to its full complement of men, led to the creation of a tenth company on September 4. "The regiment is to be re-organized today into ten companies," the *Enquirer* reported, and "is then to recruit for each Company until they leave for the war."[24]

Michael Kelly noted that each of the nine companies was "required to furnish a quota for the formation of a tenth company." This new Company K—Civil War regiments had no Company J, as that letter looked too much like an I—received automatic legitimacy through the appointment of Edward O. Peck, Wessells's deputy sheriff, to be its captain. "There couldn't be a better appointment made," a proud *Enquirer* boasted. And while Peck promised to make this the "'crack company' of the regiment," men who had enlisted with friends, neighbors and relatives were not easily convinced to leave their hometown regiments behind to join Company K. Men had to be transferred from the other nine companies to form the new company, which would, ultimately, contain soldiers from twenty-six different towns. August Fenn, one of the company's lieutenants, worried that the company would be "regarded as outcasts—a sort of Botany Bay of the regiment," referring to the British penal colony in Australia.[25]

The creation of Company K highlights one aspect of the organization of the larger regiment. The arrival of the men at Camp Dutton marked a transformation. It began to break down the walls of parochialism that led them to identify first with their town. Their backgrounds, occupations and financial statuses mattered less, as did their politics. Instead, their individual identities became associated with the unit, an association that, for many, became the high point of their lives. That association would carry them from Chestnut Hill in Litchfield to the battlefields of Virginia to that singular moment at Appomattox Court House. It would lead them to active membership in the regimental alumni association, which would record the marriages, children and ultimately the deaths of all its members in a scrapbook. And it would lead the survivors back to Chestnut Hill, fifty years after they departed, to commemorate the place where their journey began.

In a practical sense, the transformation from citizens to soldiers began with Colonel Wessells's General Orders No. 1:

The following daily Regimental Calls will be observed until further orders:

Reveille—Sun Rise	*5.30 A.M.*	*(also, flag raised...assemble for roll call)*
Police	*5.40*	
Rations	*6.00*	
Surgeon	*7.00*	*(sick call)*
First call guard mounting	*7.45*	
Second " " "	*8.00*	
Adjutant Call	*8.15*	*(Note: adj. about to form guard, battal, or reg)*
1st call for drill	*8.45*	
2nd " " "	*9.00*	
1st sergeant's call	*12.00 P.M.*	*(1st sgts report w # sick, on guard duty)*
Afternoon roast beef	*12.30 P.M.*	
1st call for drill	*2.30*	
2nd " " "	*3.00*	
Retreat	*6.15*	*(Flag Lowering)*
Tattoo	*8.30*	*(prepare for bed and secure the post)*
Taps	*9.00*	*(All lights extinguished by final note)*

This was, of course, a foreign language for the new recruits. Reveille included the daily raising of the flag over the camp. The 5:40 a.m. call for police was to be sure that no one had deserted, while the surgeon's call was to account for men who were sick. Guard mounting is better known to a twenty-first-century audience as the "changing of the guard." Guard duty was not a desirable position; men paced back and forth on the same path—rain or shine, in thunder and lightning, extreme cold or heat—for up to twenty-four hours. Their most pressing assignment at Camp Dutton was not keeping watch for Confederates but rather keeping back the hordes of visitors who assembled outside the camp every day. Still, it was vital for the men to learn the importance of guard duty. Not only did the safety of their comrades depend on it when the regiment was in the field, but abandoning—or falling asleep at—one's post also carried with it a range of severe punishments, up to execution. The adjutant's call required the men to form as a squad, battalion or full regiment. "Roast beef" was a general term for the daily lunch call in the Civil War; it did not specifically denote what the men were to eat. "Retreat" meant that the men's duty for the day was done and they were to prepare for bed. "Taps" in Wessells's order is, like its equivalent term "tattoo," derived from the Dutch phrase "tap toe." (The modern version of "Taps" was composed that summer.) Upon hearing it, men were required to extinguish their lights and cease loud talking within fifteen minutes. The days were hard, especially for new recruits. There was likely little complaint from the men about being told to go to bed.[26]

The bulk of the day for the new soldiers—up to six hours—was devoted to training. This was, of course, serious business. As such, putting the men through military training was beyond the abilities of a relative amateur like Wessells. The colonel had strengths, to be sure, but to complete this evolution required someone with experience. He arrived on August 20, a day after most of the men, "with the dust of the Peninsula and the mud of Harrison's Landing still upon him." This was Lieutenant Colonel

Camp Dutton, as it appears in 2023. *Courtesy of Luke Vermilyea.*

Elisha S. Kellogg, most recently the major of the 1st Connecticut Heavy Artillery, the "damned yeast pot" regiment that provided many of the men who filled the officer ranks of the 19th. He was thirty-nine that summer, and his service in the British merchant marine likely explains why the men of his new regiment remarked that he "sneered like a pirate." In the 1st Connecticut Heavy Artillery, Kellogg learned the military craft from that unit's commander, Robert O. Tyler, a West Point graduate. Kellogg fought with the 1st throughout the Peninsula Campaign, until he was ordered to leave Virginia and report to Litchfield.[27]

At sunset on Kellogg's first day in camp, the regiment was assembled and introduced to its new lieutenant colonel. Kellogg stepped in front of the green recruits and, with his voice booming across camp, pronounced his intentions. "You men of the Nineteenth want to be soldiers," he exclaimed, "and will obey orders and you will get along." He turned to his fellow officers and said, "I shall hold you officers to see to it." Images of the lieutenant colonel remained with the men for the rest of their lives. Decades later, one of them recorded his memory of Kellogg in the regimental scrapbook:

> *In the eyes of civilians, Colonel Kellogg was nothing but a horrid, strutting, shaggy monster. But request any one of the survivors of the Nineteenth Infantry…to name the most perfect soldier he ever saw, and Elisha Kellogg would surely be the man. Or ask him to conjure up the ideal soldier of his imagination; still the same figure, complete in feature, gesture, gauntlet, saber, boot, spur, observant eye and commanding voice, will stalk with majestic foot upon the mental visions. He seemed the superior of all superiors, and major generals shrank into pigmy corporals in comparison with him.… He could swear magnificently.…He would be in the hospital tent, bending with streaming eyes over the victim of fever, and kidding the dying Corporal Webster—and an hour later would find him down at the guard house, prying open the jaw of a refractory soldier with a bayonet to insert a gag.*

This passage highlights the problem of many sources of the Civil War era. It was drafted in a fog of nostalgia by a man who understood—after the fact—the success Kellogg had achieved in turning the recruits into soldiers and who likely remembered that June day in 1864 when Kellogg, then commanding the regiment, fell at its head on that terrible field at Cold Harbor. In the summer of 1862, it was the last phrase of this reminiscence that would likely have rang true for the men.[28]

For some of the men, their first encounter with Kellogg beyond his introductory speech came on the parade ground, where men gathered for informal drilling prior to the unit's official training sessions. Vaill remembered that an "ambitious" recruit "could prevail upon his fellows to form a squad and go through the evolutions." Kellogg stood far from these men but watched their every movement until he could stand it no longer. "[H]e stepped up to a man who was drilling with the stump of a pipe in his mouth, and said—with a look that rendered disobedience impossible and a voice that made the squad wink as though they had been struck upon the head with the butt of a musket—'TAKE THAT PIPE OUT OF YOUR MOUTH, SIR.' No shell ever left a mortar more suddenly than that pipe was ejected from the mouth of that smoker." Roberts remembered walking across the camp soon after Kellogg's introduction when "we saw a fellow soldier or walking a beat by Kellogg's order, loaded with all the empty whiskey bottles that could be procured in camp—and judging by the load, in all the surrounding towns—sweating under his load until night when he was released. He vowed he would 'never again' smuggle whiskey into camp while Col. Kellogg was in command."[29]

The men would claim—up to Kellogg's death at Cold Harbor—that he was a martinet, but he understood that discipline was needed for training to be effective and that for the unit to perform well in the chaos of combat, orders needed to be followed without question. That sense of discipline was the first thing Kellogg set about instilling in the men at Camp Dutton. He was particularly concerned about the accessibility of the camp to visitors and stationed a guard detail around the camp to both keep civilians from bringing whiskey into the camp and to prevent the recruits from sneaking out to Litchfield. This was not foolproof, however, and David Soule remembered "a middle-aged man had run the guard, or got into the camp some way and sold liquor of some sort to some of the men. I think he was a cider brandy distiller. Colonel Kellogg got into it and had him arrested." It mattered not that the offender was a civilian; Kellogg turned to Soule and ordered, "Corporal, take that d----d cuss and make a 'spread eagle.' I saluted him and said I didn't know how. The Colonel said—I will show you how…get some spikes and a hammer and some rope!" Soule, eager to impress "this great big burly soldier, with his keen eyes on me," raced around procuring the implements. Kellogg took a knife and cut the rope into four pieces of about four feet each. He then ordered Soule to drive spikes into the side of the guard house, two near the ground about five feet apart and two more directly above them at a height of six feet. Kellogg bellowed, "Now you

Punishment being administered to Civil War soldiers. *Library of Congress.*

stand the cuss up there with his back to the partition between the spikes," and Soule then "under orders tied one foot to the bottom and after tieing [*sic*] the rope around the other foot, started to draw out the spike, when the colonel politely instructed me to draw it further until his feet was nearly five feet apart." Soule proceeded to repeat this with the civilian's hands, and Soule, who was "learning fast," had to be cautioned by Kellogg to "Hold on, that's far enough." The lieutenant colonel then turned to his prisoner, berating him with, "There, you d--- cuss I'll learn you to come into my camp and sell rum." He ordered Soule to stand guard over the man strapped to the wall until Kellogg returned. As he prepared to leave, Kellogg turned to Soule and asked, "Corporal, you will remember now how to make a spread eagle?" Mobilization, Kellogg likely understood, entailed more than turning civilians into soldiers. It required those who remained civilians to understand that soldiers operate under different rules.[30]

Seemingly every member of the 19th had a story about Kellogg's severity. On August 29, Michael Kelly witnessed several men forced to march around camp with fence rails on their shoulders. Elijah Briggs of Company B was one of these men; he would go on to win the Medal of Honor, evidence of

Kellogg's ability to turn even free spirits into excellent soldiers. If Kellogg was frustrated by the behavior of the men, he was equally agitated by what he felt was civilian interference in his business. Vaill remembered that Kellogg, "though equal to any emergency in the field, was not cruel enough to set brave and noble volunteers on a sharp-backed wooden horse, twenty hands high in the presence of their sweethearts." Instead, Kellogg had Briggs carry a rail for several hours. Even then, the "tender hearted maidens were distressed, and said it was 'too bad.'" With the military situation worsening every day—Lee's army crossed the Potomac River into Maryland in early September—and the indoctrination of the new regiment stymied by civilians, Kellogg could not wait to get his men into the field.[31]

To put his men in the field, however, required more than discipline. It also required training. The 16th Connecticut—a sister regiment of the 19th—met disaster at the Battle of Antietam on September 17, 1862, because it had been put into combat without adequate preparation. The accounts from the men of the 19th that discuss their days at Camp Dutton are uniform in their recollections of Kellogg and in their memory of Wessells's absence from the camp. Part of the colonel's disappearance was due to logistical considerations. He spent a great deal of time, especially in the early days of the encampment, searching for missing supplies or the items required to equip the regiment. Then, however, illness set in, a precursor to what would plague Wessells's career with the 19th. On August 31, Kelly caught a glimpse of his commander: "Colonel L.H. Wessells here today, but looking bad after his sickness. No telling when he will be fit for duty." Kelly, however, thought there was no cause for concern. "He need not worry, he has a good substitute in Lieut. Col. Kellogg."[32]

This was an accurate statement. Kellogg was a taskmaster and a superior drill instructor, perfectly suited to oversee the transformation of the men from civilians to soldiers. This was both a collective and individual journey. Civil War soldiers were often referred to as "boys," but their indoctrination into the military through training and discipline hastened their transition to men. To many who escorted their sons to Camp Dutton on August 19 and returned to see them again for the presentation of the colors, it must have appeared that their boys had become soldiers—and men—in the blink of an eye. The change, however, was the product of weeks' worth of hard work and a carefully prescribed regimen. If there was no uniform system of training among new recruits in the Civil War, it was nonetheless a serious business focused primarily on ensuring that units could march in columns and rapidly deploy into lines for battle. Formations and maneuvers were essentially all that was taught at Camp Dutton. The men did not receive their weapons until they reached Washington City in mid-September. David Soule recalled that "what little of the manual of arms we got was in going on guard around camp, as we had a few old guns for that purpose." However, forming by squads, companies and as a whole regiment, or in line or column, were as important as loading a rifle, as were directional marching and the proper response to individual bugle calls. The introductory levels of training focused on smaller-sized units—first squads, then companies and then battalions. But before even the squad, it started with the individual soldier: how to stand at attention, how to march properly with little fingers on the seam of the trousers. To be successful, a unit needed to act with cohesion. A mistake on the battlefield could have calamitous results. This is why Kellogg put the 19th through drill after drill, for six hours a day, daily, for more than three weeks.[33]

The men got tired of it. Drill took place on the west side of Chestnut Hill, below the camp. As such, the men were invisible to the visitors who made their way to the camp every day. "About the same route," Michael Kelly wrote of camp life for a five-day stretch in August. "[D]rill twice a day and improving in our routines." On September 5, he reported that he was "So tired I can't see good" after being put through drills until 10:00 p.m., an unusual occurrence inconsistent with General Orders No. 1 but one that is suggestive of Kellogg's insistence on perfection. Kelly remembered a "fearful number of calls from Reveille to taps, in connection with all drills, guard mounting, dress parade." That night he "slept better…than any other night since I left home."[34]

While the drills were monotonous, there were episodes that stood out for the men. Perhaps most memorable were any commendations the men received from Kellogg. In early September, when drilling was at its peak and additional late-night sessions were added, Homer Curtiss beamed in a letter home that "Lt. Col. Kellogg and Ajt. Deming inspected us and our tents, praising us much, and giving an occasional hint for the future." Like any good teacher, Kellogg understood he could push his pupils only so far; sometimes they also needed to be built up. Indeed, it must have been a special thrill for the men when, on August 24, "Col. Kellogg had dress parade for first time as a full regiment," Kelly recorded. "Officers and men looked well, and everyone had new uniforms, everything else in great style."[35]

The arrival of dignitaries often resulted in a break from the routine of drill for a dress parade. "We had our exercises today," Homer Curtiss wrote home to his mother. "It was broken off by a call from Orderly Marsh with the order to prepare for inspection. You know our wardrobes are limited but we did the best we could—brushed up our pants and blouses and blackened our boots." Later, Curtiss's drill was "broken off again by dress parade. Col. Wessells was the officer of the parade but General [Robert] Tyler, Lieut. Gleason, U.S.A., Lt. Col. Kellogg and other celebrities were present. It was the finest parade we have had yet." The men slowly learned what it meant to be a soldier and recognized that they were progressing toward that goal. Perhaps Homer Curtiss best underscored this idea. "Everything is new to me and interesting," he wrote to his friend Seth, "new the daily and hourly mistakes....I am now a 'military animal' and not very brilliant at that."[36]

While Curtiss described the daily routine of drill as "being very monotonous," one episode upset the routine. On September 4, he reported to his mother that he had experienced his "[f]irst excitement of Camp Dutton—a man shot in the foot by another's revolver. Luckily no damage done as the ball was from a 'Smith and Wesson' and therefore not dangerous." Neither the victim nor the accidental assailant was identified, but the episode was serious enough for Colonel Wessells to issue Order Number 1 the next day: "No Soldier will be allowed to carry or use pistols." One must assume that since no firearms were distributed at Dutton, the pistol belonged to a volunteer who either outfitted himself at home before leaving for camp or bought it in Litchfield.[37]

The training received at Camp Dutton was predicated on instilling discipline into the raw recruits. This was partly dependent on breaking down the individual identity of the men. Effectiveness on a Civil War battlefield was largely dependent on unit cohesion Through repeated drills and harsh punishment, Lieutenant Colonel Kellogg set out to achieve this, even at the risk of being deemed a martinet by his men. The men themselves provided the evidence that Kellogg was successful. In their letters, they no longer identified themselves by town, instead referring to themselves as members of a company of the 19th Connecticut Infantry.

Chapter 10

"GO HENCE FROM OUR COMMUNITY"

Drill did not necessarily make the men feel like soldiers. After all, militia squads had existed in the county since its founding, and their members could hardly be described as soldiers. Rather, for most the line of demarcation between civilian and soldier came when they put on the blue uniform of the Union army. As Peter Carmichael has written, "The coat, hat, and accouterments were a visible connection to other soldiers, conveying a masculinity that imbued Northern and Southern recruits with a sense of manly pride that encouraged feelings of superiority." For the men of Company A, that day came when they received an inventory of equipment from Quartermaster Bradley Lee.[1]

In reviewing what was issued to Company A at Camp Dutton, the sheer size of the national mobilization effort—and how the Civil War helped ramp up the industrialization of the North—comes into focus. By August 29, the company had received:

1 sash
190 pairs stockings
98 trousers
98 great coats
196 pairs drawers
98 caps
98 hat bugles
98 numbers 1

98 numbers 9
98 haversacks
98 pairs shoes
98 blouses
196 great coat straps
1 stove
2 large mess pans
2 drip pans
100 blankets
100 sets knives forks spoons
1 pick axe and handle
1 axe and handle
1 broom
1 pail
100 plates (tin)
2 wash basins
1 spade
1 mallett
1 carver and fork
1 camp hatchet
1 camp chest
1 half axe

There were concerns that much of the equipment the men received was second rate, as illustrated by a satirical piece that appeared in the *Enquirer*:

> *We are requested by the boys now in camp, to return to the Q*[uarter] *M*[aster] *General the expression of their most sincere thanks and distinguished consideration for his thoughtful generosity in furnishing them with "Camp Kettles," somewhat old and battered and worn and rusty indeed, but made it dear to every patriot by recollections that still cling to them, and will never be rusted out, of honorable service in the wars of '76 and 1812. The boys wish sincerely that the Quartermaster General may never have his kale and potatoes boiled in newer vessels.*

If some of the equipment was old, lessons were learned. In the case of one New York regiment, 450 recruits were lost because they arrived at a training camp with no supplies; not yet sworn into service, they turned around and went home. Those supervising the mobilization of the 19th Connecticut delayed calling in the recruits until the supplies had arrived, realizing that getting men into blue uniforms a little late was better than not at all.[2]

This did not guarantee that the uniforms would fit. Edward Roberts remembered being ordered to report to the quartermaster to get his uniform. He encountered men engaged in what he called the "filling up, or the picking out of what you thought would fit. Sometimes the foot would go through the pants leg too far and again not far enough and so with the blouses; but after swapping around with other comrades you got a suit that was generally a misfit which only a local tailor could remedy." Not all the men agreed with Roberts's memory. Homer Curtiss wrote on August 22 that his friend "Austin looks first rate in his blue shirt and John looks like the Lieut. Col. only lots better."[3]

Even laden down with all their new equipment, some men believed that they needed more. This was the result of a lack of experience or knowledge about what soldiers actually required in the field. It was only with hindsight that David Soule described one episode as a "funny incident." At the time, many were serious about it. Soule wrote:

> *A party came to camp and sold quite a number of men of the different companies what was named a bullet-proof chest protector. As I recollect they were made in halves, of sheet iron, to button or hitch together up and down in the center, covering the right and left breast down to the middle or low waist, and I should say, would weigh five pounds at least. The price was some three or four dollars....A man would look well carrying one of these things around, especially at the front of the march, where every additional ounce becomes a pound. I believe that Col. Kellogg came across one of these bombproofs, and asked the soldier, "What in h--- is that?" and when told by the soldier said, "Sell it, my man, for old iron."*

With the hindsight of fifty years, Soule knew that such contraptions were an encumbrance at best and useless at worst, but he was willing to excuse those who purchased the iron vests. "[R]emember," he wrote in 1911, "war and knowledge of it is different today than in 1862." And for all the gear that was provided, the soldiers learned that there were items they were lacking. After being in camp for only a few days, Curtiss asked friends, "If you have an opportunity please send over one or two white shirts, a bar of Bronner soap, and a wash cloth."[4]

The experience of becoming a soldier was more than just receiving one's gear and learning the fundamentals of maneuvering. They also learned to live as soldiers, to eat and even sleep communally. It was the latter of these that sparked curiosity among visitors to the camp. In its September 2 edition, the *Litchfield Enquirer* reported:

> *Visitors at this camp express a great deal of puzzle, as to how ten men manage to sleep in a tent about as big as a quart mug. It would be a hard thing to do, were it not for the fact that each mess is a decemvirate of mutual admirers drawn together by the law of affinity. They lied down in a heap, "as one man," and then every hero squirms until he is either comfortable or fast asleep. It is a tight squeeze, however, and the proposed plan of taking a nurse a piece will probably have to be given up.*

Nineteenth-century American men were far more comfortable sleeping in proximity to strangers than their modern counterparts; they were also more experienced with it, as it was common practice in boardinghouses and even some hotels. Still, it was perhaps an exaggeration to say that the men were completely comfortable because they had been drawn together by an "affinity."[5]

Shortages of tents, however, meant that not all the men slept at Camp Dutton. Housed at an old knife shop more than half a mile from the camp with three other men from Warren, Homer Curtiss bunked in a small room on the second floor, devoid of furniture but "strewn with carpet bags, boxes

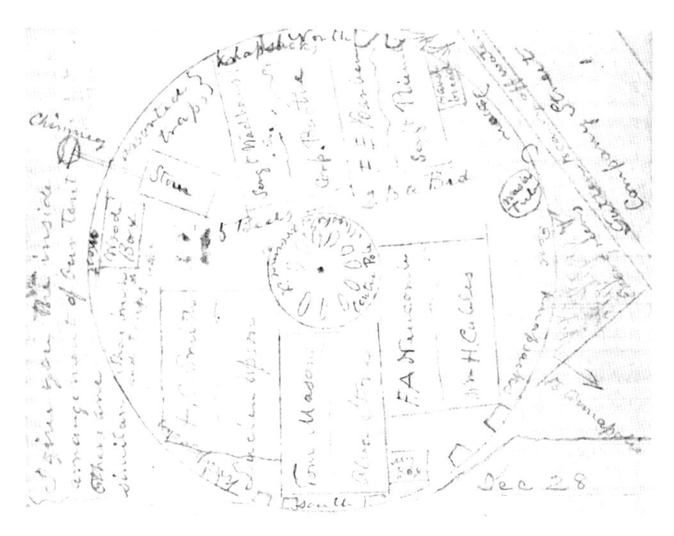

Alva Stone of the 8th Connecticut drew this layout of a Civil War camp for his daughter. *Collection of the Litchfield Historical Society, Litchfield, Connecticut.*

Homer Curtiss. *U.S. Army History and Education Center.*

of provisions, blankets, and a bed tick stuffed with enough hay for the center ornament." Curtiss slept on the bed tick, his knees pressed against a carpet bag. He shared the mattress with Homer Sackett, who was positioned in an awkward way that Curtiss described as "not on his back or his side." They got used to the conditions quickly; the next day, Curtiss wrote that "last night, Miner, Austin, Homer and I slept together, had just as good a night's sleep on our new bed as I ever had at home." Even as a raw recruit, however, Curtiss knew that his situation was not the norm. "I am going to get on well in camp," he wrote, "though this is hardly a fair specimen of camplife."[6]

If the proximity of sleeping conditions forced comradeship on the new recruits, so did the shared experience of mess. Curtiss likely wrote more about camp life than anyone else and was one of the few whose contemporaneous accounts are extant. He was thrilled with the food in camp. "Our dining has been so far the best," he wrote a few days after arriving in camp. "This morning we had our first army rations. Beefsteak! Ham, baker's bread and coffee, all very good in their way." He was, however, realistic. "We don't expect as good all year round but enjoy the present more the less on that account." Rations provided by the army were complemented by an extraordinary bounty brought to the camp daily by friends and family. "FAYDO," a pseudonym employed by the sarcastic Theodore Vaill in letters to the *Enquirer*, likened these provisions to combat. "Our sufferings have begun," he reported. "Immediately upon our arrival here, we were attacked in front, both flanks, and rear, by a murderous crossfire of pears, peaches, peaches, pears, cheese, huckleberries, honey, wedding cake, apples, sweet apples, sour apples, gentle tart apples, bug apples, little apples, ripe apples, green apples, and—apples. Also apples. The firing is yet going on." FAYDO joked that accepting the attention of these visitors made the soldiers unfaithful to the army: "The men feel very promiscuous."[7]

If the proximity of the men's homes to the training camp was beneficial to their diets, it also interfered with the business at hand. "Not hundreds, but thousands" of family and friends "visit [the soldiers] daily, from all parts of the county," reported the *Herald*. "Every road leading Litchfield-wards is crowded full of teams of every description—in the morning going in, in the evening returning. And every wagon is loaded, not with brothers and sisters only, but with goodly boxes and bundles, and in some cases bottles, which speedily find their way under the canvas in to the knapsack of the 'bold volunteer.'" In their study of Northern society in the war, Paul Cimbala and Randall Miller wrote:

> *Patriotism could also be fun, as military camps provided some diversion to the normal routines of life. Throughout the war, civilians found it entertaining to watch soldiers engage in drill, while the recruits happily showed off for the young women in the crowds. People living near the military camps also had opportunities to attend free concerts performed by military bands, and they enjoyed the excitement that military units gave to their local celebration.*

Camp Dutton was Litchfield's only military camp, and county residents made sure that they made the most of it.[8]

Enlistment in the military was a transformative experience, especially in the way it accelerated boys becoming men. One sign of this was the attention soldiers received from young women. Scores of women were at the camp every day, lavishing attention and affection on the soldiers. Social mores seemed to have gone out the window, as the hugging, kissing and squeezing of strangers became acceptable if that stranger were a soldier. Romances sprang up at Camp Dutton. Homer Curtiss could not help but notice that his lieutenant, Frederick Berry, spent "all this p.m. and evening with Miss Alice Marsh, the most beautiful lady that has visited our camp. Fred and I agree that the Lieut's [bars] were good for a permanent investment....I was quite fascinated by Miss Alice the very first time I saw her...and as I think Lieut Berry the finest looking man in our regiment, it is not strange to think that I should wish there might be a <u>Mrs. Lieut B.</u> from New Milford before we go."[9]

The specter of departing for the front sparked relationships—even engagements and marriages—among men and women who did not know each other very well. Sarah Jane Wadhams visited the camp with other members of her church to minister to the soldiers and distribute religious tracts. With only one left, she found a soldier without one and placed it in his hands. They struck up a conversation and began writing to each other once the regiment departed. Wadhams and the soldier, Fred Lucas, were both from Goshen and members of the same church but barely knew each other. When the war ended, Fred asked Sarah's father for her hand in marriage. The two were married for nearly forty years.[10]

Of course, not all visitors were there for romance; the sheer numbers of spectators were far too great for that. "Camp Dutton is particularly lively with visitors from out of town now-a-days," the *Litchfield Enquirer* announced. "The friends of the boys take advantage of these pleasant days to make them visits while they can." Michael Kelly reported that Camp Dutton was so full of visitors every day that "it would seem that all Litchfield Co. was here." Four days later, he wrote in his diary, "Visitors as usual, many; we are getting used to all sorts." Edward Roberts repeatedly made references to visitors in his diary. Charles Andrews, the young attorney from Kent, had many friends in the regiment and had presided over the swearing in of many more soldiers. Poor health precluded his own enlistment, but his diary records six visits to Camp Dutton in twenty days, a remarkable number considering it is more than twenty miles between Kent and the camp. He had "supper with the boys" and watched their parades. Many Civil War soldiers felt great homesickness while at training camp, but this was not the case at Camp Dutton. After six days in camp, Michael Kelly recorded "we are all pretty tired of staying here, bored very much by so much talking." Even the new recruits recognized that the visitors were distracting them from the business at hand. "We cannot attend to duties so well; women, young and old asking me (First Sergeant) to be kind to husbands, lovers, &c., and so many sorts of nonsense....We are completely over done, so much to do drilling, writing, and obeying all calls and filling them out, which are many." Theodore Vaill, when a veteran, recalled the nuisance of visitors in military terms: "Camp Dutton was a beautiful spot, but no place for a regiment to learn its hard and ugly trade. Fond mothers and aunts raked the position with a galling and incessant fire of doughnuts, apples, butter, pies, cheese honey and other dainties not conducive to the suppression of the rebellion, and citizens thronged the streets and environs of the camp from morning till night." Kellogg also used military metaphors to describe the onslaught of visitors, later remarking to a soldier that at Dutton, "the women were on hand all of the time; that with 900 soldiers in camp, 9,000 women came to see them....He said that he had always been decidedly in favor of the ladies, but they outflanked him at Litchfield."[11]

The residents of Litchfield County had sacrificed much to raise the regiment—money, supplies and, of course, their loved ones—and felt a sense of ownership over the regiment. This manifested itself in the ubiquitous and enormous crowds at Camp Dutton. Yet the volunteers, rather than craving the attention of friends and family, quickly grew tired of the visitors and longed for the front. They were rapidly becoming soldiers.

If the men spent their days training under the watchful eyes of their officers and visitors, it was at night by the campfires that comradeship developed. Homer Curtiss reported that men looked "dazed" when their families left, but the process of making friends went quickly. Three days after arriving, he wrote to his mother, "I have made some new acquaintances already....Seth Taylor of Washington, a first rate boy, a little older than I—bunk mate when Homer is Gone. Frank Warner a real good boy." Curtiss was a reserved, deeply religious man, devoted to his mother, and he was happy to report that "I like Henry Noble and beside Loverbridge, Warner and Taylor there are some 2 or 3 more that are my sort. Our town boys, Miner, Homer and Austin, improve every day. Austin especially. We get on finely."[12]

Still, part of fitting in with a large unit was coming to grips with the fact that not everyone is alike. "There is really a great difference in men," Curtiss wrote home after five days in camp. He was still living at the knife shop but had seen enough of the regiment to recognize these differences. "In our company [H] the men that swear are the exception. Indeed in our 107 I don't believe there are 7 bad swearers. In the Salisbury company there are some 60 men and I think not 6 men that do not swear. 'The Mount Riga Rangers' we call the Salisbury Co." Curtiss found a way to coexist with his new comrades. "I have got on well with the roughs," he told his mother. "Have done them some little kindnesses and they seem to appreciate them."[13]

Men of different backgrounds also bonded over humor. Multiple men also recounted an episode in the first week of September in which Corporal Homer Jones of New Milford was overseeing the men sign payroll forms. Private Henry B. Hoyt, also of New Milford, failed to appear to sign, so Corporal Jones went "barreling through the street, Henry B. Hoyt, Henry B. Hoyt! Henry B. Hoyt! Henry B. Hoyt! Henry B. Hoyt! To his widest satisfaction—and probably to Hoyt's amusement as the odds are in favor of his being cozily stormed in his tent reading or writing."[14]

The men laughed with one another and at one another. Sometimes the jokes were ethnic in nature. Homer Curtiss told friends at home that he laughed every day at the "Mount Riga Rangers" and their "gallant captain with his bottle of rum for ration." He also reported that he and his friends *laugh every chance we get at Michael Splein's name—Michael is a traditional Irishman—his name is on the roll and until this morning has been regularly called Mick at every roll call as he has never yet answered. The legend is that he enlisted and the very next day went to Hartford to avoid being mustered in. There is nothing funny in his name or the legend, but the Captain's pronunciation of the name and Johnny Hutchinson's repetition of the same set the laugh going—and it has not yet stopped. Capt. calls out Michael (pronounced Mickeel) Spleen! Twice—no reply—then Johnny—he's our funny boy—calls Michael Spleen! and a shout ensues the Capt. and Lieutenants participating.*

If some of the men bonded over making fun of their Irish comrades, they also grew to deeply respect men like Kelly.[15]

Moments like these endeared officers to their men. With the exception of Kellogg, whom all the accounts describe as a martinet, the men gave their officers high marks in those early days. Wessells was described in newspaper accounts as a man of "the mildest manners" who "watches every movement, not only of his immediate subordinates, but of the soldiers themselves, with the utmost interest and solicitude." Curtiss wrote that his "Captain Geo. S. Williams is a gem. I can't describe him but he is splendid." Lieutenant Berry was "a gentleman and a very good officer indeed. Walt. Burnham 2nd Lieut is the pet officer rather, but is really no better than any of the others—but he is real popular in his way and is really rather smarter in the tactics than Capt or Berry. All are fine." Their time at Camp Dutton taught the men more than marching and maneuvering. It taught them to respect and trust their officers, a lesson that would be invaluable on the battlefield.[16]

Men bonded in ways other than humor as well. On August 27, the brass band of the 1st Connecticut Artillery visited the camp and "discoursed some very excellent music, very much to the satisfaction of the boys." Volunteers found inspiration and a joint sense of purpose in singing patriotic songs. While the songs played that particular day are unknown, it is possible they included "We Are Coming Father Abraham, 300,000 More," a popular musical response to Lincoln's call that led to the formation of the 19th Connecticut. The men would certainly have found resonance in its lyrics:

We are coming, Father Abraham, three hundred thousand more,
From Mississippi's winding stream and from New England's shore.
We leave our plows and workshops, our wives and children dear,
With hearts too full for utterance, with but a silent tear.

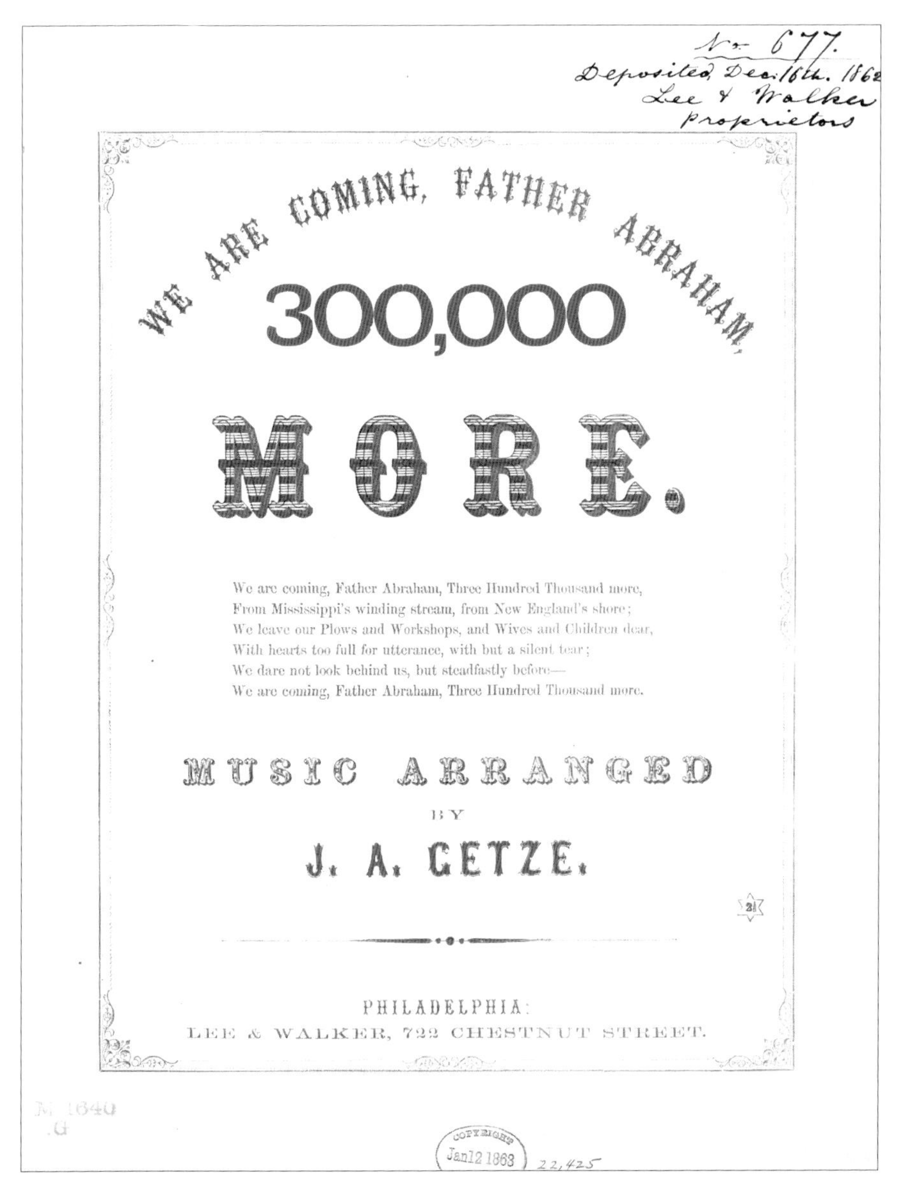

Music, like J.A. Getze's "We Are Coming, Father Abraham, 300,000 More," played an important role in Union recruiting efforts. *Library of Congress.*

We dare not look behind us but steadfastly before.
We are coming, Father Abraham, three hundred thousand more!

Sergeant James McCabe of Goshen gathered four other men from Company C—Avery Minor and George Newcomb of Goshen and Martin Judd and Alonzo Smith of Torrington—and formed a glee club that entertained their comrades at night. Other activities were more prosaic. Curtiss wrote to those at home, "You should have been here last evening and seen the greatest game of leapfrog. Yea! The boys strutted all around our street and the one below and had a splendid game." Of course, the men also got to know one another in a simpler fashion, swapping stories around the campfire at night.[17]

Even Colonel Wessells found opportunities to enjoy free time. On the evening of Sunday, September 7, Wessells hosted a gathering at his "marquee." Violinists were heard across the camp that night, and there was dancing. Homer Curtiss recalled that there was a "variety of attractions," but he, along with twenty-five or thirty other soldiers, was at a prayer meeting. One day, Curtiss reported that his company was "marched up to the ground and were rested and heard a fine sermon from Mr. Geo. Richard, text 'Who is on the Lord's side?' How fine indeed." Curtiss thought it was "just as easy to attend the prayer meeting as the dance so the fault will be our own if we don't get any good out of our camplife." Religion proved yet another way for the men of the new regiment to bond, although the various denominations present in the ranks precluded unanimity in beliefs.[18]

Training camps provided ways for men to ease into army life while maintaining their religious practices. For those like Curtiss, who had some fears that army life would expose them to immorality, camp routine allowed them access to church services. These services were very popular, as the men did not know when they would have the opportunity to attend again. The members of the 19th were furloughed on Sundays to attend church services in Litchfield, but this was not always necessary. There were plenty of services at the camp. Edward Roberts reported attending church services at Camp Dutton on Sunday, September 7; afterward, he went to Litchfield's Masonic Lodge. That same Sunday, the Young Men's Christian Association of Goshen held religious exercises at Captain Rice's tent. The *Litchfield Enquirer* reported that the "meeting was largely attended and exceedingly interesting. Heartfelt prayers and eloquent addresses were pronounced by the soldiers, as members of the Association." Michael Kelly, the one-time seminarian, recorded that a priest was in camp on September 5. An ambitious soldier,

Kelly had earlier been approached by some officers of the regiment who asked him to join the Freemasons. Aware that such affiliations could help with his advancement, he wrote to some priests with whom he was acquainted asking for their advice. As even public support for Freemasonry subjected Catholics to excommunication in 1862, the responses of the clergymen can only be imagined.[19]

Not all religious exercises at the camp were highly organized. Curtiss wrote home multiple times about prayer meetings. He informed his mother that he "noticed that a very large proportion of the attendants wore straps and stripes." Curtiss's mother had predicted that he would be an officer. Perhaps this was a way of letting her know that he was associating with the right people, or of convincing himself of that, and that he wouldn't fall in with the likes of the "Mount Riga Rangers." Families, even entire communities, feared that their sons would give in to vice and took steps to prevent this the best they could. Michael Kelly reported that the departure of the Sharon boys for Camp Dutton was delayed by "the ministers of all the churches busy giving out testaments and prayer books. It began to get tedious. We wanted to get away." Religious groups, like the one to which Sarah Jane Wadhams belonged, visited the camp regularly to hand out religious tracts. This was a scene repeated at training camps across the North. As potential death, disease and vice lurked around every corner for soldiers, wives took husbands aside and asked them to "get right with God." While religion may not have bonded all the men in the camp, it did assure men like Homer Curtiss and Michael Kelly that they had like-minded comrades and that there was a place for them in the regiment. Perhaps of equal importance, the presence of religious leaders and services at Camp Dutton made it just a little easier for parents to let go of their sons.[20]

At least two men deserted from Camp Dutton after they had been officially mustered into the army. The first known deserter was Edward Cross of Sharon, a member of Company G. He was a twenty-two-year-old house painter who lived with his mother and owned $650 in real estate and $50 in personal estate according to the 1860 census. Cross mustered into the regiment on the morning of September 11 and was gone by sundown. Could the family's financial status have led Edward to become a bounty jumper, mustering into the 19th and collecting his bounty only to desert and repeat the process with another regiment? An Edward Cross, born in

Connecticut in 1840, died of consumption in Waverly, Iowa, in 1869. He was a painter. Did the family move west with Edward's bounty money? The second deserter was Joseph Brennan, a member of Company B who enlisted from Salisbury. However, no one with the name Joseph Brennan appears in the town or county census records up to that point, raising the possibility that he was a bounty jumper, perhaps arriving in Salisbury after deserting from another regiment. He deserted three days after mustering into service.

To ease the recruits into soldiering, up to a third of the men of each company were on furlough at a time. When their soldiers came home on furlough, the women of Harwinton hosted dinners for them. Furloughs were granted to the men, ostensibly for them to go home and say goodbye, but they began weeks before the regiment's departure. Homer Curtiss used his time away from camp to visit stores in Litchfield where he bought a pocket inkstand, a fatigue cap, a book of tactics and his own rifle. Edward Roberts used his furlough not only to visit his home but also to have a photo taken for a locket. He also made several visits to someone he referenced only as "EWH." If this was the recipient of the locket, it was ultimately a failed romance; he married Lois Briggs of East Canaan after the war. He recorded on September 2 that he went from home "to Litchfield to remain for the war," and the *Herald* followed up three days later by noting, "All furloughs expire this…morning, and it is likely that few hereafter will be granted." The days when it seemed that life was as usual were rapidly drawing to a close.[21]

As Wessells saw to the organizational and logistical needs of the regiment, the other officers and noncommissioned officers learned their new roles. Few had prior military service, let alone experience in positions of such responsibility. As one of the driving forces in the formation of the 19th was a belief that Litchfield County had been slighted when it came to officer commissions, great interest was taken in these positions. The *Enquirer*, for example, boasted in its September 11 edition that thirteen of the sixteen officers and noncommissioned officers in Company A were from Litchfield. David Soule was selected as a first corporal, but he reported that this was done by the officers, "who had already appointed the sergeants" before he arrived in camp. Nervous about his new responsibilities, he "would as soon serve as a private, for little did I then know about the duties of soldiers, as I only had one thing in my mind—to obey orders." Homer Curtiss's friend Seth had predicted that Curtiss would be promoted, and the soldier wrote on September 12 that while he was "quite surprised at your prophecy—but nearly so much at that as at my nomination for 3rd Corporal." He tried to downplay his selection by arguing that "[t]he place is nothing" but accepted because "under the circumstances I thought the nomination complimentary. So if nothing [happens] to prevent I shall fulfill your prophecy and wear the chevrons out of Litchfield."[22]

There were some, of course, who were unhappy with the results of the elections. Michael Kelly recorded that he was "very much dissatisfied, but the strong side always gain or the side that is deep in the right bonds of society no matter whether he be a good person or not." Kelly had worked hard to recruit men for the regiment and suffered physical assaults in the process. He was entitled as much as any man to an officer's slot. Was he discriminated against for being Irish or Catholic? The Civil War would provide capable men like Kelly with opportunities to rise; that, however, often came when the fighting started, not in the training camps.[23]

On August 26, the noncommissioned officers met and were told of their responsibilities. Kelly, a first sergeant in Company G, reported that all the first sergeants were to review Casey's tactics and that they would meet once a week. Kelly was apparently surprised by the amount of work he faced, claiming, "Capts. and Lieuts. does [*sic*] very little in comparison to what we do." In the ensuing days, he would quickly learn just how much was expected of him: "All morning duties as usual, guard mounting detail, water detail, wood detail &c., there is no end to them, morning reports, sick reports, weekly reports, monthly reports, yearly reports, payrolls every 2 months whether we get payed or not....Oh ye skys, what an amount of writing." Certainly many, in taking on new positions, initially felt overwhelmed but adjusted quickly, and Kelly was no different. By the end of August, he could report, "Oh what a day, Quartermaster Commissary Master, every master calling like fury on the 1st Sergeants for clothing reports, ration reports, ordnance reports, and all coming pell mell on us, so we ought to be Clerks of the Pell, be we get used to it."[24]

As September approached, selectmen appeared in camp to hand out bounty money. Edward Roberts received $100 on August 30. The Sharon selectmen disbursed their funds on September 3. A second round of bounty payouts would happen as the regiment was officially mustered into the U.S. Army and the men received their money from the federal government. Following these payouts, "straightway [*sic*] the camp and its environs were beset by sutlers and peddlars innumerable." While Giles Alvord of Barkhamsted was slated to be the official regimental sutler when the unit departed for the front, the men were fair game for all who wished to ply their wares as long as they were at Camp Dutton. "Out of compassion for the overburdened warriors," the wry FAYDO reported, these sutlers

> *offered to lighten their pockets by furnishing them with army knives, forks, spoons, napkin rings, individual salt collars—all in one—army cook-stoves and army ice cream freezers, all in one—army door bells, army grindstones, foot-scrapers, cheese presses, and sideboards—all in one—each one containing little cubby holes to stick in nutmeg graters, flat irons, horse blocks, and many other little knickknacks, equally indispensable to a soldier on the march.*

If there is sarcasm in the account, it should also be remembered that these sutlers were the same who sold the soldiers havelocks, bulletproof vests and other impedimenta that would litter the roadsides of Virginia from armies on the march.[25]

Even as it became evident that the 19th Connecticut would soon depart for the front, another drama was playing out across the county. The events set in motion by Lincoln's second call for 300,000 men—this time to serve for nine months—were coming to a head. There were extraordinary challenges in this endeavor that, in some ways, made it a more formidable task for the towns of northwest Connecticut than raising the 19th had been. From Lincoln's first call for volunteers in April 1861, each appeal removed men motivated solely by patriotic impulses from the pool of available bodies. Furthermore, men like Kelly, Roberts, Bissell, Rice and Soule, who had proven quite adept at recruiting their friends and neighbors for military service, were now in the army, unable to aid in raising the new soldiers. The challenges forced the towns to once again lean heavily on bounties to produce volunteers if they were to avoid the draft threatened by the War Department regulations enacting Lincoln's proclamation. Winsted,

Harwinton, Canaan and other towns voted to extend the $100 bounty that had been offered to three-year volunteers to nine-month men. New Milford offered these men $200, and Washington "patriotically voted a bounty of $200 to each man volunteering."[26]

Men looking to score a quicker financial windfall could not help but notice stories in the papers announcing that between bounty money and monthly pay, a nine-month volunteer would make $329.59. Those drafted would earn only $117 over their nine months of service. But even such financial incentives failed to do the job, and talk turned increasingly to the likelihood of a draft. That draft was originally scheduled for August 15, but the overwhelming desire of all involved to avoid conscription led to a delay to August 27 and then to September 10.[27]

Winchester secured its quota through a spate of wheeling and dealing. On the morning of the draft, eleven volunteers were still needed to fulfill the quota. A request by citizens to delay the draft for a few hours so they could find last-minute volunteers was granted, and a procession of hourly delays followed, each one accompanied by a town meeting that increased the bounty. Finally, at 2:00 p.m. the quota was pronounced met, but not before the amount of the bounty reached $310. Still, this was considered favorable to a draft, the "aversion" to which "was almost universal." The *Herald* commented, "We never saw pocket-books open with so little reluctance as on Wednesday." High bounties in Washington and Sharon did the trick as well, with the former raising its full quota in one day and the latter oversubscribing its rolls by 160 percent.[28]

Not all towns escaped the dreaded draft. After the two statewide delays, Buckingham ordered the town drafts to be held on September 10. In anticipation, Litchfield's selectmen ran a legal notice in the *Enquirer* on September 4 declaring that they had "appointed the highway in front of the Court House in the village of Litchfield, as a place of Parade for the Inactive Militia, for the purpose of a Draft, and you are hereby ordered to appear at said place of parade, on Wednesday, the tenth day of September, 1862, at nine o'clock in the forenoon, to answer said call of the Governor."[29]

Litchfield's draft took place less than one hundred yards from the spot where the 19th would assemble later that day to receive its regimental flag. Many anticipated trouble, but none transpired. "Noisy fellows, who have a hundred times sworn they would never submit, would die on their thresholds first, have marched into camp as promptly as volunteers," the *Enquirer* reported. Others, "so zealously applied themselves to the work of procuring substitutes, that they have scarcely grumbled." Eleven names were pulled, and six of them promptly produced medical exemptions, requiring a second draft on October 27 to replace them. In Barkhamsted, eight men were drafted. None of the eight ever served in the Union army, likely having secured either a substitute or a certificate. In Harwinton, eight were still needed on draft day. Four stepped forward at the last minute when private donations augmented the town's bounty. The town then pulled the names of four men: Delos Bristol, James J. Catlin, Linus B. Castle and A.A. Scoville. Assuming their work was done, the selectmen adjourned the meeting only to see all four of the men produce medical exemptions. A new town meeting was scheduled for the fifteenth at which a $200 bounty was offered. Dennis Perkins of New York City, a Harwinton native, offered an additional $100 for each volunteer from his own pocket. Six minutes before the draft, George W. Catlin, Emory Barer, Cornelius Quin and Timothy Dewire volunteered.[30]

The "drafting machine" selected six men from Colebrook, one of whom, Anson G. Rice, was the father of eight children. None of the six men served in the army. Ultimately, at least nine towns in the county had to hold two drafts because of the number of men who produced medical exemptions. Perhaps what was most remarkable about Connecticut's 1862 draft was that it was essentially a complete bust. Statewide, 1,212 names were pulled. However, because of either exemptions of substitutions, only 135 of these men were actually mustered into the army, and 81 of them deserted before leaving the state. For all the worry and fear it caused, the September draft produced 54 Connecticut soldiers. This is somewhat reflective of a trend in the Union army for the entire war. Only 5 to 7 percent of soldiers in blue were drafted. There were too many options—either financial incentives, medical certificates, exemption fees or substitutes—to get around conscription.[31]

Most of the nine-month soldiers from Litchfield County served in the 28th Connecticut, which spent the bulk of its existence in operations against Port Hudson, Louisiana, one of the final Confederate strongholds on the Mississippi River. Other county men fought with the 27th Connecticut, which suffered 446 casualties during combat with the Union army's 2nd Corps at Fredericksburg, Chancellorsville and Gettysburg. How did the nine-month men compare to those who were training at Camp Dutton? The nine-month soldiers were older, with an average age of just over thirty, and two men from Bethlehem were Mexican-American War veterans. The same percentage, 50 percent, were married. A majority of the men were farmers, with mechanics being the second-most common occupation. It would be wrong to assume that the nine-month men were not as patriotic as the three-year men or were motivated only by the opportunity to earn a quick buck. Men served for any number of reasons. John and James Cummings were brothers who resided in Sherman and New Milford, respectively. They were, in the words of attorney Charles Andrews, "determined to go," despite the opposition of their mother. It did not matter that John was forty-three and married and James was forty-four. They were her means of support. Andrews drew up a contract by which the mother would receive the sons' bounty money, and the two brothers marched off to war with the 28th Connecticut. John died of disease one month before the regiment was mustered out of service. Age, motivations, experiences—none of these shielded a man from death in the Civil War.[32]

In a sure sign that the regiment would soon be moving out and that more strenuous days lay ahead, regimental surgeon Henry Plumb began the formal physical examinations of all the men on September 9. Army regulations ordered that the men be examined by a surgeon "as soon as a recruit joins any regiment" and be "vaccinated when it is required." They further required that

> [i]*n passing a recruit the medical officer is to examine him stripped; to see that he has free use of all his limbs; that his chest is ample; that his hearing, vision and speech are perfect; that he has no tumors or ulcerated or extensively cicatrized legs; no rupture or chronic cutaneous affection; that he has not received any contusion, or wound to the head, that may impair his faculties; that he is not a drunkard; is not subject to convulsions; and has no infectious disorder, nor any other that may unfit him for duty.*

Additionally, surgeons were to exclude men who suffered from epilepsy, rheumatism, ophthalmia or ulcers. It was not uncommon to see naked men hopping in circles on one leg or flexing their limbs or digits as part of the examination.[33]

There is no evidence that anyone other than Surgeon Plumb performed the exams, although a *Litchfield Enquirer* story hints that they may have taken place on September 9–10. However, even assuming that Plumb was aided by assistant surgeons Jeremiah Phelps and John W. Lawton and hospital steward James Averill, for four men to conduct nine hundred physical examinations—even if only five minutes each—would take nearly nineteen hours. It is possible that this was done, but the exams certainly would not have been very thorough. And to a certain extent, that proves the point. The 19th Connecticut was born out of a crisis. Soldiers were needed in the field immediately. There was neither the time to conduct thorough examinations nor additional soldiers to replace men who would be exempted.

Nor were doctors quick to reject men who wanted to serve. One soldier who was rejected was Private Albert Jones of Litchfield, who had enlisted in Company A. His exam revealed "an insignificant breach" for which army regulations mandated a discharge. Jones and his comrades were devastated, and the case was brought directly to Wessells, who intervened on the private's behalf with Plumb. The surgeon relented, the Litchfield boys celebrated, "for [Jones] was a general favorite" and the recruit was with the regiment when it departed Camp Dutton. A good soldier, Jones was promoted to corporal in February 1864. Less than four months later, he was killed in the charge against Confederate earthworks at Cold Harbor.[34]

A central component of celebrating a community's achievement in raising a regiment and the patriotism of its volunteers was the presentation of flags and a sendoff parade. These ceremonies commonly featured addresses that made clear that the men were on the right side of history as the heirs of the spirit of 1776, an entrusting of national and state flags from the community to the soldiers and a prominent role for women of the community. Thousands would gather and, with tears streaming down their cheeks, bid farewell to their loved ones. The presentation ceremony for the 19th did not culminate with the men marching off to war. Rather, afterward they returned to Camp Dutton for five more days before embarking for Washington City. In every other way, however, the 19th's sendoff matched what was taking place across the country as summer gave way to fall.[35]

Michael Kelly remarked that September 10 was "[a] great day, a change for the boys." After the morning duties were over, the assembly sounded. By that time, spectators by the thousands had been pouring into Litchfield for hours. At 12:30 p.m., the regiment departed Camp Dutton and marched "in fine order to the East Park," where a reviewing stand had been erected. A photograph of the ceremony shows them standing at attention. A tent stands along the northern side of East Park. Perhaps this was a reviewing stand, or the recruiting tent commemorated today by a marker on the Litchfield Green. If it is the latter, no documentary evidence has been found to corroborate its existence. The soldiers in the photo are standing

The 19th Connecticut Infantry, Litchfield, Connecticut, September 10, 1862. *Collection of the Litchfield Historical Society, Litchfield, Connecticut.*

at attention facing not the tent but the courthouse, suggesting that the speakers were located there.[36]

With Wessells slated to be one of the speakers, the regiment likely proceeded from the camp under Kellogg's command. Charles Andrews, in the crowd that day, recorded as much in his diary: "Saw the parade of the 19th Regiment under the command of Lt Col Kellogg." Reverend George Richards, minister at Litchfield's Congregational Church, gave the opening prayer and was followed to the platform by William Curtis Noyes, a prominent New York City attorney and Republican politician. He was chosen as the day's principal speaker because his wife, Julia Noyes Tallmadge, granddaughter of Revolutionary War hero Colonel Benjamin Tallmadge and signer of the Declaration of Independence William Floyd, was to present the unit with its regimental flag. Competition for this honor was fierce. The regiment had to politely turn down other offers of flags, including one from Charles Wolcott of Fishkill Landing, New York, a grandson of Oliver Wolcott Sr.[37]

In his address, Noyes capitalized on these familial connections to emphasize the soldiers' bonds with heroes of the nation's founding. It was a powerful speech, certainly memorable to the thousands who were present.

He began by referencing Colonel Tallmadge, the "friend and confidant of Washington," who made personal sacrifices in the war and then as a public servant. Over the course of Tallmadge's life—"more than four score years"—he had "maintain[ed] an irreproachable character for integrity and patriotism." Such traits were not unique to Tallmadge; rather, they were "coextensive with the Union." Noyes then called the crowd's attention to his wife, who as a granddaughter of both Tallmadge and signer of the Declaration William Floyd was an embodiment of the virtues of that earlier era. By presenting the colors to the regiment, she was imparting this connection to the nation's founding.[38]

Noyes was unafraid to delve into the politics of the war. "Instead of freedom and its untold blessings," he told the men, Confederates "would give you slavery and its unutterable evils." Standing between the country and this bleak future were the flags being presented that day. "Take then these standards," Noyes proclaimed, "confided to your keeping as a sacred deposit. They embody the dignity and honor of your Ancient Commonwealth, as well as the dignity and honor of the Republic, with their glorious reminiscences. They symbolize the principles for which the nation is contenting—principles which found expression in the Declaration of Independence—and upon which rest the hopes of oppressed peoples and nationalities everywhere." Through his powerful rhetoric, Noyes invested into the flags the hopes and dreams, values and virtues that impelled these men to go to war. It is not surprising that Edward Roberts wrote with pride of his being one of the

The national flag presented to the 19th Connecticut Infantry. *Collection of the Litchfield Historical Society, Litchfield, Connecticut.*

SWORD PRESENTATION!

The Sword voted by the Legislature of this State, to HENRY W. WESSELLS, will be presented at Litchfield, on Wednesday, January 23d.

By request of Major Wessells, the Sword will be received by *Colonel Thomas H. Seymour* from the hands of his Excellency *Gov. Trumbull.*

The Ceremony will take place upon the Balcony of the Mansion House, at 1 o'clock P. M.

A Procession will be formed in the following order, under the direction of

MAJOR GENERAL SHELTON,
COLONEL WM. F. BALDWIN,
Marshals of the Day.

1st Military Companies.
2nd Band.
3rd Committee of Arrangements.
4th Committee of Presentation and Reception.
5th Officers, Past and Commissioned.
6th Citizens and Strangers.

A National Salute will be fired at sunrise, and a Military Salute at the close of the ceremonies.

A general invitation is extended to the public to be present on this occasion.

A Military Ball in honor of the occasion will be given in the evening at Spencers' Hall.

Sword presentations to officers were a common ritual in regimental sendoffs. *Collection of the Litchfield Historical Society, Litchfield, Connecticut.*

color bearers that September day. Nor is it surprising that in the Civil War so many men would sacrifice their own lives to carry the flag of the regiment into battle.

This was a tough act to follow, and Wessells, already ill and likely overwhelmed with the responsibility of leading a regiment, responded only briefly. He "hesitated to receive [the flags] only because he thought such elegant testimonials of regard and confidence should be first merited by valor." Therefore, he said, they could be accepted only "in trust; promising for himself and the noble regiment which he had the honor to command that sooner than lose them they should fall beneath them, and that he trusted, at no very distant time, to bring them back with him to the Good Old State crowned with victory." Wessells concluded by thanking the "assembled representatives of Litchfield County…for the many kindnesses to the Regiment and as the Regiment must leave within a very short time, wishing them a sincere goodbye." The 19th then reformed its ranks and marched back to camp.[39]

While the ceremony was certainly the grandest and largest presentation made as the regiment prepared to depart, it was far from the only one. Towns and soldiers raised money to send the officers off to war with expensive gifts. Presentation swords, horses and other mementoes were quite common in the Civil War, and they were usually granted in recognition of exceptional bravery or leadership. In the 19th, these were also given in anticipation of what was to come. Homer Curtiss, writing to his mother, was more blunt about the purposes behind these gifts. "We got up a subscription for a sword, sash and belt for Dr Plumb yesterday," he reported. "[R]aised $40 or $50 I believe. The Dr is fine and I guess a dollar or two invested in his sword will not be a bad investment." Curtiss suggests that respect was, perhaps, transactional. Towns presented swords to the captains of their respective companies. Some of these presentation ceremonies took place in those towns when the captains were on furlough; others took place at the flag presentation on September 10. Lieutenant Colonel Kellogg was given a sword by Congressman George Woodruff. Relentlessly pursued by the press for not supporting the war effort, Woodruff may have used this very public occasion as a means of refuting such charges. After all, he was soon up for reelection, and Kellogg was a stranger to him. Kellogg pronounced it "the proudest and happiest hour of his life" and swore that he would defend it with his life, relying on friends to return it to Litchfield should he be "gobbled up." He added that he would never send them to a place he would not venture himself. For all of them, it would be "victory or death."[40]

Taken as a whole, these presentations to the departing men served several purposes. Some—like clothing or tobacco—simply sought to make men more comfortable under the trying conditions of war. In presenting swords to company commanders, towns provided a reminder that they were entrusting their children to those men. Finally, the men themselves presented gifts to their officers as an early investment, a show of respect they hoped would yield good treatment down the road.

As the men returned to camp that afternoon, there remained but one hurdle before they departed for war. They were not yet soldiers of the United States Army. This did not happen immediately upon enlistment. That made them members of Connecticut's militia; only when minimum manpower levels had been met and medical examinations completed could the men be mustered into federal service. Even then, a mustering officer needed to get to the camp. In the summer of 1862, when hundreds of regiments across the North were preparing to be federalized, that could take weeks, even months.

It was September 11 when Lieutenant Watson Webb of the 3rd United States Light Artillery arrived in camp. For Michael Kelly, this was "[t]he day, the day of all days." Webb's arrival also confirmed for Kelly why the physical examinations had been so hurried—they needed to be completed before the muster. Also arriving that day were scores of spectators, drawn once again to Litchfield by a martial ceremony. Whereas the prior day's events had been celebratory, the muster had a different tone. Major Nathaniel Smith of Woodbury remembered "many hundred, men, women and children, thronged thither, not however attracted, as usual by the stirring scenes of military duty—the flutter of flags, screaming of fifes, rattle of drums, ringing orders quickly repeated, and the swift evolutions of the drill…—but evincing, by the deep solemnity of the demeanor, a graver purpose than mere curiosity." These spectators gathered at the camp's "Field and Staff Street," where Wessells, Kellogg, Major Smith, Adjutant Deming and other members of the regimental staff had their tents. The individual companies formed in their own streets, captains and lieutenants at their heads. One by one, the companies marched forward, stopping in front of Webb, who stood with a military statute book in his hands, the regiment's field officers arrayed behind him. Wessells sent orderlies to each company commander when it was his unit's turn, and those men marched until its center was opposite Webb. There it halted and faced the lieutenant. Webb called each man's

The roll of Company H, 19th Connecticut Infantry. *Collection of the Litchfield Historical Society, Litchfield, Connecticut.*

name. The soldier took two steps forward, and this continued until each volunteer had advanced with his new comrades. They removed their caps, raised their right hands and repeated the oath of service. Their training was over. The Litchfield County boys were now soldiers.[41]

Rumors had swirled almost since the men arrived in camp that their departure for the front was imminent. On September 8, for example, Homer Curtiss began a letter to his friend Seth but was unable to finish it before the noon collection of outgoing mail, reporting that he "[s]hall have to wait until I reach Dixie land before I finish it." These rumors accelerated in the wake of the mustering ceremony, but the process of paying off the federal bounties took longer than anticipated. The *Winsted Herald* edition of September 12 repeated the rumor but hedged its bets: "The Litchfield Regiment will positively leave next Monday noon—*we guess*. Nobody seems to know." In the meantime, the men existed in a state of limbo. They had said goodbye to friends and family and had their ceremonial sendoff, but they remained at Camp Dutton, within sight of the homes of some of the men.[42]

If there was disagreement about when the men would depart, there was universal acclaim for their appearance. This began from the first day the Litchfield company assembled at their town hall, the men in two rows, "each man standing so very erect that his spine described an inward curve, painful both to himself and the spectator; and having by much tuition been enabled to master the evolution known as 'right face.'" After a few weeks of training, a reporter observed, "the regiment made a fine appearance, and few are sick; the diseases of the latter are mostly traceable, by the by, to the kind of donations of friends in the vegetable line." The message was simple: it was time for the regiment to depart.[43]

When the regiment was fully mustered and ready to depart, the *Enquirer* ran a complete roster of the unit. Despite printing one thousand extra copies, it still sold out, and another roster, with additions and corrections, appeared the following week. While the desire to obtain these rosters was primarily due to pride, this was not the case for all. Alva Stone, with the 8th Connecticut in Fredericksburg, Virginia, wrote home, "When a Company is started in your town, I want you to send me the Roll. I shall be happy to hear who are the 'patriots' and who are not." Rather than being a purely unifying act, the full mobilization of the county also provided a means by which residents could evaluate the loyalty of their neighbors.[44]

Epilogue

"The Flower of Her Youth"

The long-awaited order to depart Camp Dutton arrived on Friday, September 12. Adjutant General Williams instructed Wessells and the 19th Connecticut to leave for Washington in the early morning hours of September 15. Some men, including carpenter Anson Healey and Quartermaster Bradley Lee, left earlier to prepare the unit's new camp and supervise the unpacking of supplies. Ministers across the county devoted their sermons on Sunday, September 14, to the unit's leaving for the front. Among these was Reverend George Richards of Litchfield's Congregational Church. The sermon had special meaning for Richards, who knew that many men from the 19th would attend service at his church that day. His sermon was titled simply "19th Regt Goes Tomorrow," and he drew his inspiration from James 5:16: "The prayer of a righteous person is powerful and effective." It was intended more for those who would be left behind than for the soldiers; he articulated the idea that having offered up their sons on the altar of the nation and made financial sacrifices to fill the quota and outfit the men, all that remained was for the civilians to pray: "There are times that we can do little else.…What is left us but to look and wait for a higher will and stronger arm to interpose?" The events of the last two and a half months—from Lincoln's proclamation to this eve of departure—had demonstrated the degree to which county residents had been swept up in the whirlwind of war. "The greatness of the exigency," Richards preached, "mocks our puny and impotent exertions." Yet if men had lost a degree of agency in secular matters, they still possessed the power of prayer. And the prayers of parents could continue to protect sons, even if on distant battlefields, for "there is such a thing as a traveling prayer." Richards closed by reminding his congregation, "Our country, too, particularly needs and demands our supplications." Ministers had been active recruiters for the 19th Connecticut, and in many ways these final sermons were the culmination of their efforts. They had exhausted all the secular means available to aid the war effort and now used their spiritual offices to place the soldiers into God's hands.[1]

Reverend George Richards. *Collection of the Litchfield Historical Society, Litchfield, Connecticut.*

Volunteers for the 19th continued to arrive in Litchfield. Abby J. Hubbard, wife of John Hubbard who had been haranguing those men waiting to see Dr. Beckwith, remembered that her "servants had just gone out for the evening and I had just put the children to bed, when Mr. Hubbard came into the house, and told me that a number of enlisted men had just come to town, and that there were no preparations to receive them at Camp Dutton, and that the hotels were full. 'They must be taken care of, for they are going out to fight for us.' So I looked up all my bedding, and then went in to Miss Ogden's and borrowed of her. That night nineteen soldiers slept in our house.'" The residents of the county had provided for the men throughout the mobilization process; they would continue to do so even as the men marched off to war.[2]

Bugles blared reveille across the Litchfield countryside at 4:00 a.m. that Monday, September 15. Edward Roberts remembered the morning ominously as a "dark and gloomy one, the fog overhanging our camp, as a dark and fitting veil of our mission, that day to begin." Soon "the pack up call sounds," Michael Kelly recorded, and morning rations were issued. The men were assembled and inspected for departure. At about ten o'clock, they were permitted to say goodbye to family and friends who had gathered at the camp. "On all sides," Major Smith remembered, "a hurried party, last kisses of wives, mothers or sweethearts. The fathers or brothers handgrasped firmly for an instant, on all sides, earnest requests to write—write as soon as you get to—don't forget to write—God Bless you!—Don't fear for me! Be a good boy!" The somber scene was broken by the calls of "fall in Company," and the men scrambled to get into line. Smith remembered that "hurriedly the knapsack is thrown on, never again to be so heavy," and roll calls were taken. Adjutant Deming appeared on the parade ground with a band and markers to guide the regiment's march. From each company's street, the assembled men tentatively put one foot in front of the other, beginning their journey toward war. A temporary moment of confusion arose as companies marched in different directions, but "suddenly order comes out of chaos, as each [company] drops into place in line." Kellogg, in command, appeared at the unit's front and, summoning the color company, bestowed on them the flags that Mrs. Noyes had presented five days earlier. Finally, "in the presence of thousands of spectators," the men gave "three rousing cheers for Camp Dutton." Kellogg ordered, "Battalion Right F-A-C-E," a cry taken up by the major, adjutant and sergeant major. Drummers snapped to the ready so as to strike a beat simultaneously. Kellogg snarled, "COLUMN FORWARD" and then "Harr!" which, Smith later explained, "is military for March!" With that, approximately nine hundred men departed Camp Dutton for the Naugatuck Railroad Station in East Litchfield. Behind them came wagons of supplies, as well as carriages and other conveyances of loved ones and spectators. One estimate stated that there were three hundred vehicles, a line that stretched for a mile behind the men.[3]

As the men proceeded to the station, the fog lifted and the sun, growing higher in the sky with each minute, beat down on the men. Roberts remembered, "We were soon sweating under the loads we thought were necessary for our existence." Cresting the ridge that separates Litchfield from East Litchfield, the men likely would have seen the steam rising from the two locomotives hitched to the approximately twenty passenger cars of the special train procured to transport them to New York City. It was about 2:00 p.m. when the column reached the station. Military trappings surrounded them. Guards were posted at all entrances of the train's cars, with orders to allow only soldiers on board and to prevent them from leaving once they had boarded. Also waiting at the station were crates of Enfield rifles of the "newest patterns." These would be issued to the men once they arrived in Washington City.[4]

The men and the "multitude" (or, as the *Herald* described it, "the entire population for miles around") that followed in wagons and carriages and on foot "covered every available inch of ground around the depot." Cheers rang out from the crowd, which were answered by the soldiers. Families craned their necks for a final look at the faces of their departing soldiers. The *Herald* captured the poignancy of the moment: "A careless observer would have been electrified by the waving handkerchiefs and hats, the ringing cheers, and the band's sweet music. Looking closer, one could not fail to see the manifestation of heart agony or measuring all the funerals of a lifetime. 'Will my boy come back to me?' was the unanswered question on a thousand throats; God grant that all may!" The train slowly pulled away from the station. "Left camp for Dixie" was how Roberts remembered it, the men bound for a war from which hundreds of them would never return.[5]

The departure made many in Litchfield County consider the sacrifices made and what they meant. "It is sad to think the brave men are at length gone," the *Enquirer* noted on September 18, "and yet grateful to know that they have gone to fulfill their duty and perform their allotted work." The paper made no attempt to define what that duty was; that had been done countless times over the previous two and a half months. Rather, it reminded its readers that war meant sacrifice, and that some of the men—"the very flower and cream of our county—the best and dearest to many of us…we shall never see anymore." Rather than fill themselves with worry or dread, the *Enquirer* urged its readers to "thank God then that we live in times where we can make such sacrifices, and render such offerings."[6]

Yet the mobilization effort seemed to yield tangible results as well. In its immediate aftermath, there were calls to set aside party loyalty in favor of political unity. Litchfield Democrats and Republicans met to put forth a "Union" ticket composed of jointly nominated candidates. The *Enquirer* thoroughly approved: "In these times when all loyal men everywhere are upholding Government and lending every energy as one man, to the crushing out of the rebellion, and while all issues are out of sight, it seems proper that we should unite on one loyal ticket for officers of the town.…Let loyal men have no petty *party* issues raised in so unimportant an election." Any hopes of a Union ticket, however, were dashed with the issuance of the preliminary Emancipation Proclamation one week after the 19th departed. The *Enquirer* rejoiced at the news, declaring, "We believe the time was ripe for its appearance, and the classes north will hail its production as the omen of a victorious end of the rebellion." The Emancipation Proclamation, however, galvanized Democrats into thinking that Lincoln was making the war one of abolition and rejected the proposal of a Union ticket. Within a week, the *Enquirer* had reverted to calling Democrats "sorry," "foolish" and "miserable." The *New Haven Register* declared that the "North is not *all* abolitionized and the UNION MAY YET BE RESTORED." Many saw the election as a referendum on the Emancipation Proclamation. In Litchfield, Democrats took control of town government, but Union tickets composed of Republicans and prowar Democrats were more successful in other parts of the county, controlling the government of fifteen towns, while Democrats ran eight. Two—Barkhamsted and Woodbury—were divided.[7]

It was not long before dreams of party unity were completely gone. By early October, the Republican papers were referring to Democrats as "secesh," "red noses" or "white feathers." Democrats were also accused of besmirching the soldiers of the 19th to further their political interests. The *Enquirer* responded angrily and in terms that spoke to the communal effort of raising the regiment:

> *If the secessionists in this co*[unty] *chose to manufacture foolish and wicked lies insinuating mutinies in our Co*[unty] *Regiment…we trust no one will be silly or weak enough to believe them, and will treat the stories with the same contempt their authors deserve. Various stories of this kind…are the inventions of the enemy, and can be generally traced to sources, which to say the least, have no sympathy with the brave boys of our regiment or the cause which they have gone forth to uphold; and such stories only recoil in the end upon their contemptible authors.*

Just two weeks earlier, the *Enquirer* had hopes of setting aside party differences and working together with Democrats toward the preservation of the Union. In the wake of the preliminary Emancipation Proclamation, the Democratic victory in the local election and criticism of the officers of the 19th, Democrats were suddenly "the enemy." The raising of the Litchfield County regiment may have, in some ways, worsened the situation. Republicans and supporters of the war may have looked the other way when critics lambasted far-off targets; they simply could not abide criticisms of the local soldiers.[8]

Enormous energies had been expended raising the regiment, and many certainly hoped that the bipartisan spirit of the rallies would endure. The quick reversion to the politics of old must have been disappointing, but just as with the continued presence of baseball games and agricultural fairs, it can be seen as yet another piece of evidence that there was some normalcy to life on the Northern homefront.

The disappointment was heightened by the sacrifices made, which went beyond the men sent to war. The financial encumbrances taken on by the state and towns were enormous. For the enlistment period culminating on September 30, 1862, the town of Litchfield paid approximately $11,250 in bounties to soldiers and payments to their families. More than $5,250 of this amount was borrowed. The town of Winchester paid $6,500 just in bounties. Croffut and Morris estimated that Winchester's total expenditure for the war—including bounties, reimbursements to recruiting officers, expenses related to annual meetings, travel to Hartford to consult with the adjutant general's office and purchasing uniforms for the earliest volunteers—exceeded $60,000, nearly $2 million in 2020 dollars. These tabulations do not include the bounties offered by private individuals. For example, Elliot Beardsley, a Winsted factory owner, personally gave each enlistee from the town in the summer of 1862 $10. In total, Litchfield County towns spent $551,211.61 on bounties and support of families over the course of the war, while individuals expended $192,998.94 on private bounties or payments to substitutes.[9]

After the war, many second-guessed the effectiveness of the bounties, with the U.S. Sanitary Commission, a private relief agency that aided sick and wounded soldiers, declaring that "the Government had foolishly spent too much on bounties at enlistment, too little afterwards on upkeep for the maimed, the widows, the orphans, now destitute." Whether or not the second part of this criticism is true, the overall sentiment ignores the necessity of the bounties to fill the ranks. Simply put, it is unlikely that the 19th Connecticut would have even come close to filling its ranks without the financial inducements.[10]

When considered in national terms, this would have imperiled the war effort in the short run; historian Joseph L. Harsh has convincingly demonstrated that superior Confederate mobilization efforts and the South's early passage of a conscription act reduced the Union's manpower advantage of men in the military from 1.6:1 to 1.3:1 between January 1 and June 30, 1862, the latter being the day before Lincoln's call for 300,000 volunteers. The president's twin calls for troops in the summer of 1862, coupled with Confederate losses in the summer and fall campaigns, increased the Union advantage to 2:1 by the end of the year. At the very least, without bounties the United States government would have had to adopt a conscription act earlier, perhaps one more wide-ranging than those that went into effect in September 1862 and the summer of 1863. The result may have been even greater unrest and diminution of morale on the Northern homefront.[11]

Of course, the Union cause was ultimately triumphant. Perhaps reminding civilians that they had also contributed to the mobilization efforts that made the victory possible was the motivating factor in the erection of a commemorative marker on the Litchfield green denoting the location of the recruiting tent for the 19th Connecticut. Those who remembered the summer of 1862 knew that mobilization meant more than simply getting men to enlist. It meant convincing citizens about the worthiness of the cause, involving all residents—including women—in the war effort, marshaling economic resources for the war effort and stifling dissent.

But what of the men who left Camp Dutton for war that foggy morning? Arriving in Washington a few days later, they remained there for twenty months, guarding the capital from Virginia fortifications. In November 1863, the unit's name was changed to the 2nd Connecticut Heavy Artillery, suggesting that its station was a permanent one. The situation was frustrating for the men, fighting disease instead of rebels. In May 1864, however, the unit was summoned to join the Army of the Potomac in its Overland Campaign. Less than two weeks after reaching the front, the 2nd Connecticut Heavy Artillery charged Confederate entrenchments at Cold Harbor, suffering more than three hundred casualties in about an hour of fighting. After that battle, Lewis Bissell of Litchfield wrote, "Old Litchfield's best sons have laid their lives on the altar of their country."[12]

The regiment would see further fierce combat at Third Winchester and Fisher's Hill and in the Petersburg Campaign. Regardless of where the war took them, the men never forgot Camp Dutton. From the defenses of Washington, John Shaw of Colebrook wrote home that "we doant [*sic*] get as good feed as we got on camp dutton." Lying in a hospital bed after being severely wounded at Cold Harbor, he asked a loved one to "please let me know how things are getting along in Litchfield. I should like to be on Chestnut Hill again."[13]

When the unit's designation changed from infantry to heavy artillery, its regulation size increased from 1,000 to 1,800. Ultimately, 2,468 men served in the unit at some point. Eventually, men from all but twenty of Connecticut's towns would serve in the regiment, but its core remained from Litchfield County, with more men coming from Litchfield, Plymouth and Winchester than any other towns. Over the course of the war, 254 men of the regiment died as a result of battle, and another 181 died from disease; 19 men died in Confederate prisoner of war camps, most notably at Andersonville, Georgia, and Salisbury, North Carolina. Another 283 men were permanently disabled due to illness, injury or wounds.[14]

Of course, the county's towns sent men into regiments other than the 19th. Using Litchfield as an example, the toll the war took on communities both in the short and long term can be better understood. Litchfield had approximately 3,200 residents when the war began and sent 299 men off to war. Of these, 27 were killed or mortally wounded, another 27 died of disease and 5 died in prisoner of war camps; 47 men were discharged for disability; and 39 men deserted, a number that at first glance seems considerable. A sample of ten towns from across the North of similar size to Litchfield reveals an average desertion rate of 9.2 percent for the sample and 13 percent for Litchfield. Many of the deserters were draftees. Seven of Litchfield's deserters left the army after Lee's surrender, when they presumed the war was over. With so many dead, disabled or tainted by desertion, an entire generation of men from the county was scarred by war. Perhaps veteran and Supreme Court justice Oliver Wendell Holmes Jr. captured this best in writing that he and his comrades had "shared the incommunicable experience of war." For the men of the 19th Connecticut, that began at Camp Dutton.[15]

In looking back on the organizing of the regiment, Theodore F. Vaill remembered, "In order to raise it, Litchfield County had given up the flower of her youth, the hope and pride of hundreds of families, and they had by no means enlisted to fight for a superior class of men at home. There was no superior class at home. In moral qualities, in social worth, in every civil relation, they were the best Connecticut had to give."[16] Vaill's memory is both accurate and awash in nostalgia. There is no doubt about the sacrifices made by the men and their families. Yet while it is understandable that a veteran would tout the superiority of his own regiment, there was nothing unique about the 19th. It was generally representative of the county. In that fact, however, lies the evidence that the vast mobilization effort was successful. To further the war effort, it turned out rich and poor, college graduates and illiterate, Democrats and Republicans. Its men proved to be good soldiers and bad soldiers, heroes and cowards. Together they, along with hundreds of thousands of comrades in blue, won the war, helped free the enslaved and preserved the Union.

Notes

Introduction

1. *Bridgeport Times and Evening Farmer*, September 12, 1912, 6; Freeman, *Field of Blood*; *Winsted Herald*, August 31, 1860.

Chapter 1

1. Carley, *Litchfield*, 18; see especially Kirby, *Echoes of Iron*.
2. Niven, *Connecticut for the Union*, 14, 360.
3. *Litchfield Enquirer*, October 27, 1859.
4. Niven, *Connecticut for the Union*, 10.
5. For more on education in Litchfield County, see Vermilyea, *Hidden History of Litchfield County*.
6. Paludan, *"People's Contest,"* 10–11; Cimbala and Miller, *Northern Homefront during the Civil War*, 5.
7. White, *History of the Town of Litchfield*; Vermilyea, *Hidden History of Litchfield County*, 107.
8. Cimbala and Miller, *Northern Homefront during the Civil War*, 1.
9. Mott, *American Journalism*, 216.
10. Howe, *What Hath God Wrought*, chapter 6.
11. Phillips, "Grapevine Telegraph," 753–88; Cimbala and Miller, *Northern Homefront during the Civil War*, 23–24.
12. *Litchfield Enquirer*, February 16, 1860.
13. Warshauer, *Connecticut in the Civil War*, 43; Finan, "William A. Buckingham," 10.
14. James A. Briggs to Abraham Lincoln, February 29, 1860, Abraham Lincoln Papers, Library of Congress, https://www.loc.gov/item/mal0245900; "Speech

at New Haven, Connecticut," Basler, *Collected Works of Abraham Lincoln*, 4:13. See also Warshauer, *Connecticut in the Civil War*, 43.
15. Niven, *Connecticut for the Union*, 24.
16. "The Connecticut Election: The Result Heavy Republican Majority in the Legislature," *New York Times*, April 5, 1860.
17. Niven, *Connecticut for the Union*, 24; Brands, *Zealot and the Emancipator*, 300.
18. *Winsted Herald*, August 31, 1860; September 7, 1860.
19. *Litchfield Enquirer*, September 7; September 20, 1860; October 11, 1860.
20. *Litchfield Enquirer*, October 18, 1860.
21. *Winsted Herald*, October 12, 1860; November 2, 1860.
22. *Litchfield Enquirer*, November 8, 1860.
23. *Winsted Herald*, November 23, 1860; *Litchfield Enquirer*, November 29, December 14, December 20, 1860; *Winsted Herald*, November 23, December 21, 1860.
24. *Litchfield Enquirer*, January 3, 1861, March 29, 1861.

Chapter 2

1. *Litchfield Enquirer*, April 18, 1861; Niven, *Connecticut for the Union*, 45–46.
2. *Winsted Herald*, March 1, 1861.
3. *Litchfield Enquirer*, May 2, 1861, May 9, 1861; Rable, *God's Almost Chosen People*, 4.
4. *Litchfield Enquirer*, May 2, 1861; *Winsted Herald*, September 20, 1861; *Litchfield Enquirer*, May 16, 1861, June 6, 1861, May 30, 1861.
5. Cimbala and Miller, *Northern Homefront during the Civil War*, 45–46; *Litchfield Enquirer*, May 22, 1862.
6. *Litchfield Enquirer*, May 2, 1861, June 6, 1861.
7. Paludan, *"People's Contest,"* 15; Finan, "William A. Buckingham," 26; *Litchfield Enquirer*, February 2, 1862.
8. Paludan, *"People's Contest,"* 10.
9. *Winsted Herald*, April 26, 1861.
10. *Winsted Herald*, April 26, 1861, May 10, 1861.
11. *Winsted Herald*, May 10, 1861. Minutes of May 2, 1861, Litchfield Town Meeting; *Litchfield Town Minutes,* Vol., 49, 1840–1880, Office of the Litchfield Town Clerk.
12. White, *History of the Town of Litchfield*, 219; *Litchfield Enquirer*, May 2, 1861; *Winsted Herald*, May 17, 1861; May 24, 1861.
13. *Winsted Herald*, May 24, 1861; June 21, 1861; July 26, 1861; September 3, 1861; January 10, 1862.
14. *Litchfield Enquirer*, October 24, 1861; *Winsted Herald*, December 13, 1861; *Winsted Herald*, January 10, 1862.
15. *Litchfield Enquirer*, October 24, 1861.
16. Alva Stone to "Dear Wife, October 27, 1861," Alva Stone Letters, LHS. The censoring of some names is typical of Stone's letters.

17. *Winsted Herald*, March 7, 1862; *Litchfield Enquirer*, May 15, 1862; *Winsted Herald*, September 6, 1861.
18. Giesberg, *Army at Home*, 31.
19. Paludan, *"People's Contest,"* 105; Niven, *Connecticut for the Union*, 360; *Litchfield Enquirer*, March 27, 1862; *History of Litchfield County, Connecticut*, 223.
20. *Winsted Herald*, September 12, 1862; Adam, "Titans for a Battlefield."
21. Paludan, *"People's Contest,"* 157–58; Cimbala and Miller, *Northern Homefront during the Civil War*, 55–57; *Litchfield Enquirer*, November 15, 1861.
22. Engle, *Gathering to Save a Nation*, 47.
23. *Litchfield Enquirer*, February 13, 1862, February 27, 1862; "Charlie" to "Sister," April 2, 1862, Plumb Family Correspondence, LHS.
24. *Winsted Herald*, December 13, 1861, December 27, 1861, April 25, 1862; American Civil War Research Database.

Chapter 3

1. *Litchfield Enquirer*, May 16, 1861.
2. Ibid.
3. Paludan, *"People's Contest,"* 158.
4. Warshauer, *Connecticut in the Civil War*, 62; Seidman, "We Were Enlisted," 63; Gallman, *Defining Duty*, 195; Cimbala and Miller, *Northern Homefront during the Civil War*, 39.
5. Blevins, "Women and Federal Officeholding"; Orr, "North Mobilizes for War."
6. Warshauer, *Connecticut in the Civil War*, 90; *Litchfield Enquirer*, May 9, 1861; *Winsted Herald*, May 17, 1861.
7. *Litchfield Enquirer*, May 23, 1861, June 3, 1861.
8. Spar, *New Haven's Civil War Hospital*; *Litchfield Enquirer*, August 7, 1862; "Ladies' Benevolent Society Secretary's Book, Vol. I, 1842–1865" and "Soldier's Aid Association," Ladies' Benevolent Society of Northfield secretary's books and Soldier's Aid Association Minutes, LHS;*Litchfield Enquirer*, May 1, 1862, October 18, 1861.
9. S.H. Perkins to the Editor, *Litchfield Enquirer*, January 9, 1862; January 2, 1862.
10. *Litchfield Enquirer*, January 2, 1862; June 6, 1861.
11. *Litchfield Enquirer*, May 1, 1861; *Winsted Herald*, September 12, 1862; Katharine Bissell Borgert Roe, "Memoir of Litchfield in the 1860s," LHS.
12. *Litchfield Enquirer*, January 2, 1862.
13. *Winsted Herald*, October 18, 1861, November 15, 1861.
14. *Litchfield Enquirer*, November 7, 1861.
15. *Litchfield Enquirer*, October 31, 1861; Alva Stone to "Wife & Child," November 13, 1861, Alva Stone to "Family," December 1, 1861, Alva Stone Letters, LHS.
16. Croffut and Morris, *Military and Civil History of Connecticut*, 468; *Litchfield Enquirer*, September 11, 1862.

Chapter 4

1. *Litchfield Enquirer*, August 8, 1861; August 29, 1861; *Winsted Herald*, October 11, 1861.
2. *Winsted Herald*, October 11, 1861, January 10, 1862; *Litchfield Enquirer*, January 23, 1862.
3. Paludan, *"People's Contest,"* 88; Warshauer, *Connecticut in the Civil War*, 47, 188.
4. Gallman, *Defining Duty*, 2.
5. Weber, *Copperheads*.
6. Jeffrey, "They Cannot Expect…," 6, 9, 16.
7. Ibid., 10–11, 16.
8. *Winsted Herald*, September 6, 1861.
9. Croffut and Morris, *Military and Civil History of Connecticut*, 40; Esther Thompson memoir, Thompson Family Papers, LHS.
10. Warshauer, *Connecticut in the Civil War*, 55.
11. *Litchfield Enquirer*, June 27, 1861.
12. *Winsted Herald*, June 28, 1861.
13. Ibid.; *Litchfield Enquirer*, June 27, 1861.
14. Esther Thompson memoir, Thompson Family Papers, LHS; *Winsted Herald*, June 28, 1861.
15. *Litchfield Enquirer*, June 27, 1861.
16. *Litchfield Enquirer*, July 11, 1861, July 18, 1861.
17. Esther Thompson memoir, Thompson Family Papers, LHS.
18. *Winsted Enquirer*, August 16, 1861.
19. Croffut and Morris, *Military and Civil History of Connecticut*, 104; *Litchfield Enquirer*, August 15, 1861.
20. *Litchfield Enquirer*, September 5, 1861; Esther Thompson memoir, Thompson Family Papers, LHS.
21. Esther Thompson memoir, Thompson Family Papers, LHS.
22. *Litchfield Enquirer*, August 1, 1861.
23. Esther Thompson memoir, Thompson Family Papers, LHS.
24. *Litchfield Enquirer*, September 5, 1861.
25. Ibid.
26. Esther Thompson memoir, Thompson Family Papers, LHS; "The Arrest of Ellis B. Schnabel," *New York Times*, September 1, 1861; *Litchfield Enquirer*, September 5, 1861.
27. Engle, *Gathering to Save a Nation*, 101.
28. Alva Stone to "Dear Wife," October 8, 1861; Stone to "Dear Wife and Child," October 11, 1861; Alva Stone to "Dear Wife," November 17, 1861, Alva Stone Letters, LHS.
29. Neely, *Fate of Liberty*; *Litchfield Enquirer*, January 16, 1862.

Chapter 5

1. *Winsted Herald*, August 8, 1862.
2. Hines, *Civil War Volunteer Sons of Connecticut*.
3. United States Department of War, *War of the Rebellion* (hereafter *OR*), series III, vol. 2, 3; Hartwig, *To Antietam Creek*, 138.
4. Miller, *States at War*, 76–77; *Winsted Herald*, June 20, 1862.
5. Winsted Herald, May 30, 1862; *New York Times*, July 2, 1862.
6. Charles Andrews Diary, June 24, 1862, Charles B. Andrews Papers, LHS.
7. McPherson, *Battle Cry of Freedom*, 491; Thompson, "Altoona Was His," 91; *Collected Works of Abraham Lincoln*, 5:297.
8. Croffut and Morris, *Military and Civil History of Connecticut*, 223; Engle, *Gathering to Save a Nation*, 179; Harsh, *Taken at the Flood*, 20.
9. Croffut and Morris, *Military and Civil History of Connecticut*, 456.
10. *Winsted Herald*, July 18, 1862.
11. *OR*, series III, vol. 2, 123, 186.
12. Niven, *Connecticut for the Union*, 78.
13. Miller, *States at War*, 79.
14. Croffut and Morris, *Military and Civil History of Connecticut*, 240–49.
15. *Litchfield Enquirer*, July 17, 1862.
16. Cothren, *History of Ancient Woodbury, Connecticut*, 1,191.
17. *Winsted Herald*, July 11, 1862; *Litchfield Enquirer*, July 31, 1862; McPherson, *Battle Cry of Freedom*, 491.
18. Giesberg, *Army at Home*, 36; *Litchfield Enquirer*, July 31, 1862; McPherson, *Battle Cry of Freedom*, 492; Murdock, *One Million Men*, 4–5.
19. *Litchfield Enquirer*, July 17, 1862; *Winsted Herald*, July 18, 1862.
20. *Winsted Herald*, July 18, 1862; Vaill, *County Regiment*, 12.
21. *Winsted Herald*, July 18, 1862; *Litchfield Enquirer*, July 17, 1862.
22. Cimbala and Miller, *Northern Homefront during the Civil War*, 36.
23. *Winsted Herald*, July 18, 1862.
24. *Housatonic Republican*, July 26, 1862; *History of Litchfield County, Connecticut*, 349.
25. *Winsted Herald*, July 27, 1862.
26. *Litchfield Enquirer*, July 24, 1862; *Winsted Herald*, July 27, 1862.
27. *Litchfield Enquirer*, July 24, 1862; *Housatonic Republican*, July 26, 1862; Charles Andrew diary, July 22, 1862, Charles B. Andrews Papers, LHS.
28. *Litchfield Enquirer*, August 1, 1862; Cothren, *History of Ancient Woodbury, Connecticut*, 1,190.
29. *Litchfield Enquirer*, August 8, 1862.
30. Vaill, *History of the Second Connecticut*, 10–12; Alva Stone to "Wife and Child," July 30, 1862, Alva Stone Letters, LHS.

Chapter 6

1. *Winsted Herald*, August 1, 1862; Boatner, *Civil War Dictionary*, 624.
2. Alva Stone to "Wife and Child," July 27, 1862, Alva Stone Letters, LHS.
3. *Winsted Herald*, August 8; Smith, *Old Nineteenth*, 9.
4. Weld, *Connecticut Physicians in the Civil War*, 47.
5. John Brinsfield, William C. Davis, Benedict Maryniak and James I. Robertson, eds., *Faith in the Fight: Civil War Chaplains* (Harrisburg: Stackpole Press, 2008), xvi; *Litchfield Enquirer*, September 11, 1862.
6. *Litchfield Enquirer*, August 21, 1862.
7. Vaill, *History of the Second Connecticut*, 15.
8. *Housatonic Republican*, July 26, 1862; *Winsted Herald*, July 27, 1862.
9. *Litchfield Enquirer*, August 7, 1862.
10. Alva Stone to "Wife,"July 21, 1862, Alva Stone Letters, LHS.
11. *Litchfield Enquirer*, August 1, 1862.
12. *Litchfield Enquirer*, August 8, 1862; August 21, 1862.
13. *Winsted Herald*, July 27, 1862; Alva Stone to "Wife," July 27, 1862, Alva Stone Letters, LHS.
14. McPherson, *For Cause and Comrades*, 20.
15. Manning, *What This Cruel War Was Over*; Seth Plumb to "Friends," June 7, 1862, Seth Plumb to Lemira, September 2, 1862, Plumb Family Correspondence, LHS.
16. Rable, *God's Almost Chosen People*, 70.
17. *Winsted Herald*, August 1, 1862, August 8, 1862; Vaill, *County Regiment*, 8.
18. Paludan, *"People's Contest,"* 180; Marvel, *Lincoln's Mercenaries*, 17–18, 20.
19. Marvel, *Lincoln's Mercenaries*, 25, 116.
20. Giesberg, *Army at Home*, 59, 19; Alva Stone to "Wife," November 25, 1861, Alva Stone Letters, LHS.
21. "Comptroller's Records of Returns from Towns and Payments to Soldiers and Families during the Civil War.
22. Ibid.
23. *Winsted Herald*, August 15, 1862.
24. *Winsted Herald*, July 27, 1862; Murdock, O*ne Million Men*, 9; Smith, *Old Nineteenth*, 316.
25. *Winsted Herald*, September 15, 1862, August 8, 1862.
26. Seth Plumb to "Friends," August 10, 1862, Plumb Family Correspondence, LHS; Cothren, *History of Ancient Woodbury, Connecticut*, 1,189.
27. "Litchfield Awake!," American Civil War Printed Ephemera, LHS; *Litchfield Enquirer*, July 31, 1862.
28. "Colonel Wessells' Regiment," American Civil War Printed Ephemera, LHS; Prices and Wages by Decade: 1860–1869, "Wages for Four Common Occupations in 1860, by State."
29. Paludan, *"People's Contest,"* 179.

30. Vaill, *County Regiment*, 7; Schweiger, "Literate South," 333; Homer Curtiss to "Ma," September 15, 1862, Bernhard Knollenberg Collection, Manuscripts and Archives, Yale University Library (hereafter Yale).

Chapter 7

1. Alva Stone to "Wife & Child," August 2, 1862, Alva Stone Letters, LHS.
2. Vaill, *History of the Second Connecticut*, 10; Special Orders 53, RG 13, CSL; also, Smith, *Old Nineteenth*, 6.
3. *Litchfield Enquirer*, July 27, 1862; Smith, *Old Nineteenth*, 9.
4. Croffut and Morris, *Military and Civil History of Connecticut*, 224; *Litchfield Enquirer*, September 5, 1862.
5. Smith, *Old Nineteenth*, 33.
6. Michael Kelly diary, Manuscript Collection, Connecticut Historical Society. (Hereafter CHS.)
7. Michael Kelly diary, CHS.
8. Edward S. Roberts diary, CHS.
9. David Soule, "Recollections of the Civil War," *New Milford Gazette*, June 30, 1911.
10. Croffut and Morris, *Military and Civil History of Connecticut*, 720; Stone to "Wife and Child," July 27, 1862, Alva Stone Letters, LHS; *Winsted Herald*, August 8, 1862, August 15, 1862 and August 22, 1862.
11. *Winsted Herald*, August 1, 1862; *Utica Daily Press*, June 5, 1920.
12. Stephen Fenn to Horace Fenn, July 22, 1862, CH; Rable, *God's Almost Chosen People*, 70; *Litchfield Enquirer*, August 8, 1862; Stephen Fenn to Horace Fenn, September 9, 1862, CHS.
13. Alva Stone to "Wife and Child," August 8, 1862, Alva Stone Letters, LHS.
14. Engle, *Gathering to Save a Nation*, 203; Marvel, *Lincoln's Mercenaries*, 109.
15. *Housatonic Republican*, July 27, 1862.
16. Murdock, *One Million Men*, 9; Gallman, *North Fights the Civil War*, 61; Niven, *Connecticut for the Union*, 83; Geary, *We Need Men*, 39.
17. *Hartford Courant*, August 11, 1862; Niven, *Connecticut for the Union*, 85.
18. Niven, *Connecticut for the Union*, 84.
19. *Winsted Herald*, September 19, 1862.
20. *Litchfield Enquirer*, September 4, 1862.
21. *Litchfield Enquirer*, August 7, 1862.

Chapter 8

1. A more detailed version of this chapter appeared in the Fall 2022 issue (Volume 61:2) of *Connecticut History Review*.
2. Leone, "Peace Movement in Litchfield," 19–21; Beckwith, *Beckwiths*, 155–56.
3. McGaugh, *Surgeon in Blue*, 75–98; Murdock, *One Million Men*, 121–23.

4. *Winsted Herald*, August 8, 1862.
5. *Winsted Herald*, August 8, 1862; Niven, *Connecticut for the Union*, 83; *Litchfield Enquirer*, August 14, 1862.
6. *Winsted Herald*, August 8, 1862; Croffut and Morris, *Military and Civil History of Connecticut*, 243.
7. *Winsted Herald*, August 8, 1862.
8. Croffut and Morris, *Military and Civil History of Connecticut*, 242; *Litchfield Enquirer,* August 14, 1862. It should be noted that in a February 15, 1861 letter to his father, Josiah Beckwith hints that he may have been facing financial troubles. "Must work or lose my practice & family," he wrote, "need all that I can earn." Could this have been a motivating factor for what was to transpire in the summer of 1862? "Treasure Discovered Beneath the Floorboards," *On the Drawing Board*, May 27, 2011, https://blog.crisparchitects.com/2011/05/treasure-discovered-between-the-floorboards-you-have-to-crack-some-eggs-5.
9. Josiah Beckwith account books, Beckwith Family Papers, LHS.
10. Ibid.
11. "List of Certified Cowards in Woodbury! As Per Surgeon's Certificates," Broadside Collection, CSL.
12. For more on vigilantism in Litchfield County, see Vermilyea, *Wicked Litchfield County*; "John H. Hubbard," *Litchfield Enquirer*, August 1, 1872; Croffut and Morris, *Military and Civil History of Connecticut*, 243.
13. *Housatonic Republican*, August 16, 1862.
14. *Litchfield Enquirer*, August 14, 1862.
15. *Winsted Herald,* August 15, 1862.
16. Ibid.; soldier data from American Civil War Research Database.
17. "List of Certified Cowards in Woodbury! As Per Surgeon's Certificates," Broadside Collection, CSL.
18. Ibid.
19. Ibid.
20. *Litchfield Enquirer*, August 28, 1862.
21. Seth Plumb to "Friends," August 10, 1862, Plumb Family Correspondence, LHS; Alva Stone to "Wife & Child," August 16, 1862, Alva Stone Letters, LHS.
22. Vaill, *History of the Second Connecticut*, 14.
23. *Winsted Herald*, August 15, 1862.
24. Ibid.; *Litchfield Enquirer*, August 14, 1862; *Winsted Herald*, August 15, 1862; Smith, *Old Nineteenth*, 10.
25. *Litchfield Enquirer*, August 14, 1862.
26. Ibid.
27. Ibid.
28. Gallman, *North Fights the Civil War*, 71; *Litchfield Enquirer*, August 27, 1863; August 13, 1863.

Chapter 9

1. *Winsted Herald*, August 8, 1862; *Litchfield Enquirer*, August 1, 1862; Rufus Smith to Quartermaster, August 1862, Small Acquisitions, LHS.
2. *Litchfield Enquirer*, August 27, 1862.
3. Luman Wadhams pension records, National Archives and Records Administration, Washington, D.C. (Hereafter NARA); Seth Plumb to ___, January 5th, 1862, Plumb Family Correspondence, LHS; *Connecticut War Record*, v. 2, no. 11, September 1864, 276.
4. Smith, *Old Nineteenth*, 474, n.22; Second Connecticut Regimental Order Book, Regimental Order and Descriptive Books, Record Group 094, NARA.
5. Roberts, "War Reminiscences," *Connecticut Western News*, May 18, 1911.
6. Michael Kelly diary, August 11, 12, and 21, 1862, Manuscript Collection, CHS.
7. Homer S. Curtiss to "Ma," August 22, 1862, Yale.
8. *Litchfield Enquirer*, August 18, 1862; Soule, "Recollections…," *New Milford Gazette*, July 7, 1911.
9. Homer S. Curtiss to "Ma," August 22, 1862, Yale.
10. *Litchfield Enquirer*, August 18, 1862.
11. Homer S. Curtiss to "Ma," August 22, 1862, Yale.
12. Ward, "Civil War Tour of Litchfield County"; *Litchfield Enquirer*, August 21, 1862.
13. *Litchfield Enquirer*, August 21, 1862.
14. Taylor, *Philadelphia in the Civil War*, 136; Wisconsin Historical Society, "Camp Randall (MADISON, WIS.)."
15. Soule, "Recollections…," *New Milford Gazette*, July 7, 1911.
16. Cothren, *History of Ancient Woodbury, Connecticut*, 1,194.
17. 19th Connecticut Enlistment Papers, RG 13, Box 30, CHS.
18. "Lieutenant George Benjamin Hempstead, Second Connecticut Heavy Artillery," Civil War Soldier Reminiscences and Remembrances Collections, LHS.
19. Smith, *Old Nineteenth*, 6.
20. Barker, *Dear Mother from Your Dutiful Son*, 12.
21. Keefe, "East Litchfield Men."
22. Civil War Veterans Record Book, LHS.
23. Smith, *Old Nineteenth*, 7; 19th Connecticut Enlistment Papers, RG 13, Box 30, CHS; Shepherd, *Litchfield*, 77
24. Homer S. Curtiss to Seth, September 12, 1862, Yale; *Litchfield Enquirer*, September 4, 1862.
25. Michael Kelly diary, August 21, 1862, CHS; *Winsted Herald*, September 12, 1862; Smith, *Old Nineteenth*, 6.
26. Second Connecticut Regimental Order Book, Regimental Order and Descriptive Books, Record Group 094, NARA; Heiser, "Life of a Civil War Soldier."
27. Vaill, *History of the Second Connecticut*, 11; Smith, *Old Nineteenth*, 15.

28. Rudd, *Men of Worth of Salisbury Birth*, 212; Civil War Veterans Record Book, LHS.
29. Vaill, *History of the Second Connecticut*, 11.
30. Ibid.; Roberts, "War Reminiscences," *Connecticut Western News*, May 18, 1911; July 7, 1911.
31. Michael Kelly diary, August 29, 1862, CHS; Vaill, *History of the Second Connecticut*, 14.
32. Michael Kelly diary, August 31, 1862, CHS. On the 16th Connecticut see, Lesley J. Gordon, *A Broken Regiment: The 16th Connecticut's Civil War* (Baton Rouge: LSU Press, 2014).
33. Carmichael, *War for the Common Soldier*, 20; Hess, *Civil War Infantry Tactics*, 61; Soule, "Recollections…," *New Milford Gazette*, July 7, 1911.
34. Michael Kelly diary, September 5, 1862, CHS.
35. Ibid., August 24, 1862, CHS.
36. Homer S. Curtiss to "Mother," September 4, 1862, Yale; Homer S. Curtiss to Seth, September 12, 1862, Yale.
37. Homer S. Curtiss to "Mother," September 4, 1862, Yale; Second Connecticut Regimental Order Book, Regimental Order and Descriptive Books, Record Group 094, NARA.

Chapter 10

1. Carmichael, *War for the Common Soldier*, 20.
2. List of Quartermaster's Stores &c. Issued by B.D. Lee, Quartermaster, 19th Conn Volunteers to Wm Bissell Captain Company A 19th Conn Volunteers at Camp Dutton, August 29, 1862, Bissell Family Collections LHS, *Litchfield Enquirer*, August 21, 1862; Orr, "North Mobilizes for War."
3. Roberts, "War Reminiscences," *Connecticut Western News*, May 18, 1911; Homer S. Curtiss to "Ma," August 22, 1862, Yale.
4. Soule, "Recollections…, "*New Milford Gazette*, July 14, 1911; Homer Curtiss to "Friends," August 24, 1862, Yale.
5. *Litchfield Enquirer*, September 2, 1862.
6. Homer Curtiss to "Ma," August 22, 1862, Yale; Homer Curtiss "Ma," August 23, 1862, Yale.
7. Homer Curtiss to "Friends," August 24, 1862, Yale; *Litchfield Enquirer*, August 28, 1862.
8. *Winsted Herald*, September 12, 1862; Cimbala and Miller, *Northern Homefront during the Civil War*, 44.
9. Linderman, *Embattled Courage*, 5; Orr, "North Mobilizes for War"; Homer S. Curtiss to "Mother," September 4, 1862, Yale.
10. Barker, *Fred and Jennie*, 8; Barker, *Dear Mother from Your Dutiful Son*, 22.
11. *Litchfield Enquirer*, August 28, 1862; Michael Kelly diary, August 25, 1862, CHS; Vaill, *History of the Second Connecticut*, 13; *Winsted Herald*, October 3, 1862.
12. Homer S. Curtiss to "Ma," August 23, 1862, Yale.

13. Homer S. Curtiss to "Ma," August 22, 1862, Yale; Homer S. Curtiss to "Ma," August 23, 1862, Yale.
14. Homer S. Curtiss to "Mother," September 4, 1862, Yale.
15. Homer S. Curtiss to "Friends," August 24, 1862, Yale, 450; *Winsted Herald*, September 5, 1862.
16. Homer S. Curtiss to "Seth," September 12, 1862, Yale.
17. Stephen Collins Foster and J.S. Gibbons, "We are Coming, Father Abra'am, 300,000 More" (New York: S.T. Gordon, 1862), Notated Music, https://www.loc.gov/item/2011567050; Smith, *Old Nineteenth*, 16; Homer S. Curtiss to "Mother," September 4, 1862, Yale.
18. Homer Curtiss to "Mother," September 4, 1862, Yale.
19. Rable, *God's Almost Chosen People*, 70; *Litchfield Enquirer*, September 11, 1862; Michael Kelly diary, August 25, 1862, CHS.
20. Homer Curtiss to "Ma," September 7, 1862, Yale; Michael Kelly diary, July 22, 1862, CHS; Rable, *God's Almost Chosen People*, 70.
21. Homer Curtiss to "Ma," August 22, 1862, Yale; Edward S. Roberts diary, September 2, 1862, CHS; *Winsted Herald*, September 5, 1862.
22. *Litchfield Enquirer*, September 11, 1862; Soule, "Recollections…," *New Milford Gazette*, July 7, 1911; Homer Curtiss to Seth, September 12, 1862, Yale.
23. Michael Kelly diary, July 23, 1862, CHS.
24. Ibid., August 27, 1862, CHS; August 28, 1862, CHS.
25. General Orders 74, *Litchfield Enquirer*, August 8, 1862; *Litchfield Enquirer*, September 4, 1862.
26. *Litchfield Enquirer*, September 11, 1862.
27. Ibid., August 28, 1862; September 11, 1862; *Housatonic Republican*, August 16, 1862; *Winsted Herald*, August 22, 1862.
28. *Winsted Herald*, September 12, 1862.
29. *Litchfield Enquirer*, September 4, 1862.
30. *Litchfield Enquirer*, September 19, 1862.
31. Ibid.; Niven, *Connecticut for the Union*, 86–87; Frank, *With Ballot and Bayonet*, 7.
32. Charles Andrews diary, September 15, 1862, Charles B. Andrews Papers, LHS.
33. *Revised United States Army Regulations of 1861*, 313; National Museum of Civil War Medicine, "Surgeon's Role in Enlisting Civil War Soldiers."
34. Vaill, *History of the Second Connecticut*, 14.
35. Orr, "North Mobilizes for War."
36. Williams, "Litchfield Civil War Recruiting Tent."
37. Charles Andrews diary, September 10, 1862, Charles B. Andrews Papers, LHS; *Litchfield Enquirer*, August 28, 1862.
38. William Curtis Noyes, quoted in *Litchfield Enquirer*, September 11, 1862.
39. *Litchfield Enquirer*, September 11, 1862; Edward S. Roberts diary, September 10, 1862, CHS; Leverett Wessells, quoted in *Litchfield Enquirer*, September 11, 1862.

40. Homer Curtiss to "Mother," September 4, 1862, Yale; *Litchfield Enquirer*, September 11, 1862.
41. Michael Kelly diary, September 11, 1862, CHS; Cothren, *History of Ancient Woodbury, Connecticut*, 1,195; *Winsted Herald*, September 12, 1862; *Litchfield Enquirer*, September 18, 1862.
42. Homer Curtiss to "Ourfolk," September 8, 1862, Yale; *Winsted Herald*, September 12, 1862; Homer Curtiss to "Seth," September 12, 1862, Yale; *Winsted Herald*, September 12, 1862.
43. Vaill, *History of the Second Connecticut*, 10.
44. Alva Stone to "Wife and Child," July 27, 1862, Alva Stone Letters, LHS.

Epilogue

1. Smith, *Old Nineteenth*, 122; Civil War Soldier Reminiscences and Remembrances Collections, LHS; "19th Regt Leaves Tomorrow," George Richards Collection, LHS.
2. Boswell, *Litchfield Book of Days*, 150–51.
3. Roberts, "War Reminiscences," CHS; Michael Kelly diary, September 15, 1862, CHS; Nathaniel Smith quoted in Cothren, *History of Ancient Woodbury, Connecticut*, 1,198; *Litchfield Enquirer*, September 18, 1862; Vaill, *History of the Second Connecticut*, 13; Nathaniel Smith quoted in Cothren, *History of Ancient Woodbury, Connecticut*, 1,198; *Winsted Herald*, September 19, 1862.
4. Roberts, "War Reminiscences," CHS; *Winsted Herald*, September 19, 1862; *Litchfield Enquirer*, September 18, 1862.
5. *Winsted Herald*, September 19, 1862; *Litchfield Enquirer*, September 18, 1862; Edward S. Roberts diary, September 15, 1862, CHS.
6. *Litchfield Enquirer*, September 18, 1862.
7. Ibid.; September 25, 1862; October 9, 1862.
8. *Litchfield Enquirer*, October 8, 1862.
9. Croffut and Morris, *Military and Civil History of Connecticut*, 849.
10. Finan, "Litchfield County in the Civil War," 37.
11. Harsh, *Confederate Tide Riding*, 12–13.
12. Olcott and Lear, *Civil War Letters of Lewis Bissell*, 250.
13. John W. Shaw to "Dear Sir," October 7, 1862, August 8, 1864, Civil War Soldier Reminiscences and Remembrances Collections, LHS.
14. Hines, *Civil War Volunteer Sons of Connecticut*, 71.
15. The towns included in the sample are Enfield, Groton, Simsbury, Southbury and Watertown, Connecticut; Battle Creek, Michigan; Belchester, Massachusetts; Columbus, Indiana; Decatur, Illinois; Londonderry, New Hampshire; and Rockland, Maine. The numbers of deserters and populations of the town were found at the American Civil War Research Database; Posner, *Essential Holmes*, 93.
16. Vaill, *History of the Second Connecticut*, 13.

Sources

Manuscript Collections

Hartford, Connecticut
Connecticut Historical Society
James Deane Papers
Stephen Fenn Papers
Michael Kelly Papers
Edward S. Roberts Papers
Salisbury, Connecticut, Civil War Bounty Records

Connecticut State Library/Connecticut State Archives
Broadside Collection
Record Group 8: Records of the Comptroller, 1758–1887
Comptroller's Records of Returns from Towns and Payments to Soldiers and Families during the Civil War, 1861–66
Record Group 13: Military Department, 1776–1986
19th Connecticut Infantry Enlistment Papers

Litchfield, Connecticut
Helga J. Ingraham Library, Litchfield Historical Society
American Civil War Printed Ephemera
Charles B. Andrews Papers
Beckwith Family Collection
Bissell Family Collection
Civil War Soldier Reminiscences and Remembrances Collections
Civil War Veterans Record Book

Rufus King to Quartermaster General, August 1862
Ladies' Benevolent Society of Northfield Secretary's Books and Soldier's Aid Association Minutes
Plumb Family Correspondence
George Richards Collection
Katharine Bissell Borgert Roe Memoir
John W. Shaw Collection
Small Acquisitions Collection
Alva Stone Letters
Thompson Family Papers

LITCHFIELD TOWN HALL
Litchfield Town Minutes, vol. 49, 1840–80, Office of the Litchfield Town Clerk

NEW HAVEN, CONNECTICUT
Yale University Manuscripts and Special Collections
Bernhard Knollenberg Collection, Manuscripts and Archives, Yale University Library

WASHINGTON, D.C.
Library of Congress
Abraham Lincoln Papers
Notated Music Collection

National Archives and Records Administration
Record Group 15, Records of the Department of Veterans Affairs
Pension Records—Luman Wadhams
Record Group 94, Records of the Adjutant General's Office, Book Records of Volunteer Union Organizations, Civil War, 2nd Connecticut Heavy Artillery, Order Books

Private Collections

Keefe, Daniel. "East Litchfield Men Serving in the Union Army." Unpublished manuscript. Author's collection.
Ward, David A. "Civil War Tour of Litchfield County." Unpublished manuscript. Author's collection.
Williams, Fenton. "Litchfield Civil War Recruiting Tent." Unpublished manuscript. Author's collection.

Newspapers

Bridgeport Times and Evening Farmer
Connecticut War Record
Connecticut Western News
Hartford Courant
Housatonic Republican
Litchfield Enquirer
New York Times
Utica Daily Press
Waterbury American
Winsted Herald

Books

Barker, Ernest B. *Dear Mother from Your Dutiful Son: Civil War Letters, September 22, 1862 to August 18, 1865; Letters by Frederick A. Lucas to His Mother*. Goshen, CT: Purple Door Gallery Press, 2003.

———. *Fred and Jennie: A Civil War Love Story*. Goshen, CT: Purple Door Gallery Press, 2002.

Basler, Roy P., ed. *The Collected Works of Abraham Lincoln*. New Brunswick, NJ: Rutgers University Press, 1953.

Beckwith, Paul. *The Beckwiths*. Albany, NY : James Munsell's Sons, 1891.

Boatner, Mark. *The Civil War Dictionary*. New York: Vintage Press, 1991.

Boswell, George Copeland. *The Litchfield Book of Days: A Collation of the Historical, Biographical, and Literary Reminiscences of the Town of Litchfield, Connecticut*. Litchfield, CT: Alex. B. Shumway, 1900.

Brands, H.W. *The Zealot and the Emancipator: John Brown, Abraham Lincoln, and the Struggle for American Freedom*. New York: Doubleday, 2020.

Carley, Rachel. *Litchfield: The Making of a New England Town*. Litchfield, CT: Litchfield Historical Society, 2011.

Carmichael, Peter S. *The War for the Common Soldier: How Men Thought, Fought, and Survived in Civil War Armies*. Chapel Hill: University of North Carolina Press, 2018.

Cimbala, Paul A., and Randall M. Miller. *The Northern Homefront during the Civil War*. Santa Barbara, CA: ABC-Clio, 2017.

Cothren, William. *History of Ancient Woodbury, Connecticut, from the First Indian Deed in 1659 to 1872*. Woodbury, CT: William Cothren, 1872.

Croffut, W.A., and John M. Morris. *The Military and Civil History of Connecticut during the War of the Rebellion*. New York: Ledyard Bill, 1868.

Engle, Stephen D. *Gathering to Save a Nation: Lincoln and the Union's War Governors*. Chapel Hill: University of North Carolina Press, 2016.

Frank, Joseph Allan. *With Ballot and Bayonet: The Political Socialization of Civil War Soldiers.* Athens: University of Georgia Press, 2016.

Freeman, Joanne B. *The Field of Blood: Violence in Congress and the Road to Civil War.* New York: Farrar, Straus and Giroux, 2018.

Gallman, J. Matthew. *Defining Duty in the Civil War: Personal Choice, Popular Culture, and the Union Home Front.* Chapel Hill: University of North Carolina Press, 2015.

———. *The North Fights the Civil War: The Home Front.* New York: Ivan R. Dee, 1994.

Geary, James W. *We Need Men: The Union Draft in the Civil War.* Chapel Hill: University of North Carolina Press, 1991.

Giesberg, Judith. *An Army at Home: Women and the Civil War on the Northern Home Front.* Chapel Hill: University of North Carolina Press, 2009.

Harsh, Joseph L. *Confederate Tide Riding.* Kent, OH: Kent State University Press, 1998.

———. *Taken at the Flood: Robert E. Lee and Confederate Strategy in the Maryland Campaign of 1862.* Kent, OH: Kent State University Press, 1999.

Hartwig, D. Scott. *To Antietam Creek: The Maryland Campaign of September 1862.* Baltimore, MD: Johns Hopkins University Press, 2012.

Hess, Earl J. *Civil War Infantry Tactics: Training, Combat, and Small-Unit Effectiveness.* Baton Rouge: Louisiana State University Press, 2015.

Hines, Blaikee. *Civil War Volunteer Sons of Connecticut.* Thomaston, ME: American Patriot, 2002.

History of Litchfield County, Connecticut, with Illustrations and Biographical Sketches of its Prominent Men and Pioneers. Philadelphia, PA: J.W. Lewis & Company, 1881.

Howe, Daniel Walker. *What Hath God Wrought: The Transformation of America, 1815–1848.* New York: Oxford University Press, 2007.

Kirby, Ed. *Echoes of Iron in Connecticut's Northwest Corner.* Sharon, CT: Sharon Historical Society, 1998.

Linderman, Gerald F. *Embattled Courage: The Experience of Combat in the American Civil War.* New York: Free Press, 1987.

Manning, Chandra. *What This Cruel War Was Over: Soldiers, Slavery and the Civil War.* New York: Alfred A. Knopf, 2007.

Marvel, William. *Lincoln's Mercenaries: Economic Motivation Among Union Soldiers during the Civil War.* Baton Rouge: Louisiana State University Press, 2018.

McGaugh, Scott. *Surgeon in Blue: Jonathan Letterman, the Civil War Doctor Who Pioneered Battlefield Care.* New York: Arcade, 2013.

McPherson, James M. *Battle Cry of Freedom: The Civil War Era.* New York: Oxford University Press, 1988.

———. *For Cause and Comrades: Why Men Fought in the Civil War.* New York: Oxford University Press, 1997.

Miller, Richard. *States at War.* Vol. 1, *A Reference Guide for Connecticut, Maine, Massachusetts, New Hampshire, Rhode Island, and Vermont in the Civil War.* Lebanon, NH: University Press of New England, 2013.

Mott, Frank Luther. *American Journalism: A History of Newspapers in the United States through 250 Years, 1690–1940*. New York: MacMillan Company, 1941.

Murdock, Eugene C. *One Million Men: The Civil War Draft in the North*. Madison: State Historical Society of Wisconsin, 1971.

Neely, Mark E. *The Fate of Liberty: Abraham Lincoln and Civil Liberties*. New York: Oxford University Press, 1991.

Niven, John. *Connecticut for the Union: The Role of the State in the Civil War*. New Haven, CT: Yale University Press, 1865.

Olcott, Mark, and David Lear, eds. *The Civil War Letters of Lewis Bissell: A Curriculum*. Washington, D.C.: Field School Educational Foundation Press, 1981.

Paludan, Philip Shaw. *"A People's Contest": The Union and the Civil War, 1861–1865*. New York: Harper and Row, 1988.

Posner, Richard. *The Essential Holmes: Selections from the Letters, Speeches, Judicial Opinions, and Other Writings of Oliver Wendell Holmes Jr*. Chicago: University of Chicago Press, 1992.

Rable, George C. *God's Almost Chosen People: A Religious History of the American Civil War*. Chapel Hill: University of North Carolina Press, 2010.

Revised United States Army Regulations of 1861, With an Appendix Containing the Changes and Laws Affecting Army Regulations and Articles of War to June 25, 1863. Washington, D.C.: Department of War, 1863.

Rudd, Malcolm Day. *Men of Worth of Salisbury Birth: The Salisbury Quadramillenium Edition*. Salisbury, CT: Salisbury Association, 1991.

Seidman, Rachel Filene. "'We Were Enlisted for the War': Ladies' Aid Societies and the Politics of Women's Work During the Civil War." In *Making and Unmaking Pennsylvania's Civil War*. Edited by William Blair. University Park: Pennsylvania State University Press, 2001.

Shepherd, Henry L., ed. *Litchfield: Portrait of a Beautiful Town*. Litchfield, CT: Litchfield Historical Society, 1969.

Smith, Richard W. *The Old Nineteenth: The Story of the Second Connecticut Heavy Artillery in the Civil War*. Lincoln, NE: iUniverse Inc., 2007.

Spar, Ira, MD. *New Haven's Civil War Hospital: A History of Knight U.S. General Hospital, 1862–1865*. Jefferson, NC: McFarland, 2013.

Taylor, Frank H. *Philadelphia in the Civil War, 1861–1865*. Philadelphia, PA: City of Philadelphia, 1913.

United States Department of War. *The War of the Rebellion: A Compilation of the Official Records of the Union and Confederate Armies*. Washington, D.C.: Government Printing Office, 1894.

Vaill, Dudley Landon. *The County Regiment: A Sketch*. Litchfield, CT: Litchfield University Club, 1908.

Vaill, Theodore F. *History of the Second Connecticut Volunteer Heavy Artillery: Originally the Nineteenth Connecticut Vols*. Winsted, CT: Winsted Printing Company, 1868.

Vermilyea, Peter C. *Hidden History of Litchfield County*. Charleston, SC: The History Press, 2014.

———. *Wicked Litchfield County*. Charleston, SC: The History Press, 2016.

Warshauer, Matthew. *Connecticut in the Civil War: Slavery, Sacrifice, and Survival*. Middletown, CT: Wesleyan University Press, 2012.

———. *Inside Connecticut and the Civil War: Essays on One State's Struggles*. Middletown, CT: Wesleyan University Press, 2014.

Weber, Jennifer L. *Copperheads: The Rise and Fall of Lincoln's Opponents in the North*. New York: Oxford University Press, 2008.

Weld, Stanley B. *Connecticut Physicians in the Civil War*. Hartford: Connecticut Civil War Centennial Commission, 1964.

White, Alain. *The History of the Town of Litchfield, 1720–1920*. Litchfield, CT: Litchfield Historical Society, 1920.

Wilson, Mark R. *The Business of Civil War: Military Mobilization and the State, 1861–1865*. Baltimore, MD: Johns Hopkins University Press, 2006.

Articles

Blevins, Cameron. "Women and Federal Officeholding in the Late 19th Century U.S." *Current Research in Digital History* 2 (August 23, 2019).

Finan, W.J. "Litchfield County in the Civil War." *Lure of the Litchfield Hills* 15, no 2 (June 1958): 6–7, 35–36.

———. "William A. Buckingham: Civil War Governor of Connecticut." *Lure of the Litchfield Hills* 21, no. 1 (June 1961): 10–11, 26–27.

Jeffrey, Julie Roy. "'They Cannot Expect…That a Loyal People Will Tolerate the Utterance of Such Sentiments': The Campaign Against Treasonous Speech during the Civil War." *Civil War History* 65, no. 1 (March 2019): 7–42.

Leone, Julie Frey. "The Peace Movement in Litchfield." *Connecticut History Explored* 9 no. 2 (Spring 2011): 18–21.

Phillips, Jason. "The Grapevine Telegraph: Rumors and Confederate Persistence." *Journal of Southern History* 72, no. 4 (2006): 753–88.

Schweiger, Beth Barton. "The Literate South: Reading Before Emancipation." *Journal of the Civil War Era* 3, no. 3 (September 2013): 331–59.

Thompson, Kees D. "'Altoona Was His, and Fairly Won': President Lincoln and the Altoona Governors' Conference, September 1862." *Gettysburg College Journal of the Civil War Era* 7, no. 7 (2013): 85–108.

Lectures

Orr, Timothy. "The North Mobilizes for War." Lecture. Gettysburg College Civil War Institute. Gettysburg, Pennsylvania, June 27, 2011.

Online Resources

Adam, Abigail. "Titans for a Battlefield: Horatio Ames and His Colossal Cannon." *Gettysburg Compiler*, March 28, 2021. https://gettysburgcompiler.org/2021/03/28/titans-for-a-battlefield-horatio-ames-and-his-colossal-cannon.

American Civil War Database. civilwardata.com.

Heiser, John. "The Life of a Civil War Soldier." Anchor: A North Carolina History Resource. https://www.ncpedia.org/anchor/life-civil-war-soldier.

The Ledger. Litchfield Historical Society. https://ledger.litchfieldhistoricalsociety.org/ledger.

National Museum of Civil War Medicine. "A Surgeon's Role in Enlisting Civil War Soldiers." https://www.civilwarmed.org/enlist.

Prices and Wages by Decade: 1860–1869. "Wages for Four Common Occupations in 1860, by State." University of Missouri Libraries. https://docs.google.com/document/d/1E1H_BNIkSChANXCUAnph9qx6Os6wM1sZ8IdY3AQanxA/edit.

Wisconsin Historical Society. "Camp Randall (MADISON, WIS.), as It Appeared in 1862." https://www.wisconsinhistory.org/Records/Image/IM1875.

About the Author

Courtesy of Luke Vermilyea.

Peter C. Vermilyea teaches history at Housatonic Valley Regional High School in Falls Village, Connecticut. A graduate of Gettysburg College, he is the director of the student scholarship program at his alma mater's Civil War Institute. Vermilyea is the author of *Hidden History of Litchfield County* (The History Press, 2014), which received the 2015 CultureMax Award, and *Wicked Litchfield County* (The History Press, 2016), as well as more than two dozen articles, mostly on Civil War history. He lives in Litchfield, Connecticut, with his wife and two sons.